AF251628

THE ECONOMICS OF INDUSTRY

Alfred Marshall
and
Mary Paley Marshall

With a new Introduction by
Denis O'Brien

© Thoemmes Press 1994

Published in 1994 by

Thoemmes Press
85 Park Street
Bristol BS1 5PJ
England

ISBN 1 85506 320 4

This is a reprint of the 1879 Edition

© *Introduction* Denis O'Brien

Publisher's Note

These reprints are taken from original copies of each book. In many cases the condition of those originals is not perfect, the paper, often handmade, having suffered over time and the copy from such things as inconsistent printing pressures resulting in faint text, show-through from one side of a leaf to the other, the filling in of some characters, and the break up of type. The publisher has gone to great lengths to ensure the quality of these reprints but points out that certain characteristics of the original copies will, of necessity, be apparent in reprints thereof.

THE ECONOMICS OF INDUSTRY[*]

Introduction

The origins of this small, but highly important, book lie in the education and early career of Mary Paley Marshall (1850–1944), the wife of the great Alfred Marshall (1842–1924). Mary Paley, as she then was, had taken the Tripos examinations in December 1874 and began lecturing in Cambridge in 1875 to women students. She accepted 'with too light a heart' a suggestion that she should write a textbook for the Cambridge University Extension Lectures. In May 1876 she became engaged to Alfred Marshall, and in October of that year the pair of them began to sketch the outline of the book (M. P. Marshall, 1947, p. 20). The book was planned to be one of a pair – the second volume was to be the *Economics of Trade and Finance*. This was (sadly) never written – and one particular reason for regret that it never appeared is that the monetary chapter (III (i)) of the present book indicates that a full discussion of monetary topics had been reserved for the companion volume. Alfred Marshall was still promising this other book to Macmillans in 1887 (Whitaker, 1975, I, p. 89) but it fell victim both to Marshall's dislike of the first book and also to the delays in publication of his work on macroeconomics which persisted until the penultimate year of his life.

[*] I am extremely grateful to Dr Julia Stapleton and to Professor John Creedy for comments on an earlier draft of this introduction.

In 1877, faced with the loss of his Cambridge Fellowship as a result of marriage, Marshall became Principal of Bristol University and it seems to have been there that the book, which was published in 1879, was very largely written (M. P. Marshall, 1947, p. 23; Whitaker, 1972, pp. 119, 128).

Mary Paley Marshall, the great granddaughter of the famous arch-deacon William Paley (1743–1805) has given a delightful account of her up-bringing in the posthumously published *What I Remember* (1947). She was born on 24 October 1850, the daughter of the Rector of Ufford near Stafford in Lincolnshire whom Keynes described as 'an evangelical clergyman of the straightest Simeonite sect' (1944, p. 269). She was educated at home (where she acquired a fluent command of German which was later to prove an academic asset – M. P. Marshall 1895) and then – perhaps rather surprisingly, given the narrowness of her father's outlook – allowed to go to the University of Cambridge. She possessed both beauty and intelligence (Clough and Strachey 1944; Keynes, 1944) despite Beatrice Webb's catty reference to her being 'badly dressed with protruding teeth, weak eyes, and quickly changing colour' (Webb, 1982, p. 285), a description which may well have been motivated by the evident dislike felt by its author for Alfred Marshall (*eg.* Webb, 1983, p. 25). (There is some hint that Mary Paley was herself not a whole-hearted admirer of Beatrice Webb in M. P. Marshall 1896.) Mary Paley seems to have inspired affection in those with whom she had dealings – affection is indeed the characteristic which shines most clearly through Keynes's memoir of her. She was also a productive artist (Clough and Strachey 1944; Constable 1960). (A number of her paintings were presented to the Marshall Library by C. R. Fay.)

Induced by a friend to attend lectures on economics – her original interests were Latin, history, literature and logic – she encountered Marshall (whom she had previously met, and to whom she was evidently attracted – Keynes believed it to have been love at first sight) as a lecturer. Marshall encouraged her to enter for the Tripos, in which she was successful though the examiners were unable to agree on whether she should be placed in the First or Second Class. Marshall seems to have been a hard-working and enthusiastic teacher (1947, pp. 17–18) though his lectures appear to have been of a rather moralizing kind, at least at that date, covering such matters as dancing, marriage, betting and smuggling, leading his wife to remark in her memoir that 'He was a great preacher' (1947, p. 20). But he seems to have entered enthusiastically enough into the education of his female students and was indeed one of the so-called 'runners' who brought the examination papers to the place set aside for the (at that time irregular) examination of women students – the drawing room of a house in Bateman Street owned by the famous classicist Kennedy.

Mary Paley lectured at Cambridge (Clough and Strachey, 1944) and (during Marshall's time as Principal) at Bristol – which in 1928 awarded her an honorary doctorate – as well as at Oxford. The vast majority of this teaching was to women students. She had, very unusually for a woman at that date, a full length academic career (Groenewegen, 1993). But in 1896 Alfred Marshall was one of those who opposed the introduction of degrees for women and this, coupled with various anecdotes – notably one by C. R. Fay which implied that Marshall treated his wife as a domestic servant, even though this is clearly not the case – has led to a view of their marriage through late-twentieth century eyes which is perhaps rather an unkind one.[1] Lionel Robbins, indeed, in a phrase itself reflecting a less sensitive age, wrote that Marshall 'was obviously a bit of a Turk at home' (1970, p. 64). Yet Mary Marshall was clearly devoted both to Alfred and, after 1924, to his memory and, equally clearly, saw the great good which could come out of marriage – she believed that Keynes's marriage was the best thing he ever did and regretted that Pigou did not marry (Skidelsky, 1992, pp. 217, 282). Although the Marshalls' marriage was not a partnership such as that of the Webbs, as Keynes observed, it was still an intellectual partnership for all that, and it was also a practical partnership with Mary managing the family finances. A touching piece of evidence of his devotion to her came to light many years later with the publi-

---

[1] The Marshalls marriage has been the subject of comment, much of it impertinent in the most literal sense, which has no parallel anywhere in the history of economics. The literature in this field proceeds, on the flimsiest of evidence, to conclusions which sometimes border on the hysterical. The origins of this deplorable development lie in the denigration, personal as well as professional, of Marshall which manifested itself in Cambridge in the decade and a half following his death (for an authentic manifestation of this see Robinson, 1948) and which must have been acutely hurtful to his widow. But it has now assumed a life of its own. The ascertainable facts, however, are that the couple were mutually devoted, that this devotion survived Marshall's opposition to degrees for women (which was itself in such contrast to his earlier attitudes, which included the surreptitious removal of the word 'obey' from the marriage service and his enthusiastic participation in the development of women's education in Cambridge) and that, despite inevitable social disapproval (which the thin-skinned Alfred must have felt acutely), Mary Paley enjoyed a full-length academic career (as noted above), retiring in the same year as her husband, 1908 (Groenewegen, 1993). This was a remarkable achievement for the era, and one rendered all the more remarkable by the fact that she published (M. P. Marshall, 1895, 1896, 1902) at a time when this was far from automatic for academics; and it is an achievement which would certainly not have been possible if her husband had been as oppressive, or she as oppressed, as later detractors would have us believe.

cation of the letters of Sidney and Beatrice Webb (1978, p. 310) where it was revealed that in 1891 Marshall had, by mistake, sent a letter to E. R. A. Seligman beginning 'My own dear darling' – it was intended for Mary.

The Writing of the Book

According to Mrs Marshall's own account, the book 'was published in our joint names in 1879. Alfred insisted on this, though as time went on I realized that it had to be really his book, the latter half being almost entirely his and containing the germs of much that appeared later in the *Principles*' (1947, p. 22). It was also the opinion of Marshall's nephew Claude Guillebaud that the book 'ended up being very much Marshall's own work' (1961, vol. II, p. 12). A careful reading, however, indicates that the situation is rather more complicated than this.

There are substantial parts of the book for which Mary Paley was clearly more responsible than Alfred. This is particularly true of the whole of Book I 'Land, Labour and Capital'; and there can be very little doubt also that Mary Paley wrote much of the labour economics material – material which Keynes thought particularly valuable – contained in chapters v, vi and viii, as well as chapter ix on co-operation, in Book III. (It is perhaps worth mentioning that all three of her independent publications listed in the bibliography are concerned with labour economics.) It also seems likely that she wrote at least a first draft of chapter iii of Book III 'Local Variations of Prices and Wages. Influence of Custom.' Some of this material – and this is a topic to which we shall return below – passed beyond friendliness towards trade unions into serious naivety. It is difficult to believe that anyone familiar with even the elements of nineteenth-century labour history could have written of strike pickets that

> they now confine themselves almost entirely to explaining to workmen who may be seeking employment, the nature and cause of the strike. The pickets appeal to their feelings of class patriotism, and endeavour to dissuade them from siding with the employers against the employed; offering them on the part of the union the repayment of all the expenses to which they may be put by abandoning their purpose.
>
> (p. 198)

It is surprising to learn that intimidation by pickets had, it seemed, become rare by 1879 (p. 197).

Marshall's own intervention in the text shows up in various ways. Firstly, even in Book I, there are paragraphs inserted in square brackets – with instructions to beginners to omit these – which subtly, and sometimes substantially, qualify the argument in the unbracketed text. We also find rather less subtle qualifications by Alfred of statements in the text which seem to have been written by Mary. This is particularly obvious in the case of the treatment of capital (pp. 16–17) and of the 'arithmetical' and 'geometric' ratios of Malthus although the most striking example occurs late in the book (p. 201) where a plainly incorrect statement in the text (involving simple interest where compound was implied) is corrected in a footnote.

Secondly there are insertions reflecting Marshall's particular preoccupations. An example is the attack on the American economist Carey (p. 79) with whom Marshall had clashed when in the United States. Thirdly there are characteristic Marshallian concepts –

notably 'abstinence', which, deriving from Senior as the supply price of capital, became in the *Principles* 'waiting'. Indeed it is apparent at one point that Marshall had failed to notice that the concept had not been introduced in Book I as he believed (compare pp. 13–20, 73). Fourthly, there are, scattered about the book, a number of Marshall's particular (and sometimes quasi-philosophical) themes which occur elsewhere in his writings. Most obviously there is the matter of motherhood, to which he attached such importance, as well as questions of moral character, general and technical education, physical vigour, national moral habits, eugenics, the role of selective poor relief, and an interest in the detail of industrial processes.

Perhaps most strikingly of all there is a fairly clear inconsistency over the treatment of entrepreneurship. In the *Principles,* Marshall was to make 'organization' a fourth factor of production, alongside land, labour and capital. By contrast Book I of *The Economics of Industry* does not do this but treats the entrepreneur as a supplier of skilled labour. But then in chapter ix of Book II 'Supply of Business Power' we have an approach which is much more in line with that of the *Principles.* Indeed the case of business power is said explicitly to differ from that of skilled labour (p. 117).

Some of these tensions within the text, as was explained in the preface to the second edition of 1881, arose because of the use of the process known as 'stereotyping' which involved making up complete plates for printing. Nineteenth-century authors habitually used proofs as later authors used a typescript – a provisional text which could be altered at will to produce a finished text. But this could not be the case where the proofs were from plates rather than movable type. This certainly made it difficult for Marshall to alter, at a later date, what his wife had written and led him to qualify it in footnotes and in extra material.[2] Perhaps the most clear-cut example of such qualification is to be found in the section of the book dealing with labour economics. Chapter vi of Book III 'Influence of Trades Unions on Wages', which is distinctly classical and contains noticeable traces of the wage fund, does appear to have come from the pen of Mary Marshall in the first instance though, at the end of the chapter, material from J. S. Mill – actually from his 'recantation' of the wage fund (Mill, 1869), although no source is given – seems to have been added by Alfred. But this chapter is followed by another of the same title which uses a general equilibrium analysis consistent with the distribution theory of the book as a whole to demonstrate the ultimate futility of attempting to raise wages and pursue sectional interests.

The Success of the Book

The book was produced in painfully small print. As one of Marshall's contemporaries wrote, 'the attempt... to crowd into a limited space a great amount of matter

---

[2] This point is made explicitly in the preface to the second edition of 1881 (p. vi). However there certainly were some changes between editions. One acknowledgement to Jevons, with regard to capital theory, was added to the second edition (p. 124) and the two 'Laws' (of demand for capital and of supply of capital) on pp. 124–6 of the first edition were removed from the second. In addition there were changes between the two editions on pp. 59 and 62–3 (on peasant proprietorship and Irish tenancy respectively), the first reinforcing the argument and the second modifying the critical tone. In addition the text did not remain completely unchanged after the second edition. The 1888 reprinting refers (p. 64) to 'recent events (1885)', and the material is significantly expanded compared with the first edition reprinted here.

...resulted in the use of a type so small as to try the eyes even of the fortunate possessors of more than average eyesight' (Price, 1892, p. 13). Yet it enjoyed astonishingly successful sales and, according to the bibliography which Mrs Marshall assembled for the Pigou volume *Memorials of Alfred Marshall,* total sales were 15,000 by the time the book was suppressed which, as John Whitaker has pointed out, yielded a total royalty of £312–10s, a sum which may be compared with the £300 which would have been regarded at that date as 'a tolerable annual stipend for a university lecturer' (1975, vol. I, pp. 60–1). The book was published in 1879, and was reprinted ten times in all before it was finally suppressed after the publication of the *Principles* in 1890. It was subsequently replaced by *Elements of the Economics of Industry,* which was largely made up of material taken from the *Principles* to which was added some material on trades unions. Partly because of the stereotyping, the changes between editions are minimal although some were introduced even after the second edition of 1881. But Marshall felt obliged – with his usual excessive sensitivity to criticism – to deal with the complaint (from Cliffe Leslie) that no formal definition of 'free competition' had been given in the text; he did this in the preface to the second edition rather than by alteration in the text.

Given the high sales, it is rather paradoxical that the book itself seems to be rare. Marshall actually took the trouble to seek the withdrawal of copies when the *Principles* was published. Claude Guillebaud recalled that Marshall required Guillebaud's father to return (for destruction) his copy of the book when Marshall sent him a complimentary copy of the first edition of the *Principles* (Guillebaud 1961, II, p. 12n).

In later years Marshall developed a well-marked – even exaggerated – dislike of the book, a dislike which it certainly did not merit. Mary Marshall recalled that

> He never liked the little book for it offended against his belief that 'every dogma that is short and simple is false', and he said about it 'you can't afford to tell the truth for half-a-crown' (1947, p. 22).

Marshall told Seligman that it was a book 'in which truth was economized for the benefit of feeble minds' (Whitaker, 1975, I, p. 80) and elsewhere he referred to it as being 'forcibly simplified for working class readers' (Guillebaud, 1963, II, p. 7). According to Keynes he revolted 'from the thought of Economics as a subject capable of being treated in a light and simple manner for elementary students by half-instructed extension lecturers aided by half-serious books'. Keynes quotes a letter to a Japanese translator in which Marshall said that 'the central doctrines of Economics are not simple and cannot be made so' (Pigou (ed.), 1925, p. 38).

Marshall had had no intention of writing an elementary book and seems to have been drawn into the work on the *Economics of Industry* purely because it was a commitment by the wife he loved. He later regretted that the statement of doctrines in it was not made clear enough. He seems ultimately to have become really touchy about the book; Lionel Robbins told the present writer that, after a lunch at which Edwin Cannan had praised the book, Mary Marshall took him on one side and asked him not to do this as it upset Alfred.

Yet the suppression of the book, and Marshall's later attitude towards it, struck his contemporaries and successors as not only ungenerous but actually harmful.

L. L. Price, reviewing its successor *Elements of the Economics of Industry* in the *Economic Journal* in 1892 regretted the loss of the earlier book 'for, in common no doubt with many others, we date the inauguration of a new era in our economic knowledge to the perusal of the earlier book. We then first began to see what the *Principles of Economics* has since taught us more fully' (1892 in Wood, IV, p. 13). In Keynes's view, Marshall's attitude did

> an injustice to the book. It won high praise from competent judges and was, during the whole of its life, much the best little textbook available. If we are to have an elementary textbook at all, this one was probably, in relation to its contemporaries and predecessors, the best thing of the kind ever done – much better than the primers of Mrs Fawcett or Jevons or any of its many successors. Moreover the latter part of Book III on Trade Combinations, Trade Unions, Trade Disputes and Co-operation was the first satisfactory treatment on modern lines of these important topics (Pigou (ed.), 1925, pp. 38–9).

As a much more recent commentator has noted 'Indeed there were elements of happy expression in the little book which the big one [the *Principles*] somehow lacked' (Robertson (1976) in Wood, vol. I, p. 448). The view that the *Economics of Industry* was better written had also been expressed by a leading economist of an earlier generation. F. W. Taussig said of it that 'Compact tho [sic] it was, it showed the marks of an acute, independent, forward-looking mind.... As a piece of exposition, it has qualities not surpassed, not always maintained, in the later writings; and it remains good to read and to ponder on' (Taussig 1924 in Wood, vol. I, p. 71).

It may well be that an element in Marshall's decision to suppress the book was its attitude towards trades unions which has already been commented on. This has been suggested by a later commentator (Petridis, 1973). But, despite the book's many merits, the elements of inconsistency introduced by the combination of dual authorship and stereotyping was such as to make a perfectionist like Marshall, who polished his *Principles* through eight editions, deeply dissatisfied with the work. Its replacement volume was, itself, a considerable success, running through four editions up to 1913, and this no doubt made it easier to bury the earlier one. According to Mrs Marshall's bibliography, it sold 81,000 copies (Pigou (ed.), 1925, p. 504).

The Intellectual Background to the 'Economics of Industry'

The starting point for the book is undoubtedly the education in economics received at Cambridge by Mary Paley. Overwhelmingly, as she explained in *What I Remember*, this meant J. S. Mill. Indeed the preface to the book says that 'It is an attempt to construct on the lines laid down in Mill's *Political Economy* a theory of Value, Wages and Profits, which shall include the chief results of the work of the present generation of Economists'. This was a general position which was perfectly acceptable to Alfred who had, in the *Fortnightly Review* in April 1876, presented a defence of Mill's theory of value, a defence which is cited (with reference to the journal in which it appeared but not with any acknowledgement of its authorship) in the present book (p. 97). The preface to the second edition (1881) of this book, which shows every sign of coming from the hand of Alfred, makes the statement that 'there is but little in the careful exposition of it [classical theory] given by John Stuart Mill which is not, when properly interpreted, true as far as it goes' (p. v). Mary Paley wrote of her education in economics that

> In those days books were few. There were no blue books or Economic magazines and very few text-books. Mill was the mainstay, with Adam Smith and Ricardo and Malthus in the background. Hearn's *Plutology* was thought well of for beginners. Later we read Jevons' *Principles*, Cairnes' *Leading Principles* and Walker on *Wages* (1947, p. 20).

These influences are evident in the book, and all but Hearn and Cairnes are cited by name. It seems likely also that Mary Paley was responsible for the references to the much underrated Bastiat (though he is also cited in the *Principles*) and to Cliffe Leslie – the latter does not appear in the *Principles* but his influence is particularly evident in the chapter (Book III, chapter iii) 'Local Variations of Prices and Wages. Influence of Custom' which seems to have come from the pen of Mary Paley.

The references to Babbage are consistent with the Millian background while those to Sargant (on saving), acknowledged as an important source for Book I chapter vi, and Holyoake (an important source for the material on co-operation in Book III) are the sort of things that the bright undergraduate Mary Paley would have picked up.

But, much more fundamentally, there is throughout the book a stress on the continuity of the book with classical economics, something which was to be an essential theme of Marshall's own work. This shows not only in the reference to Mill from the second edition preface already quoted but also in the way in which the analysis (as in that of wages in Book II, chapter xi) takes classical themes and develops them. For instance the classical idea of equilibrium wages as those that keep population stable is applied (pp. 131–2) to each sub-group within the labour force.

The stress on continuity in economics, combined with the importance of J. S. Mill's work in Mary Paley's own education in economics, ensured that the influence of J. S. Mill on the text is very much in evidence. The book is in fact Millian in two different ways. Firstly, it reflects Mary Paley's aim to write an up-dated Fawcett-type book for the extra-mural classes. That explains the nature of the quotations from, and references to, Mill (of which more below) and other clear Millian influences such as repeated references (pp. 40, 59, 61, 63) to the merits of peasant proprietorship. Secondly it is Millian because it accurately reflects Marshall's own development as he worked from his 1874 material on economic growth, which Whitaker has republished (Whitaker 1974), towards the *Principles*. Perhaps the most fascinating aspect of this book is, however, the interaction between these two facets – the keen student expositor (Mary Paley) and the original theorist (Alfred). A nice example of this is provided by a statement in Book I chapter iii (pp. 16–17) of Mill's famous fourth proposition on capital which was then qualified by Alfred with material which showed how far beyond Mill he had progressed.

This interaction between the two authors is also reflected in the nature of the citations from Mill (and it should be noted that not all the Mill quotations are listed in the index and there are some unattributed quotations which are in fact from Mill). The straightforward citations from Mill are in the early chapters; of the 19 passages referring to Mill (of which six are indexed) 12 occur in Book I which seems to be Mary Paley's work in origin. The later quotations and references are not only much more scattered but also reflect a rather more distant attitude – for instance Mill is corrected in his analysis of engrossing (p. 183), and a passage on the wage fund from Mill, though not referenced (p. 204) is actually from the famous 'recantation' by Mill, not from the statement of the doctrine itself in Mill's *Principles*. The Mill influences on Book I are substantial – especially on chapter vi 'Growth of Capital'. But where the influence of Alfred predominates, the Mill influences are subject to the process of digestion and reconstruction which Marshall was applying to the whole of economics at that time.

Nowhere is this more dramatically illustrated than in Marshall's mathematical growth system which Whitaker disinterred from the Marshall papers. As he suggests, there is every sign that this system of equations has its origin in Book IV of Mill's *Principles* (1975, vol. II, p. 306). This model employs the concept of net national product (*ibid*. p. 307); and although Marshall was later (1898) to attribute this concept to Thünen, there is clear evidence, both in the growth equations and in the *Economics of Industry* (p. 36), that it originated in Mill. Marshall was later to claim (in 'Distribution and Exchange', *Economic Journal*, 1898) that the distribution theory in the *Economics of Industry* was written under the influence of Thünen and that the Earnings and Interest Fund (national income minus rent) came from the same source. As Whitaker (whose two volumes are an indispensable source for a study of the evolution of Marshall's thought) has noted, there is little in the papers 'to suggest why Marshall came to feel that he had been strongly influenced by Thünen' (1975, vol. II, p. 249) even though in an unpublished manuscript of 1919 Marshall claimed that his debt to Thünen was greater than to any previous writer except Smith and Ricardo.

The *Economics of Industry* is a radical book – this is apparent from the difficulty which some of the classically training American critics had in grappling with its contents. Part of its novelty lies in the repeated insistence on the essential unity of value and distribution. As the preface to the second edition put it

> In this volume an attempt is made...to show that there is a unity underlying all the different parts of the theory of prices, wages and profits (p. v).

This certainly went beyond Mill; and Whitaker's guess (1975, vol. II, pp. 249–50) is that what Marshall really derived from Thünen was 'the perception of the possibility of a symmetrical treatment of capital and labour'. It is this which is referred to in the 1898 article, and it was indeed an important step.

If the influence of Thünen is problematical, that of Jevons is more clear cut. The treatment of demand (Book II, chapter i) follows Jevons not only in defining a market as an area of common price but also in its treatment of marginal ('Final') utility (pp. 67–70. Jevons is acknowledged elsewhere in the book – notably with reference to the suggestion to include consumer goods as part of capital (pp. 99–100) and an acknowledgement in relation to capital theory more generally was added to the second edition (p. 124) – but it is the demand theory where the Jevonian influence is most marked.

It is the distribution theory which is at once novel and radical. The wage fund is firmly rejected. At one point where Mary Paley appears to be straying towards the wage fund, the correcting hand of Alfred descends gently but firmly (p. 17 and note). It is firmly explained in the book that wages are *not* paid out of pre-accumulated capital (p. 203). What in fact the *Economics of Industry* contains is a developed (if sometimes opaquely expressed) marginal productivity theory. As Stigler observed, in the *Economics of Industry* 'Marshall advanced the marginal productivity theory in England for probably the first time since Longfield and Butt wrote' (1941, p. 344). The book contains a complex and subtle distribution theory which is, in all its essentials, the same as that in the *Principles*; yet it is hard not to feel that it must have caused its readers very considerable difficulties. Schumpeter has remarked, even of the *Principles*, that it is only the fully informed reader who understands what Marshall is saying. We now have our understanding of that great book to aid us in the interpretation of the *Economics of Industry*. But one wonders what on earth its early readers can have made of it, even those who were professional economists. What the intended students in extra-mural classes could have made of it is even more difficult to imagine. Yet it became a book which members of the aspiring intelligentsia like Beatrice Webb read (1938, p. 337; 1982, p. 174), though it is difficult to escape the feeling, especially in seeing her later comments on the *Principles*, that she did not understand it very well (1978, pp. 163, 165–6).

But in this she was hardly alone. Taussig, as already noted, thought it a book 'to ponder on'. It contained much of the *Principles*; not only in the distribution theory but also arguments, and even material – such as that about the rich man's and the poor man's shilling which appears both in the *Economics of Industry* (p. 70) and in the *Principles*' discussion of consumer surplus – which Marshall later reused. Guillebaud has drawn attention to some of these overlaps (1963, vol. II, pp. 648–9, 658) dealing with earnings of management and economies of scale. Other instances include the argument (p. 70) that though one individual would not have a continuous demand curve for carpets, the aggregation of individuals would ensure that the market demand curve was continuous; the theory (p. 108) of step by step chain reaction producing labour mobility; the statement (p. 148) that while Ricardo was incorrect to say that cost of production determines value others (such as Jevons, though he is not named) were just as incorrect to make utility alone the basis of value; and the treatment of aggregate demand (pp. 154–7) which is clearly paralleled in the *Principles* (Guillebaud, 1963, vol. I, pp. 709–12). Even the treatment of monopoly (Book III, chapter iv) foreshadows that in the *Principles*.

All this indicates clearly enough the radical nature of the book. The professional economists, at least in England, seem to have appreciated this. Leslie reviewed the book in *The Academy* (8 November, 1879) and drew attention both to the book's radicalism and to the subtle nature of that radicalism.

> The book before us makes greater changes in economic method and doctrine, compared with previous text-books, than might be perceived at first sight; for they are made without sound of trumpet, and for the most part without controversy (1888, pp. 73–4).

Jevons, despite the dig in the book at his one-sided treatment of value (p. 148) is reported by Edgeworth to have praised the book (Pigou (ed.), 1925, p. 66). Indeed Edgeworth himself, it has been suggested (Creedy 1986, pp. 47–9), may well have been influenced by the book's discussion of indeterminacy in wage bargaining; and he clearly saw the link between the little book and the great *Principles* (Pigou (ed.), 1925, p. 41).

It was with the American readers that the book encountered difficulty; and, given that Marshall felt compelled to reply to criticisms by American economists, despite his deep dislike of controversy, this may well have been the deciding factor in souring his attitude towards the little book. While Laughlin, MacVane and Walker all acknowledged the importance of the book, their discussions, especially those of the first two, betrayed a degree of misunderstanding which Marshall must have found very galling. Laughlin (1887) managed to build a criticism of the book on a complete failure to understand its marginal productivity analysis. MacVane's laborious and muddled discussion makes it clear that he also had failed to understand this and that he was completely wedded to a wage fund analysis (see especially, MacVane, 1887, pp. 24 and 35). Marshall replied to these contributions with restraint and admirable clarity (Marshall 1887a, b, 1888). But it was an episode which was probably decisive in his decision to suppress the book once his theories had been fully stated in the *Principles* which he was then nurturing and which appeared in 1890.

The Economics of 'The Economics of Industry'

The book is divided into three separate parts. Book I 'Land, Labour and Capital' (pp. 1–64) is much the most classical, in the sense that the classical material is little different to that in the classical authors themselves and has not been through Alfred Marshall's reconstructive process.

After some interesting material on methodology, reflecting a tradition stemming from Senior and, in particular, Cairnes, succeeding chapters deal with the means of production – land, labour and capital. The material on capital leans, despite inserted qualifications by Alfred, very largely on Mary Paley's reading of J. S. Mill although it introduces one of the persistent (and neglected) themes of this book, human capital. Chapter iv of the first book then introduces the concept of diminishing returns; a marginal statement of this is confused with a proportionate one and there are signs of tensions between the views of the two authors. Chapter v on the growth of population, Malthus and the Poor Laws, is a mainstream orthodox discussion although it stresses some standard Marshallian themes – the 'standard of comfort' (or psychological subsistence level) and the mechanics of poor relief. After the growth of population comes a chapter on the growth of capital which reflects very clearly J. S. Mill's treatment of the same topic; willingness to save depends on foresight, family affection, ambition, habits of thrift, and security as well as on the rate of interest, with the judgement that, despite Sargant ('target saving') effects (p. 41), the interest elasticity of saving is, on balance, positive. Chapter vii then deals with the organization of industry; organization is not here treated as a separate factor of production. Chapter viii 'Division of

Labour' is conventional material and in this chapter, as indeed throughout the book, there is a persistent confusion in treating 'Increasing Returns' (which is really a proposition about scale) and 'Decreasing Returns' (which is a proposition about factor productivity) as if they were of the same kind. Chapter ix on the 'Tenure of Land' is notable mainly for its borrowings from Mill and for its enthusiasm about peasant proprietorship.

The meat of the book, and by far the most interesting part analytically, is Book II dealing with 'Normal Value'. In this we have the maximising model as giving rise to 'normal' results; and the competitive model which is at the centre of the *Economics of Industry* is the core of this Book. The treatment is essentially a verbal exposition of general equilibrium, with mutual determination (the parallel with balls in a bowl which was to appear later in the *Principles* makes its appearance) and with economic actors pursuing enlightened (and Marshall was insistent upon that) self-interest.

Book II begins with demand. We have the concept of the negatively sloped demand curve with, for each individual, price equal to marginal utility. Chapter ii then deals with supply, with supply prices being equal to expenses of production. The expenses of production include the opportunity costs of factors and boil down to 'efforts and abstinences'. Efforts involve the supply of skilled, unskilled and managerial labour while abstinence regulates the supply of capital. Competitive behaviour leads to a positive relationship between quantities supplied and price, while the coupling of this with a negative relationship between quantity demanded and price leads to market clearing. Normal

Value is that existing at market clearing, with negative feedback to ensure that market price tends towards the long-run equilibrium price.

Chapter iii then discusses rent, and introduces the idea of rent as the area under the marginal product curve less the marginal product of capital multiplied by the amount of capital employed.

> The Law of Rent then is:– If a farmer applies as much capital to his land as he profitably can, his rent is what remains after deducting from his total produce the return to his last dose multiplied by the number of doses he applies (p. 83).

Though rent is generalized to include rent of ability, and account is also taken of the classical debate over the effect of improvements on rent, the key interest in the chapter centres on the marginal productivity approach to rent. But then chapter iv perpetuates a classical confusion, which was carried over into the *Principles*, over whether or not rent enters into price. The message which comes over clearly is that rent is price-determined not price-determining, but there is a fleeting recognition (p. 90) of the fact that, because land has transfer earnings in different uses, the cost of land-use enters into the expenses of producing any particular product. The discussion then reverts to the influence of demand on value, in chapter v, and here we find not only the usual problem over increasing and decreasing returns but also the elementary mistake that the supply of Old Masters is of zero price elasticity. (As Wicksteed pointed out (1910, p. 506) it depends on the sellers' own demand curve.) However the main point of the chapter is to indicate that market price fluctuates around the long run normal price.

In chapter vi, however, the analysis becomes more sophisticated. This chapter 'Distribution' introduces the concept of net national income made up of earnings, interest, rent and taxes, deducts the last two items and ends up with a 'Wages and Profits Fund'. The problem of distribution is then the problem of dividing the wages and profit fund. However this can be simplified. Earnings of management can be classified with wages, and the division is now that of the Earnings-and-Interest Fund. The remainder of Book II is then devoted to explaining the division of this fund on the basis of factor valuation: the factor valuation itself depends upon the supply of factors and on the demand for them which in turn depends upon their marginal revenue product.

Chapter vii begins this process by analysing the supply of unskilled labour, and using the classical inheritance of equalization of net advantage; and chapter viii then follows this with a discussion of the supply of skilled labour with, as throughout the book, an emphasis upon human capital. It is in this treatment that the Marshallian concept of step-by-step labour mobility makes its appearance – the movement of skilled labour into an *adjacent* occupation is what provides responsiveness of labour supply. Parents take decisions about investing in the human capital of their children; but they have limited access to capital, they do not reap the benefit of the investment, and 'the rate of interest at which parents discount future advantages to their sons increases with the narrowness of their own education and the pressures of immediate want' (pp. 112–113). Government must thus become involved in education, and will gain from the resulting rise in GNP precisely in proportion to its own share of GNP through taxation. Chapter ix, in contrast to the earlier discussion, now treats business power much more in line with the treatment in the *Principles*, distinguishing (p. 117) the supply of this from the supply of skilled labour.

The discussion in chapter x then moves on to the question of interest. This depends upon the supply of capital and the demand for capital, reflecting, principally, its marginal productivity although there is also a demand for consumption loans. Market clearing of the capital market ensures the establishment of a Normal Rate of Interest which is estimated (p. 126) at four per cent. Chapter xi deals with wages, with the demand for labour dependent upon its marginal productivity. As a first approximation, the argument is advanced (p. 133) that wages tend to be equal to the discounted value of marginal product, an argument rapidly qualified by reference to such matters as cross-partial derivatives of the production function (to put the matter in more modern terms), although the suspicion remains that it had not been properly worked out. Chapter xii then deals with earnings of management which are determined in the same way as those of skilled labour, with the difference – in effect fundamental – that managers have to have control of, or access to, capital. The role of capital considerably alters the picture; those working with borrowed capital may accept lower earnings of management (pp. 136–7) while a high ratio of fixed to variable capital is also likely to bring about lower earnings of management. These lower earnings fall below 'Normal' values; exceptional entrepreneurs, on the other hand, can earn rent of ability. The Normal level of profits can be expected to fall over time; interest rates will fall over time with the exhaustion of investment opportunities, while earnings of management will fall over time because of an increased supply of managers.

Book II concludes with a chapter 'Relation of Normal to Market Value' which provides a summary of the distribution theory before restating the proposition that market values fluctuate around the long run equilibrium values. This chapter is however designed to provide a lead into Book III which carries the title 'Market Value'. The first two chapters of this Book deal with market fluctuations. The first of them, 'Changes in the Purchasing Power of Money', is Marshall's fullest statement of macroeconomics (apart from official evidence) until *Money, Credit and Commerce* appeared in the penultimate year of his life. As such this chapter is full of interest in its discussion of the trade cycle and of aggregate demand. Chapter ii 'Market Fluctuations' then deals with fluctuations in the markets for particular commodities, but takes the opportunity to restate the basic model in which Normal Value is a long-run equilibrium value, with changes in output around the equilibrium altering the marginal supply price.

Thus we see how the Law that Normal value is determined by Normal Expenses of production is consistent with the fact that market fluctuations of value are the cause and not the consequences of market fluctuations of Expenses of production. If Ricardo and Mill had taken more pains to make clear the distinctions between the theory of Normal value and that of Market value, there could not have been as much controversy as there has been on the question whether value is governed by Expenses of production, or Expenses of production by value (pp. 166–167).

Chapter iii of the final book then deals with 'Local Variations of Prices and Wages' and contains some excellent economic analysis. It bears the signs of having been written, initially at least, by Mary Paley. It is then followed by a chapter 'Monopolies. Combinations' which deals with positions of *producer* market power. While this foreshadows the treatment in the *Principles*, particularly in its discussion of monopoly profit maximization and also (p. 181) of imperfect competition ('partial monopoly'), there is also a good deal of perceptively handled institutional material.

The discussion then passes to the matter of *labour* market power in chapter v. This contains the friendly, not to say romantic, material already referred to. It is followed by chapter vi which deals with the influence of trades unions on wages and which appears to have been written by Mary Paley with corrections (and at one point – p. 201 – a flat contradiction) by Alfred. The chapter is distinctly sympathetic towards the aspirations of trades unions to raise wages. But it is then followed by chapter vii on the same subject which appears to have been written by Alfred and which seeks to minimize the power of trades unions to affect wages. The book concludes with a chapter on arbitration and conciliation and one on co-operation. That on arbitration appears to have been written by Mary Paley and contains straightforward, if optimistic, material while that on co-operation also appears to have come from her pen despite the fact that this was one of Alfred's life-long interests.

Conclusion

At the end of a detailed reading of the *Economics of Industry* it is hard to escape the feeling that this is a flawed, though deeply interesting, book. The tensions between the two authors' treatments are never fully resolved. In part – probably a major part – this is undoubtedly due to the strait-jacket imposed by stereotyping to which the preface to the second edition refers. But the difficulties run deeper than that. Even the order of the chapters is a little odd – certainly when compared with the architectural structure of the *Principles* – and the book is full of 'Laws', a concept from which the *Principles* shows a marked retreat. Thus we have 'Laws' of the increase of the produce of land ('diminishing returns'), of the increase of labour, and of the increase of capital (p. 36); of the equalization of profit rates adjusted for net advantages (p. 48); of division of labour and of 'increasing returns' (p. 57); of demand (pp. 65, 71); of Normal Value (pp. 77–8, 93); of Demand for, and Supply of, Capital (pp. 124–6 – these were omitted from the second edition); of the Normal Rate of Interest (p. 126); of Normal Wages (p. 131); of Increasing Returns (pp. 141–2); and of Normal Earnings of Management (p. 143).

Virtually all of these 'Laws' simply amount to propositions about which functions are of positive slope and which of negative, or to statements about competitive market clearing. While they lend a spurious scientism to the text, they also, because of their actual content, reflect the competitive maximizing marginalist model which is at the centre of the book and they are of interest for this reason. It is however unfortunate that this competitive marginalist maximizing model was not fully worked out. For there really is no justification for applying a supply-and-demand marginal-product analysis to labour and capital in order to divide an 'Earnings and Interest' fund while at the same time putting rent and the earnings of land to one side. This is a classical hangover which certainly cannot be justified in terms of the analytical apparatus in the book, particularly as marginal productivity is applied to the rent analysis. It is moreover a classical hangover which cannot be blamed on Mary Paley; it continued to dog Marshall in his writing of the *Principles* although the treatment is more symmetrical there.

But for all these difficulties the *Economics of Industry* remains a book of outstanding interest. If it is true as George Stigler (1962) remarked – and it is certainly a view to which I would subscribe – that Marshall's *Principles* is the second greatest book in economics (after the *Wealth of Nations*), then this little book is a fascinating insight into the way in which his thought evolved on the way to the *Principles*. By 1879 he had made enormous strides in developing a general equilibrium marginalist model which was capable of providing significant insights by freezing some of the variables and employing partial equilibrium analysis. The latter was to receive more emphasis in the *Principles*; but it is the *Economics of Industry* which shows us how Marshall had, starting from the work of J. S. Mill, developed a fully modern model of the economy.

Denis O'Brien
University of Durham, 1994

BIBLIOGRAPHY

Becattini, G. (1987) 'Marshall, Mary Paley (1850-1944)', pp. 363–4 in J. Eatwell, M. Milgate, P. Newman (eds.), *The New Palgrave*, London: Macmillan.

Clough, B. A. and Strachey, J. P. (1944) 'Mrs Alfred Marshall (Mary Paley) 1850–1944', *The Cambridge Review*, 6 May, p. 300.

Creedy, J. (1986) *Edgeworth and the Development of Neoclassical Economics*, Oxford: Blackwell.

Constable, W.G. (1960) 'Art and Economics in Cambridge', *Eagle*, (April), pp. 23–26.

Groenewegen, P. (1993) 'A Weird and Wonderful Partnership. Mary Paley and Alfred Marshall 1877–1924', *History of Economic Ideas*, I, pp. 71–109.

Guillebaud, C.W. (1960) 'Mary Paley Marshall', *Eagle* (April), pp. 27–8.

Guillebaud, C.W. (ed.) (1961) *Alfred Marshall. Principles of Economics*. 9th (Variorum) Edition. 2 vols. London: Macmillan for the Royal Economic Society.

Keynes, J.M. (1944) 'Mary Paley Marshall (1850–1944)', *Economic Journal*, 54, pp. 268–284.

Laughlin, J. Lawrence (1887a) 'Marshall's Theory of Value and Distribution', *Quarterly Journal of Economics*, I, pp. 227–232.

Laughlin, J. Lawrence (1887b) Reply to Marshall 1887a (no title), *Quarterly Journal of Economics*, I, pp. 361-362.

Leslie, T. E. Cliffe (1888) *Essays in Political Economy*, 2nd ed., London: Longmans.

MacVane, S. (1887) 'The Theory of Business Profits', *Quarterly Journal of Economics*, II, pp. 1–36.

MacVane, S. (1888) 'Business Profits and Wages; A Rejoinder', *Quarterly Journal of Economics*, II, pp. 453–468.

Marshall, A. (1887a) 'Note by Professor Marshall', *Quarterly Journal of Economics*, I. pp. 359–361.

Marshall, A. (1887b) 'The Theory of Business Profits', *Quarterly Journal of Economics*, Vol. I, pp. 477–481.

Marshall, A. (1888) 'Wages and Profits' *Quarterly Journal of Economics,* Vol. II, pp. 218–223.

Marshall, A. (1890) *Principles of Economics*, London: Macmillan.

Marshall, A. (1892) *Elements of the Economics of Industry,* London: Macmillan.

Marshall, A. (1898) 'Distribution and Exchange', *Economic Journal*, 8, pp. 37–59.

Marshall, A. (1923) *Money, Credit and Commerce,* London: Macmillan.

Marshall, Mary Paley (1895) Review of M. Wettstein-Adelt *Viertehalb Monate Fabrikarbeiterin* (Berlin: Deutsche Schriftsteller Genossenschaft), *Economic Journal*, 5, pp. 401–4.

Marshall, Mary Paley (1896) 'Conference of Women Workers', *Economic Journal*, 6, pp. 107–109.

Marshall, Mary Paley, (1902) Review of C. Collet *Educated Working Women* (London: King), *Economic Journal*, 12, pp. 252–257.

Marshall, Mary Paley (1947), *What I Remember*, Cambridge: Cambridge University Press.

Mill, J. S. (1869) 'Thornton on Labour and Its Claims', *Fortnightly Review*, May 1869 reprinted pp. 632-668 in *Essays on Economics and Society* ed. J. M. Robson, Toronto: University of Toronto Press, 1967, *Collected Works of John Stuart Mill*, Vol. V.

Petridis, A. (1973) 'Alfred Marshall's Attitudes to and Economic Analysis of Trade Unions: A Case of Anomalies in a Competitive System', *History of Political Economy*, 5, pp. 165–98.

Pigou, A.C. (ed.) (1925) *Memorials of Alfred Marshall*, London: Macmillan.

Price, L. L. (1892) Review of A. Marshall *Elements of the Economics of Industry, Economic Journal*, II, pp. 316–20, repr. in Wood (1982), Vol. IV, pp. 11–16.

Robbins, L. (1970) *The Evolution of Modern Economic Theory*, London: Macmillan.

Robertson, H. M. (1976) 'Alfred Marshall' reprinted in Wood (1982), Vol. I, pp. 442–452.

Robinson, E.A.G. (1948) Review of Mary Paley Marshall *What I Remember* (Cambridge: Cambridge University Press) *Economic Journal*, 58, pp. 122–124.

Skidelsky, R. (1992) *John Maynard Keynes. The Economist as Saviour 1920–1937*, London: Macmillan.

Stigler, G.J. (1941) *Production and Distribution Theories*, New York: Macmillan.

Stigler, G.J. (1962) 'Marshall's *Principles* after Guillebaud', *Journal of Political Economy,* 70, (1962), pp. 282–286.

Taussig, F.W. (1924) 'Alfred Marshall' *Quarterly Journal of Economics,* 39, pp. 1–14, repr. in Wood (1982), Vol. I, pp. 71–9.

Walker, F.A. (1887) 'The Source of Business Profits', *Quarterly Journal of Economics,* Vol. I, pp. 265–288.

Webb, B (1938) *My Apprenticeship*, London: Pelican.

Webb, B. and Webb, S. (1978) *The Letters of Sidney and Beatrice Webb* ed. N. MacKenzie, Cambridge: Cambridge University Press.

Webb, B. (1982) *The Diary of Beatrice Webb*, Vol. I, 1873–1892, ed. N. & J. MacKenzie, London: Virago.

Webb, B. (1983) *The Diary of Beatrice Webb*, Vol. II, 1892–1905, ed. N. & J. MacKenzie, London: Virago.

Whitaker, J. K. (1972) 'Alfred Marshall: The Years 1877 to 1885', *History of Political Economy,* Vol. 4, pp. 1–61, reprinted in Wood, Vol. I, pp. 98–147.

Whitaker, J.K. (1974) 'The Marshallian System in 1881: Distribution and Growth', *Economic Journal,* 84, pp. 1–17.

Whitaker, J.K. (ed.) (1975) *The Early Economic Writings of Alfred Marshall, 1867–1890,* New York: Free Press, 1975.

Wicksteed, P. H. (1910) *The Common Sense of Political Economy,* ed. L. Robbins, London: Routledge, 1933, repr. 1949.

Wood, J. Cunningham (ed.) (1982) *Alfred Marshall. Critical Assessments*, 4 vols., London: Croom Helm.

THE
ECONOMICS OF INDUSTRY

BY

ALFRED MARSHALL,

PRINCIPAL OF UNIVERSITY COLLEGE, BRISTOL;
LATE FELLOW OF ST JOHN'S COLLEGE, CAMBRIDGE;

AND

MARY PALEY MARSHALL,

LATE LECTURER AT NEWNHAM HALL, CAMBRIDGE.

London:
MACMILLAN AND CO.
1879

[The Right of Translation is reserved.]

PREFACE.

THIS book was undertaken at the request of a meeting of Cambridge University Extension lecturers, and is designed to meet a want which they have felt.

It is an attempt to construct on the lines laid down in Mill's *Political Economy* a theory of Value, Wages and Profits, which shall include the chief results of the work of the present generation of Economists. The main outlines of this theory have been tested during many years in lectures at Cambridge, and more recently at Bristol.

An inquiry into the subjects of Banking, Foreign Trade and Taxation is deferred to a companion volume on the "Economics of Trade and Finance."

The authors wish to acknowledge their obligations to Mr H. Sidgwick, Mr H. S. Foxwell and the Rev. W. Moore Ede for suggestions and aid in preparing the book for the press.

CONTENTS.

BOOK II.

NORMAL VALUE.

CHAPTER I. DEFINITIONS. LAW OF DEMAND.

CHAPTER II. LAW OF SUPPLY.

CHAPTER III. RENT.

CHAPTER IV. RENT IN RELATION TO VALUE.

CHAPTER X. INTEREST.

CHAPTER XI. WAGES.

CHAPTER XII. EARNINGS OF MANAGEMENT.

CHAPTER XIII. RELATION OF NORMAL TO MARKET VALUE.

BOOK III.

MARKET VALUE.

CHAPTER I. CHANGES IN THE PURCHASING POWER OF MONEY.

CHAPTER II. MARKET FLUCTUATIONS.

CHAPTER III. INFLUENCE OF CUSTOM. LOCAL VARIATIONS OF PRICES AND WAGES.

CHAPTER IV. MONOPOLIES. COMBINATIONS.

CHAPTER V. TRADES UNIONS.

CHAPTER VI. INFLUENCE OF TRADES UNIONS ON WAGES.

CHAPTER VII. INFLUENCE OF TRADES UNIONS ON WAGES (CONTINUED).

CHAPTER VIII. ARBITRATION AND CONCILIATION.

CHAPTER IX. CO-OPERATION.

*_** A few discussions are included in square brackets
to show that they should be omitted by beginners in the
first time of reading. Words used in a technical sense are
printed with capital initial letters.

BOOK I.

LAND, LABOUR, AND CAPITAL.

CHAPTER I.

INTRODUCTORY.

§ 1. "Rousseau has said, 'Much philosophy is wanted for the correct observation of things which are before our eyes.' And such are the events and customs of every day social life. Habit has so familiarized us with them that we fail to observe them, unless something striking and exceptional forces them on our notice.

"Let us take, by way of illustration, a man in the humble walks of life—a village carpenter, for instance—and observe the various services he renders to society, and receives from it; we shall not fail to be struck with the enormous disproportion between them.

"This man employs his day's labour in planing boards, and making tables and chests of drawers. What does he receive from society in exchange for his work?

"First of all, on getting up in the morning, he dresses himself; but he has himself made none of his clothing. In order to put at his disposal this clothing, simple as it is, an enormous amount of labour, and many ingenious inventions, must have been employed. Americans must have produced cotton, Indians indigo, Englishmen wool and flax, Brazilians hides; and all these materials must have been transported to various towns where they have been worked up, spun, woven, dyed, etc.

"He sends his son to school, and the simple teaching which is given there, is itself due to the work of many thousand minds.

"If he undertakes a journey, he finds that, in order to save him time and exertion, other men have removed and levelled up the soil, filled up valleys, hewed down mountains, united the banks of rivers, and brought the power of steam into subjection to human wants.

"It is impossible not to be struck with the measureless disproportion which exists between the enjoyments which this man derives from society, and what he could obtain by his own unassisted exertions. The social mechanism then must be very ingenious and very powerful, since it leads to this singular result, that each man, even he whose lot is cast in the humblest condition, obtains things every day which he could not himself produce in many ages.

"The study of that mechanism is the business of Political Economy[1]."

In other words, we may say that Political Economy examines the Production, the Distribution and the Consumption of wealth. It seeks for the causes which determine wages, profits, and rent; it inquires how far these causes are fixed by unchangeable natural laws, and how far they can be modified by human effort. Last, but not least, it traces the connexion that there is between the character of the workman and the character of his work. "As a man thinketh, so is he"; as the work is, so is the worker; as the worker is, so is the work.

The nation used to be called "the Body Politic." So long as this phrase was in common use, men thought of the interests of the whole nation when they used the word "Political"; and then "Political Economy" served well enough as a name for the science. But now "political interests" generally mean the interests of only some part or parts of the nation; so that it seems best to drop the name "Political Economy," and to speak simply of **Economic Science**, or more shortly, **Economics**.

The present volume is called The Economics of Industry because it treats of the affairs of producers, both employers and workmen. The discussion of banking, foreign trade and finance is deferred to the companion volume.

§ 2. Economics is a science because it collects, arranges, and reasons about one particular class of facts. A science brings together a great number of similar facts and finds that they are special cases of some great Uniformity which exists in nature. It describes this Uniformity in a simple and definite statement, or Law.

---

[1] Bastiat's *Harmonies of Political Economy.*

A Law of Science states that a certain result will be produced whenever a certain set of causes are present[1].

[2]Science traces the connexion between different Laws, often
shewing that some of them are explained by, or contained in
others. It reasons from these Laws, applying them to new
cases of gradually increasing difficulty, and finds out the conclusions to which they point. It then inquires how far these
conclusions are consistent with observation, so as to verify its
work. If necessary, it goes back to its original Laws, and
corrects, or modifies or adds to them, so as to make them
represent Nature more truly. Thus gradually science becomes
able to predict future events with increasing confidence and
accuracy[3].

But this is all that a science can do; it cannot claim to be a
guide in life, or to lay down rules for the practical conduct of
affairs. That is the task of what in old times used to be called
an Art. An Art considers some important practical end, and
directs men in their efforts to obtain it. First it inquires generally into the various conditions of the case. Then taking one
of them at a time it seeks out the science whose special business
it is to answer questions relating to this particular class of conditions, and demands of this science an answer to a question,
which bears directly on the end in view. Having collected such
answers from many sciences, Art puts them together; and says,
Since we are told by the sciences that such and such effects
will follow from such and such causes, therefore it is best to
pursue such and such a course: this course will, all things
being considered, lead us up to, or near to, our desired end, so
as to cause as much good and as little evil as possible.

Thus the railway engineer is a man who devotes himself
to the Art of making railways: and when it is decided that a
railway is to be made from one town to another, he consults
Geology and other sciences and obtains their answers to certain
definite questions before he decides which route to adopt.

[1] It is unfortunate that the word Law is used in this sense, and also
in the sense of a command by authority. The law which speaks in the
Indicative mood, and says, A is a cause of B, is as different in character from a Law which speaks in the Imperative mood, and says "Do this,
Avoid that," as a bat that flies is from a bat that is used at cricket.

[2] Beginners should omit all passages contained in square brackets.

[3] Science, when obtaining new Laws, is said to be Inductive; when
reasoning from them and finding how they are connected with one another, it is said to be Deductive; its third task, that of Verification, has just
been described. There has been a controversy as to whether Economics
is an Inductive or a Deductive Science. It is both: its Inductions continually suggest new Deductions; its Deductions continually suggest new
Inductions.

But the statesman or the financier who decides that these two towns are to be connected by a railway is a man of Art in a yet broader sense of the term.   For he has to consider not only what it will cost to make the railway but also what nett profit it will bring in, and perhaps what will be its indirect political, social and moral effects.   In doing this he has to make many inquiries of Economics; for this science examines the laws that determine the growth of trade in particular channels, and the cost of making and working the railway.

Economics then cannot by itself be a guide in the practical affairs of life; but it answers a number of difficult questions which must be asked of it by the statesman, the man of business, and the philanthropist.   Economics is to be classed with the Moral or Social Sciences; because it deals only incidentally with inanimate things.   Its main purpose is to seek for the moral and social Laws by which men's conduct is determined in the every day work of their lives: the motives which cause them to seek one trade and occupation rather than another, and which govern their behaviour to others with whom their trade brings them into contact.   Economics investigates the causes which determine the work of a man's daily life, the manner in which he spends his income, and the influence which his work exerts on his character.

§ 3.   Social sciences have made slower progress than physical sciences.   One reason of this is that men have only recently begun to apply to social sciences those methods of classification, and that systematic study of each class of truths, which have been so successful in the physical sciences. But now that men have set themselves to study each separate group of social facts by itself, these sciences too are beginning to advance steadily.

In any history of the physical sciences we may read how men failed to make rapid progress so long as they persisted in the vain attempt to discover some simple explanation of all the various natural phenomena.   The ancients used to be continually starting new theories for the explanation of the universe, which succeeding ages had to cast away.   As time went on, men learnt that they must separate the study of inorganic life from that of organic, the study of chemistry from that of mechanics, and so on.   And when men had thus begun to concentrate their attention on one particular class of natural phenomena at a time, to trace by careful and steady work their Laws, they made solid progress.   Of course they seldom obtained results that were completely true.   But the new results were always nearer the truth than those which they displaced, so that each generation started from a more advantageous position than its predecessors; and thus by gradual steps man has obtained a command over nature similar to that which fancy used to attribute to the fairy or the magician.

At the same time it is true that in the Moral Sciences, even more than the physical, a man who confines himself entirely to one narrow branch of inquiry is not likely to make good progress in it. The economist should know something of the history of manners and customs and laws, and of the principles of mental, moral, legal and political science. He must avoid the error of regarding "the present experience of mankind as of universal validity, mistaking temporary or local phases of human character for human nature itself, having no faith in the wonderful pliability of the human mind; deeming it impossible in spite of the strongest evidence that the earth can produce human beings of a different type from that which is familiar to him in their own age and even perhaps in his own country. The only security against this narrowness is a liberal mental cultivation... A person is not likely to be a good economist who is nothing else. Social phenomena acting and reacting on one another, they cannot rightly be understood apart; but this by no means proves that the material and industrial phenomena of society are not themselves susceptible of useful generalisations, but only that these generalisations must necessarily be relative to a given form of civilisation and a given stage of social advancement[1]."

Thus the economist must pause sometimes to consider the connexion between that element of well-being with which he is chiefly concerned, and the other elements; for it is only by this means that he can ascertain the real significance of his own results, and can learn in what direction it is most important to extend his inquiries.]

§ 4. This account of Economic science may be summed up in the following definitions:

> Those portions of human conduct which are directed towards the acquirement of material wealth, and those conditions of human well-being which directly depend on material wealth, are called **Economic**.
>
> **The Science of Economics** collects, examines, arranges and reasons about the facts which are connected with the economic habits and conditions of well-being in various countries at various times.

§ 5. The subject-matter of Economics is Wealth. But there is some difficulty in ascertaining the meaning of this word.

Wealth must be distinguished from well-being.

All things which are useful or pleasurable are elements of Well-being, whether they are material things, or human faculties and capacities for enjoyment.

---

[1] Mill, *On Comte*, pp. 81—83.

But though some of these human qualities should not be included under the term wealth ; yet this term should not be confined to those things which can be bought and sold in the market. For in estimating the wealth of a country every one would include the market-value of the power of work possessed by a cart-horse or a slave. And it seems unreasonable to exclude that of a free man simply because he cannot be sold, and so has no market-price.

But we want some term which will fitly describe such things as are capable of being exchanged and of having their value definitely measured; and we find such a term in "Material Wealth."

> **Wealth** then may be said to consist of Material wealth and Personal or non-material wealth.

> **Material Wealth** consists of the material sources of enjoyment which are capable of being appropriated and therefore of being exchanged.

Thus it includes not only commodities (or things the possession of which can give enjoyment directly), but also machinery and other things which are made or appropriated in order to aid man in producing commodities.

> **"Personal"** or **"non-material wealth"** consists of those human energies faculties and habits, physical mental and moral, which directly contribute to making men industrially efficient, and which therefore increase their power of producing material wealth.

Thus manual skill, intelligence, and honesty may be included in the personal wealth of a country.

> All other human faculties and qualities which it is an advantage to have, and all other sources of enjoyment, are elements in the well-being of a man, but are not included under the term wealth.

Thus the power of appreciating and deriving pleasure from music is an element of well-being, but it is not called wealth ; because generally speaking it does not make men's work efficient in the production of material wealth.

§ 6. The term Productive has been used by Economists in many senses, and has caused much misunderstanding. It seems best that Productive when used simply as a technical term should mean productive of wealth.

> Labour is **Productive** when it produces wealth, whether Personal or Material.

But whenever there is any room for doubt, mention will be made of the particular kind of thing which is produced. Thus it may be said that labour is "productive of wealth," or to anticipate the use of terms which will soon be defined, "productive of capital," or "productive of wage-capital," etc.

Productive labour cannot generally be divided off by a clearly defined line from Unproductive. A minister of religion is often classed as an Unproductive labourer, but if by exerting moral influence he makes labourers more sober, honest and efficient, he is so far productive of Personal wealth. Again, since some recreation is necessary for the highest efficiency of labour, it is quite possible that a musician may indirectly increase the wealth of a nation, and be indirectly Productive.

The word Productive is often applied not only to labour, but also to consumption. This is indeed somewhat inaccurate, for it is labour that produces; and consumption can have no further claim to being productive than that it supports the labour which is productive.

CHAPTER II.

AGENTS OF PRODUCTION.

§ 1.   MAN when producing wealth acts upon the things which Nature supplies. The gifts of Nature to man are firstly materials such as iron, stone, wood, etc., and secondly, forces such as the power of the wind, and the heat of the sun, the source whence all other powers are derived.

All that man's hands can do is to move things. A carpenter for instance takes some planks, cuts them up and fits them together in the form of a box; he does not in the strict sense of the word make, or create; he only arranges. "If we examine any case of what is called the action of man or nature we shall find" that it consists merely in "putting things into fit places for being acted upon by their internal forces and by those residing in other natural objects. . . man only moves one thing to or from another. He moves a seed into the ground; and the natural forces of vegetation produce in succession a root, a stem, leaves, flowers and fruit. He moves a spark to fuel and it ignites, and by the force generated in combustion it cooks the food, melts or softens the iron, converts into beer or sugar the malt or cane juice, which he has previously moved to the spot. He has no other means of acting upon matter than by moving it. Motion or resistance to motion are the only things which his muscles are constructed for[1]."

Since then production does not mean creation but only re-arrangement, it is a mistake to suppose, as some have done, that the work of those who carry or sell goods cannot be Productive. The carpenter who makes a box, takes certain boards from an arrangement in which they were of little use, and puts them together in an arrangement in which they are of greater use.

---

[1] Mill, *Principles of Political Economy*, Book I. chap. I, § 2.

So the carrier or the trader takes the box from the manu-factory where it is made, and where it is of little use, and delivers it to the purchaser. It is true that the carrier and the trader make no permanent change in the form of the box; but that does not prevent them from being Productive, for they as well as the carpenter contribute to render the material which is provided by nature more useful to man.

§ 2. As civilisation advances the relative importance of mental to manual labour changes. Every year mental labour becomes more important, and manual labour less important. With every fresh invention of machinery work is transferred from the muscles, or vital force, to natural force. Even with the imperfect machinery we now have, one pound of coal will raise a hundred pounds twelve thousand feet high; and the daily work of a man cannot exceed this even if we make him a mere working machine, and obtain instead of a man's life so much pulling and pushing, and hewing and hammering. With an ordinary tide, the water rushing in and out of a reservoir of a mile in area, even if three-fourths of its force were wasted through imperfections of machinery, would do as much work in a day as the muscles of a hundred thousand men.

§ 3. The agents of production are then Nature's forces, and Man's force; man's force being generally most efficient when it is so applied as to control and direct nature's forces, rather than to counteract them. And the wealth of a country depends upon the manner in which nature's forces and man's force work together in the production of wealth.

Let us first regard the wealth of a country in so far as it depends on the liberality of nature. This consists not only in her gifts of fertile land and rich mines, but also in a convenient arrangement of her gifts. Before the invention of railways, a district could not have a prosperous trade unless it had easy means of communication by river or by sea. Iron mines are of comparatively little value if there is no coal near them. England's present position in the world is in a great measure due to the fact that she not only has coal mines and iron mines, but also her coal and iron mines are near together.

In the course of generations man works on the face of nature, and improves her gifts, or wastes them. The patient industry of the Dutch has turned their barren sands into fertile meadows; while the wasteful carelessness of the slave-owning cotton-planters of Southern America has turned some of the richest districts of the world into a wilderness.

§ 4. Turning next to the efficiency of man's labour in pro-duction, we may classify the conditions on which it depends as (i) his physical strength and energy, (ii) his knowledge and mental ability, and (iii) his moral character.

Firstly, with regard to man's physical strength and energy. While man is altering the face of nature, nature is ever changing the quality of man. A healthy invigorating climate is one of the most important of the gifts that nature bestows. Extreme heat enervates man; and in tropical countries makes him lend a ready ear to the suggestion that he should live in idleness on the fruits that nature showers down upon him. In many places even in the temperate zones work is almost entirely suspended during the extreme heats of summer. And in some parts of America men are not only prone to take a holiday during "the heated term," but are also prevented from doing such work as that of carpenters in the open air during the extreme severity of winter. England is fortunate in having a climate in which men can work with vigour out of doors almost all the year round; and which, by thus fostering energetic and steady habits of labour, contributes much to her greatness.

The physical power and energy of man is of course partly dependent upon inherited race-qualities. But modern science shews that the character of a race may be greatly modified by changes in its habits of living, in diet, in cleanliness, in houseroom, etc. Thus the physical vigour of a race depends partly on its wealth. To him that hath, to him is given.

It must be remembered that the average efficiency of labour in a country depends not only on the efficiency of the labourer in the prime of life, but also on the number of years during which he is really efficient. It is better even as regards material wealth that a man should work with moderate energy up to the age of sixty, than that he should overwork himself so as to become an old man at forty.

§ 5.   Next with regard to knowledge and mental ability.

It has already been remarked that the skill and intelligence which are required for commanding and directing the forces of nature are growing in importance relatively to the brute strength by which uncivilised races struggle with nature. Indeed a thorough general education, together with a special training for some particular employment, is becoming more necessary to the working man every year. There is scarcely any work which does not need some mental effort. Even in agriculture machinery is being introduced, the management of which requires much skill and intelligence.

A man does work that does not need skill all the better if he knows more than is actually required for him. Education makes him quick to understand whatever directions may be given to him : if his machinery gets out of order, or the plan of his work miscarries in any other way, he can set things to right at once and thus prevent much loss. In this and

other ways, every increase in the intelligence of the workman diminishes the amount of supervision required from the
employer and his foremen.   And as civilisation advances,
further progress becomes more and more dependent upon
the diffusion of education among the working classes.

This education may be classed as *general* and *technical*.
As Mill says, "the aim of all intellectual training for the
mass of the people, should be to cultivate common sense, to
qualify them for forming a sound practical judgment of the
circumstances by which they are surrounded.   Whatever in the
intellectual department can be superadded to this is chiefly
ornamental; while this is the indispensable groundwork on
which education must rest.   An education directed to diffuse
good sense among the people, with such knowledge as would
qualify them to judge of the tendencies of their actions, would
be certain, even without any direct inculcation, to raise up a
public opinion by which intemperance and improvidence of every
kind would be held discreditable."

General education should then aim at causing a man to form
an intelligent opinion with regard to the ordinary matters of life,
and to be full of resources for meeting new emergencies.

Technical education should aim at enabling him to understand the processes and the machinery of the special work in
which he is engaged.   It should help him to understand the
reason of everything that goes on in his trade, and thus enable
him to accommodate himself to new machinery or new modes of
production.   And it should train him in the use of his fingers.
This technical education should be begun at school, but a
great deal of the education that is wanted in many trades can
only be got in workshops.

§ 6.   Next with regard to moral character.

Uprightness and mutual confidence are necessary conditions for the growth of wealth.   "Wherever there is a great store
of wealth, there must be a people living to a considerable degree
under moral restraint, and possessed of a more or less accurate
code of duty; and a land dotted with bursting stack-yards,
mapped out into well-tilled fields, and noisy with the hum of
looms and the clang of hammers, is evidence that there is at
hand no small portion of the stuff out of which martyrs and
heroes are formed.   Though fine names may not be given to
the qualifications of a busy people, skilled in many crafts and
trades, producing articles cheaply and well; it is patience and
sobriety, faithfulness and honesty that have gained for them
eminence[1]."

---

[1] Macdonell, *Survey of Political Economy.*

The character of a nation depends chiefly on that of the mothers of the nation—on their firmness and gentleness and sincerity. It is in childhood, and at home, that the workman must learn to be truthful and trusty, cleanly and careful, energetic and thorough, to reverence others and to respect himself.

Finally, industry cannot attain full freedom and efficiency unless, as Mill says, it is protected *by* the Government and *from* the Government.

We have now seen how land and labour are two of the requisites of production, the third requisite is capital.

CHAPTER III.

CAPITAL.

§ 1. IN a savage state man thinks only of satisfying his immediate wants ; in a civilized state he devotes much labour to preparing the roads, buildings, tools, materials, etc. which may be of service to him in the future. He abstains from seeking immediate enjoyment from the whole produce of his labour, and devotes some part of it to producing things which will assist him in his future work. These requisites of production are called Capital.

> **Capital** is the result of labour and abstinence. It consists of all wealth which is destined to be employed Productively[1].

We say "destined" or devoted, because it is not always possible to tell whether a thing is capital or not, without knowing how the owner intends to use it. Thus oats are capital if they are to be given to a cart-horse, but not if they are to be given to a racehorse. Again, many things are used sometimes for business, therefore as capital; sometimes for pleasure, and therefore not as capital. A French peasant's cart is used as capital in the field, but not as capital when it carries him and his family for a jaunt on a holiday. Again, it is not always clear to what extent a doctor's house and his carriage should be regarded as capital required for his business.

"To familiarise ourselves with the conception, let us consider what is done with the capital invested in any of the branches of business which compose the productive industry of a country. A manufacturer, for example, has one part of his capital in the form of buildings, fitted and destined for carrying on his branch of manufacture. Another part he has in the form of machinery.

---

[1] See Chap. i. § 6.

A third consists, if he be a spinner, of raw cotton, flax, or wool; if a weaver, of flaxen, woollen, silk or cotton, thread; and the like, according to the nature of the manufacture. Food and clothing for his operatives, it is not the custom of the present age that he should directly provide; and few capitalists, except the producers of food or clothing, have any portion worth mentioning of their capital in this shape. Instead of this each capitalist has money, which he pays to his workpeople, and so enables them to supply themselves : he has also finished goods in his warehouses, by the sale of which he obtains more money, to employ in the same manner, as well as to replenish his stock of materials, to keep his buildings and machinery in repair, and to replace them when worn out. His money and finished goods, however, are not wholly capital, for he does not wholly devote them to these purposes : he employs a part of the one, and of the proceeds of the other, in supplying his personal consumption and that of his family, or in hiring grooms and valets, or maintaining hunters and hounds, or in educating his children, or in paying taxes, or in charity. What then is his capital? Precisely that part of his possessions, whatever it be, which is to constitute his fund for carrying on fresh productions. It is of no consequence that a part or even the whole of it is in a form in which it cannot directly supply the wants of labourers[1]."

The land itself and natural agents, such as waterfalls, are not called capital; because they are not made by man, and they are not saved by him. We are not dependent on the labour and abstinence of our forefathers for our supply of land, or of water power. But all the improvements that are made in land are capital; for they are the result of labour and abstinence : the labour by which they were made was devoted not to producing the means of immediate enjoyment, but to doing things which will assist man in his future work of production. Thus canals are capital; but the Thames, which is a far more important source of wealth than any canal, is not capital. It may be a question whether capital should not be so defined as to include all those natural agents and resources for the production of wealth, which are capable of being appropriated. If we used the word in this sense, the capital of America would be immensely greater than that of England. But economists have agreed to define capital so as to exclude all things that are not made by man. And when thus defined the capital of America is probably less than that of England.

§ 2. Capital is the result of labour and abstinence; it is saved. But it is also used.

---

[1] Mill, *Principles*, Bk. I. Ch. iv. § I.

It is true that some wealth is hoarded; and that while being hoarded it is not being used; but hoarding has gone out of fashion in civilized countries. An Englishman, when he saves capital, intends either to use it himself, or to lend it out to be used by others; and capital when it is used is almost always spent: but it is so spent as to be reproduced : it is spent Productively.

We may find a good instance of that Productive expenditure which is really *saving* in the career of the great Duke of Bridgewater. In his time English industries were sadly hampered by the enormous cost of carrying goods from one part of the country to another. None of the roads leading into Manchester were passable by carts. Coals, corn, cloth and other things were carried on horses' backs in summer. But in winter, when the roads were bad, Manchester was like a beleaguered town. The duke conceived the daring project of making canals to connect the manufactures of Manchester with the coal districts on the one hand, and with the sea at Liverpool on the other. He devoted all his wealth and energies to the work. He lived in the plainest manner, had long consultations with Brindley the engineer in rough log huts; and derived from the excitement of his enterprise a keener pleasure than he would have obtained from spending his wealth in luxury. He bequeathed vast wealth to his descendants, but in the act of saving it he gave employment to vast numbers of working men. His canals are a source of the prosperity of his country, and afford permanent employment to thousands.

Capital devoted to making things that are to be consumed unproductively does indeed sustain labourers during the process, but it does not produce a fresh supply of capital which will in its turn support and assist labour. A man who employs people in making lace or in laying out ornamental grounds, sustains them while they are at work, and then this means of support comes to an end. On the other hand a man who invests capital in a coal mine not only benefits labourers during the time, but prepares a store of coal which may again be used as capital : his expenditure has the after effect of increasing the amount of those things which either support or assist labour.

§ 3. And now we may pause to consider Bastiat's distinction between those effects of an action *which are seen* and those *which are not seen*. When a spendthrift is wasting his substance it is easy enough for his neighbours to see how he gives employment to cooks and valets and horse-jockeys. But when a man saves his money and invests it, say in a new canal or railway, it is not so easy to see that his wealth employs navvies and other workmen in the present, and will go on affording employment to other labourers in other generations. Though his wealth is spent, it is not spent by himself: so that his neighbours do not see that it is spent at all. And though the future effect of his spending will be to increase the means of employing labourers, these effects are not seen: but they may be foreseen. "In the department of economy, an act, a habit, an institution, a law, gives birth not only to an effect but to a series of effects. Of these effects the first only is immediate; it manifests itself simultaneously with its cause; *it is seen.* The others unfold in succession—they *are not seen;* it is well for us if they are *foreseen.* Between a good and a bad economist this constitutes the whole difference: the one takes account only of the *visible* effect: the other takes account of the effects which are seen and also of those which it is necessary to *foresee.* Now this difference is enormous, for it frequently happens that when the immediate effect is favourable, the ultimate consequences are fatal and conversely. Ignorance surrounds mankind in its cradle; then its actions are determined by their first consequences, the only ones which in its first stage it can see. It is only gradually that it learns to take account of the others. It has to learn this lesson from two very different masters—experience and foresight. Experience teaches effectually but brutally. It makes us acquainted with all the effects of an action by causing us to feel them, and we cannot fail to finish by knowing that a fire burns when we have burned ourselves. For this rough teacher I should like if possible to substitute a more gentle one—I mean Foresight. For this purpose I shall examine the effects of various economical phenomena by placing in opposition to each other those which are seen and those which are not seen." There are, as Bastiat goes on to shew, many important consequences of men's action which are not seen, but which may be foreseen by the aid of economic principles.

One of the most important of these principles has been expressed by saying "Industry is limited by Capital[1]." But when so stated it is often misunderstood. It means that :—

> Labour requires support and aid from capital. The demand for labour in a district cannot in the long run be increased by any device that does not lead to an increase of the supply of capital in it.

[If the efficiency of labour were to be doubled by a magician's wand, while the material capital in the country were unchanged

---

[1] The sentence "Industry is limited by Capital" is the first of Mill's four "fundamental propositions about Capital." His fourth proposition expresses another side of the same truth; it is "Demand for commodities" (payment for them being made after they are finished as is usually done) "is not demand for labour" (payment for it being made beforehand, as is usually done). Mill's second proposition is to a similar effect; it is "Capital is the result of saving." This and his third proposition "Capital is consumed" have already been explained.

there would be a great immediate rise in the real wages of labour, that is in the necessaries, comforts and luxuries which each labourer could purchase by his wages. The stores of capital already in existence would be distributed among the labourers more rapidly than they would otherwise have been; and the increased efficiency of work would speedily replenish the diminished stores. The fact is that increase in the efficiency of labour would really lead to an increase in the supply of capital. The overstrained interpretation of the proposition—Industry is limited by Capital—has caused many errors[1].]

§ 4. Let us now look at some conclusions which follow from this proposition. Firstly:

The destruction of things is not good for trade.

For instance, it is not good for trade to have dresses made of material which wears out quickly. For if people did not spend their means on buying new dresses, they would spend them on giving employment to labour in some other way. The dressmaking trade will be as much benefited by their ordering new dresses for the poor as by their ordering new dresses for themselves to the same amount. But it is true that if there were a sudden falling off in the demand for dresses, dressmakers would suffer through being compelled to seek a new occupation. This brings us to the question whether it is right to make work for those who are out of employment.

It may be right, if the suspension of work is temporary, to relieve those who are in distress by making work for them; because this method of relief does not injure their self-respect. If however the distress in a trade is not merely temporary, it is not true kindness to dissuade people from leaving it. A great mistake was made by those who tried to bolster up the trade of hand-weaving, after it had been proved that the hand-loom must in the long run give place to the power-loom. Those who doled out poor relief to supplement the miserable wages of the hand-weavers would have done better by helping them to earn their living in another way.

But while it is not good for trade to spend money on dress ostentatiously, or to change the fashions rapidly, it is true that those who dress well add, if not to the wealth, yet to the well-being of the nation. A service is done to society by every one who provides the means of refined pleasure without unnecessary expenditure. When a man buys a good picture he devotes wealth to one of its best ends; and a really artistic dress educates taste just as a picture does. A time may come when it will be thought absurd for a woman to display her wealth by

---

[1] These have chiefly appeared in various forms of what has been called the "Wages fund theory." See Book III. chap. VI.

carrying about a great quantity of expensive materials and embroidery; just as a painter who advertised the price he had paid for the paints on his picture would be thought vulgar.

It may be noticed that some acquaintance with luxuries seems to be a necessary condition of progress. Many nations have been aroused from a state of sluggish apathy by a desire to obtain foreign luxuries, which has made them exert themselves. But every increase in the consumption of luxuries, unless it leads to increased energy in the production of wealth, diminishes saving and so checks the accumulation of wealth.

§ 5. The fundamental truth, that the employment of labour cannot in general be increased by any artificial device that does not increase the supply of capital, shews us that:—

> It is not in the long run good for trade to prevent goods from coming freely into the country so as to cause an artificial demand for some kinds of home productions.

Bastiat tells a story of the candlemakers, who petition the authorities to pass a law ordering the shutting up of all windows and openings, by which the light of the sun can come in. This, they say, will create such a demand for artificial light that their manufactures will be greatly encouraged: being prosperous they will be able to purchase the goods made by other trades, so that the plan will benefit trade generally. Doubtless government could thus give employment to many industries: the effects which *were seen* would be beneficial. But the candlemakers did not *foresee* that the capital which came into their industry must be subtracted from some other industry, say, that of growing corn, in which it was giving good employment to labour; and that the corn growers would have purchased from other trades just as much as the candlemakers would. Government would not then increase the employment of labour; but would only cause it to be employed in producing candles that were not wanted instead of corn which was wanted.

Bastiat wrote this story for the instruction of the French Government, who often imposed heavy duties on manufactured commodities in order to give a premium to domestic manufacturers, and then plumed themselves on the "multitude of tall chimneys" they had called into existence. They did not see that the capital invested in such industries was not an addition to that which existed in the country; they did not see that it had been artificially drawn into these industries at the expense of others. We shall find that many of the most important practical conclusions of Economics are contained in the statement :—

> Regulations which prevent men from doing whatever they are best qualified to do cannot benefit the country

as a whole, whether they are made by Governments, by Professions or by Trades-Unions.

§ 6. Labour requires support and aid from capital. It is convenient to have separate names for that portion of capital which supports, and that portion which aids labour.

> **Remuneratory Capital** or **Wage-Capital** consists of the food, clothes, shelter, etc. which support labour.

> **Auxiliary Capital** is that which aids labour. It consists of tools, machines, factories and other buildings that are used for trade purposes, railways, canals, roads, ships, etc.; also raw materials.

A very rapid conversion of Remuneratory into Auxiliary Capital may temporarily injure labourers.

Suppose for instance that a great amount of labour and capital is diverted from agriculture to making railways or steam engines. The corn which would have fed farm labourers while growing corn, now feeds some of the same labourers who have left their farms, and gone to work on railways or in machine shops. At the end of the year there will be more railways or steam engines in existence than would otherwise have been, but less corn: and in consequence labourers may for the time have a scanty supply of food. But this injury will be only temporary.

At the time of the "Railway mania" capital was sunk in railways on such a gigantic scale that there was not enough left for carrying on the general business of the country, and the Railway panic of 1847 caused much suffering. Yet in the long run railways have conferred great benefits on the working classes of England by increasing that general wealth of the country on which their wages depend. The amount that is now subtracted in a year from the capital of the country for building new railways is slight in comparison to the addition which the railways make to the Remuneratory capital of the country.

§ 7. This distinction between Remuneratory and Auxiliary Capital is closely connected with one that must be made between Circulating and Fixed Capital.

> "Capital which fulfils the whole of its office, in the production in which it is engaged, by a single use, is called **Circulating Capital**."

> "Capital which exists in any durable shape and the return to which is spread over a period of corresponding duration, is called **Fixed Capital**[1]."

These terms have sometimes been used as though they were convertible with Remuneratory and Auxiliary capital respectively. But the cottage which a farm labourer has rent free is

---

[1] Mill, Book I. chap. VI.

Remuneratory Capital, but not Circulating.   Again raw materials are Circulating capital, but not Remuneratory.

We shall presently see the importance of the distinction between Fixed and Circulating Capital.   We shall also see the importance of a third distinction for which these names are sometimes used, but for which other names seem to be required.

Whenever capital has been designed for use in one trade there is some difficulty in diverting it to another; if this difficulty is great the capital is **Specialised,** if not great, the capital is **Non-specialised**[1].

No clearly defined line can be drawn between these two kinds of capital.   Labourers' food and clothing, many kinds of tools, and such materials as wood and metals are Non-specialised, for they can be employed in a number of different ways.   Again, many kinds of offices and commercial buildings and workmen's dwellings in towns are Non-specialised.   But agricultural improvements, including farm labourers' cottages, cannot often be used except for their original purposes.   So also railroads, docks, ironworks, and again printing and reaping machines may be considered as Specialised capital.   But it is often difficult to decide whether such machinery should be called Specialised, or Non-specialised : a factory fitted up with a steam engine and "over-head gear," can scarcely be called Specialised capital, because it may be almost equally adapted to many branches of the textile trades, and of the lighter metal and wood trades.

§ 8.   Almost all Personal Wealth is or may be Personal Capital.   As Adam Smith says :—"The acquisition of all useful abilities, by the maintenance of the acquirer during his education, study or apprenticeship, always costs a real expense, which is a capital fixed and realised, as it were, in his person.   Those talents, as they make a part of his fortune, so do they likewise of that of the society to which he belongs.   The improved dexterity of a workman may be considered in the same light as a machine or instrument of trade which facilitates and abridges labour, and which, though it costs a certain expense, repays that expense with a profit."

---

[1] Compare Jevons' *Theory of Political Economy*, pp. 232—234.

CHAPTER IV.

LAW OF DIMINISHING RETURN.

§ 1.   WE have seen that the requisites of production may be classed as land, labour and capital.   We have now to seek for the Law of fertility of land, the Law of the increase of population, and the Law of the growth of capital.   The latter two Laws depend on the first, which goes by the name of the Law of Diminishing Return.

We may explain the meaning of this name by an illustration. We shall presently see that the Law does not apply to all new countries in which, though the land is fertile, the population is very sparse.   But let us suppose that in a certain district there are twenty agricultural labourers to the square mile, and that in the seasons in which they grow wheat they raise 2000 quarters, which is at the rate of 100 quarters per man.   If now the population increases so that there are thirty agricultural labourers to the square mile, there will of course be an increase in the produce raised, but not a proportional increase.   Perhaps the produce may now be 2600 quarters, so that the amount due to the labour of the additional ten labourers is 600 quarters, which is at the rate of 60 quarters per man.   Now let there be a further increase in the population, till there are thirty-five agricultural labourers to the square mile: there will again be an increase in the total produce raised, but again not a proportional increase. Perhaps the produce may now be 2850 quarters, so that the amount due to the labour of the last five labourers is 250 quarters, which is at the rate of 50 quarters per man.

That increase in the amount of corn raised which is due to the labour of each additional labourer may be called the Return due to his labour; and we may then say, that in this case the greater the number of men employed on the land, the less is the Return which would be due to the labour of an additional man.   This result illustrates the meaning of the Law of Diminishing Return.

§ 2.   But so far no account has been taken of the fact that the cultivation of land requires the farmer's capital as well as the labourer's toil. It is indeed best to look at the matter from the point of view of the farmer: for since he generally advances the wages of the labourer, the produce may be regarded as due to his capital—to his Auxiliary capital in the form of implements, seed, cattle, etc. and to the Remuneratory capital with which he pays his labourers' wages.

The previous illustration represented the farmer as sending additional labourers into the farm, and then noticing the increase of produce due to their labour, or the Return to their labour. We may now suppose that he increases by successive doses[1] the capital he applies to the land, and then notices the increase due to each successive dose, or as we may say *the Return due to each Dose*. Suppose, for instance, that by expending in one way or another four doses of £1 each, on an acre of land he can raise from it 20 bushels of wheat, which is at the rate of five bushels for each dose of capital. If he applies a fifth dose of £1 to the acre, whether in the form of extra manure or extra ploughing or what not, the produce of course will be increased, but not by as much as 5 bushels. Probably he may now obtain 24 bushels from each acre, the return due to the fifth dose of capital being 4 bushels. If he applies a sixth dose of capital, and with the expenditure of £6 obtains 27 bushels an acre, the return due to the sixth dose will be 3 bushels, and this perhaps would not remunerate him for the outlay. If so, he will not apply more than £5 to the acre.

§ 3. Thus, as the experience of every English farmer tells us, when land is already well cultivated the application of additional doses of capital will cause a less than proportionate increase in the return; or, as we may say, they will obtain a Diminishing Return.

We may then state the **Law of Diminishing Return** thus :—

> After a certain amount of capital has been applied to Land every increase in produce is obtained by a more than proportionate increase of capital ; unless the arts of agriculture are meanwhile improved[2].

The Law contains two qualifying conditions, one relating to the progress of the arts of agriculture, and the other to the special circumstances of a new country in which but very little capital is applied to land. We may consider these separately.

---

[1] This term was applied by James Mill to denote equal amounts of capital applied to land.

[2] The statement that after a certain number of doses have been applied to any given piece of land, the return due to each additional dose

§ 4. Firstly, with regard to progress in the arts of agriculture.
New methods of cultivation are from time to time discovered,

will be less than those due to the preceding doses, may be illustrated
by figures.

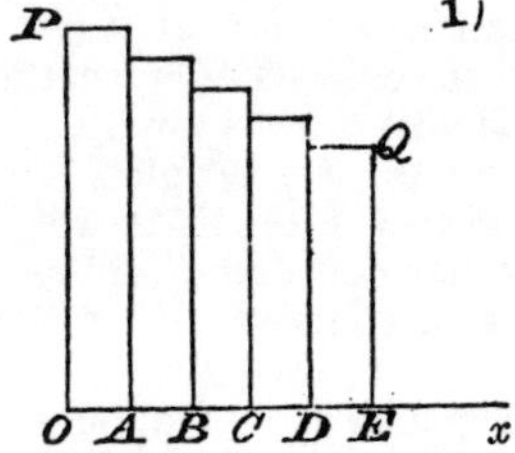

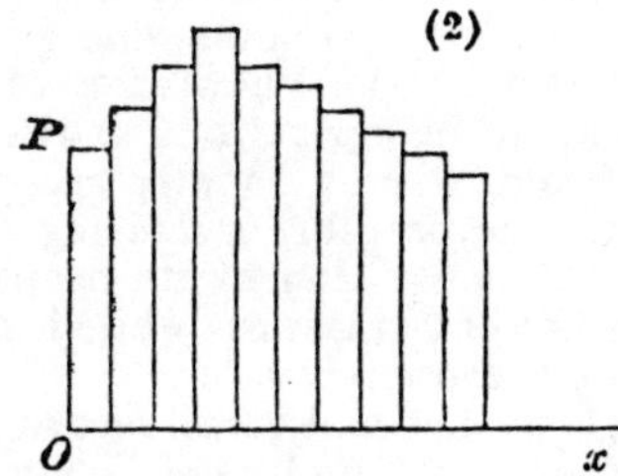

Let the line Ox be divided into equal parts, the divisions representing
equal doses of capital, and let them be called OA, AB, BC, etc., each
successive dose gives a return which may be represented by a rectangle
at right angles to Ox, and as thick as the corresponding division of Ox.

Then if five such doses, represented by OE, have been applied, the
returns are shewn by the figure $OPQE$. The Law of Diminishing Return states that after a certain number of these doses have been applied,
the corresponding rectangles are shorter.

But the Law of Diminishing Return does not state that this diminution will in every case commence at once ; the returns to the first few
doses may be small, and the returns to the later doses may be larger,
as they are in fig. 2. All that the Law states is that after a great
number of doses have been applied, the return must diminish.

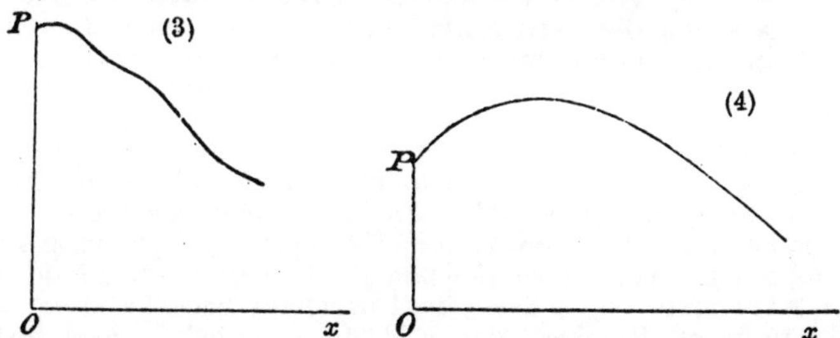

We may make the divisions in Ox as small as we please, so that the
rectangles become what may be called thick straight lines.

The tops of these straight lines will lie on curves, the shapes of
which are represented in figs. 3 and 4. Fig. 3 represents the increase
of produce of land, the return from which always diminishes : and fig.
4 that of land the return from which first increases and then diminishes.

new rotations of crops, new methods of draining land. Science gives instruction in the feeding and breeding of cattle, and in the application of different manures to different kinds of land. Machinery is being invented which lightens the work of agriculture—weeding, mowing and reaping machines ; steam ploughs, steam threshing and chaff-cutting machines. Meanwhile, the education and energy of the farmer and labourer are increasing. The knowledge of new inventions and methods is diffused by agricultural shows and farmers' newspapers.

Again, when a country becomes very thickly peopled it has great facilities for organising a supply of food from abroad, and the emigration of its people to other countries. Thus the progress of civilisation, while it presses on the resources of land, enlarges those resources.

[§ 5. Secondly, with regard to the special circumstances of a new country. The Law of Diminishing Return has been disputed by Mr Carey, who is at the head of a set of Economists calling themselves the American school. Mr Carey's arguments against the Law appear to be founded on a misconception of its real nature; and the practical conclusions for which he contends have not much application to a densely peopled country such as England is. But yet the writings of the American school are in many ways suggestive, and their opinions have attracted much attention on the continent of Europe, so that it may be well to say something about them here.

These economists argue that history shews that the best lands are not those which are cultivated first, but that the order of settlement of new countries is the passage from poorer to richer soil. The causes of this are various. Mountain districts have sometimes been selected on account of the means of defence which they offer against enemies ; but more often the steep and self-draining mountain sides were chosen because the low rich lands, until they are drained, are infested by malarious fevers.

In fact, if land is very rich, full of luxuriant undergrowth or marshy, it is not possible to cultivate it at all with only a small expenditure of capital and labour. But when the growth of population and the advance of civilisation give the means of bringing such land under the plough, the return which it gives will abundantly repay the pains that have been spent on it. The tasks of draining marshy lands and freeing them from malaria, and of making roads and railways, are not easily performed when the population is thin and scattered. And American writers have done good service in insisting on the fact that up to a certain point, the greater the numbers in a country the greater will be the power of organizing labour and capital, and the greater therefore will be the return from land. It may

be conceded to them that until this point is reached, land may
be said to yield an Increasing, not a Diminishing Return; and
that perhaps more than half of the richest land in the globe is
yet uncultivated.

But this fact is not inconsistent with the Law of Diminishing
Return which merely asserts that the return to capital applied
to land diminishes, provided that there is already a dense and
rapidly increasing population, and comparatively little improvement in the arts of cultivation.

One cause of this difference of opinion between American
and English Economists is probably that in America there is,
and in England there is not a large amount of rich land waiting
to be cultivated.]

§ 6. We may next consider the Law of increase of mineral
produce. The Law of Diminishing Return is said to apply to
mineral as well as to agricultural produce. This is not strictly
true: at least there is a fundamental difference between the two
cases. The richness of cultivated lands is likely to increase:
so that if the demand for produce were to remain stationary,
it could be satisfied with continually diminishing effort. But
every mine is being impoverished by being worked. And when
the richest mineral strata have all been discovered, the difficulty of satisfying the demand for mineral produce must increase, even if the demand should remain stationary. Improvements in the arts of mining may retard the operation of
this Law, but cannot entirely prevent it.

Another difference between agriculture and mining is this.
It is impossible to raise by any amount of labour ten times the
ordinary produce from a well-cultivated garden in one year.
But the produce raised in a year from a mine might be increased
tenfold without increasing more than tenfold the labour employed on it; provided that there were a sufficient supply of
mining plant and skilled miners. But in fact the difficulties
and dangers of mining deter those who have not been accustomed to them from childhood. A rapid increase in the supply
of coal can only be obtained by paying high wages to new men
for unskilful work. Again, the machinery, shafts and galleries
that are required for opening up new seams cannot be provided
without some delay. It is owing to these causes that a sudden
increase in the demand for coal forces its price up very high.
These causes would act even if there were an unlimited supply
of good mines ready to be opened; they are independent of the
Law of Diminishing Return. The gradual exhaustion of our
coal mines has very little to do with the sudden rise in the
price of coal in 1873. This rise was caused by a sudden increase of demand; as is shewn by the facts that it attracted a
large amount of capital and labour to the coal mining trade,

and the consequent increase in the supply of coal forced down prices below their old level.

But though the Law of Diminishing Return does not apply to mineral produce in the same way as it does to agricultural, yet the exhaustion of the mineral strata of the earth's surface may ultimately exert a most serious influence on the history of the world.

When steam power becomes expensive, science will doubtless teach us to substitute for it the forces of the air and water. In the wind and waves, in tides and waterfalls, we are supplied with forces many thousand times as great as can ever be required by the whole population of the globe. At present coal is preferred to these sources of power, because coal can easily be carried wherever it is wanted and any quantity of steam power can be obtained whenever it is wanted; but the forces of Nature cannot. Means will however probably be discovered of transmitting the power that is supplied by Nature from place to place, so that it may be applied wherever it is wanted, and of storing up this force in reservoirs so that it may be used whenever it is wanted ; and then we shall be able almost to dispense with the use of steam power.

But there seems to be no prospect of obtaining any important cheap substitute for coal as a means of producing warmth. And it is quite possible that in the colder portions of the earth's surface the growth of population will ultimately be restrained by the need of warmth, more than by the need of food.

§ 7. While considering the influence of the Law of Diminishing Return on the difficulty of obtaining raw produce, it must not be forgotten that the arts of manufacture are constantly progressing ; so that there may be a continual diminution in the difficulty of obtaining such things as lace, cutlery and watches, in the cost of which the price of the raw material is not an important element. But such commodities are consumed more by the rich than by the poor. "The wife of a common labourer may wear fabrics which would once have excited the admiration of a court. But after all the great bulk of the consumption of the labouring classes must be in coarse forms of agricultural produce simply prepared."

CHAPTER V.

GROWTH OF POPULATION. MALTHUS. POOR-LAWS.

§ 1. THE Law of Diminishing Return tells us that when population has reached a certain density, an additional amount of labour and capital will not raise a proportionately increased supply of food. The operation of this Law is delayed by the progress of the arts of agriculture and manufacture, and by bringing fresh land under cultivation. It is possible that when the whole world is well cultivated, it may afford support for five or even ten times as many people as there are acres in the earth's surface. But a limit to the growth of population must be reached at last.

The surface of the globe, including sea and land, is about 600,000,000,000,000 square yards. If we suppose that each yard allows standing room for four persons, this calculation gives room for 2,400,000,000,000,000 persons. Next, looking at the rate of increase of the population of England and Wales, we find that it doubled between the years 1801 and 1851. At this rate of increase population would in

100 years	multiply itself by		4
200 ,,	,,	,,	16
400 ,,	,,	,,	256
500 ,,	,,	,,	(1024, say) 1000
1000 ,,	,,	,,	1,000,000
2000 ,,	,,	,,	1,000,000,000,000
3000 ,,	,,	,,	1,000,000,000,000,000,000.

At this rate the descendants of a single pair would in 3,000 years form a solid column covering the surface of the globe more than eight hundred deep.

These facts shew that sooner or later the growth of population must receive a check; but they do not shew that it need be checked at present. The question whether there is such a need is a difficult one, and we shall be occupied during the greater part of the present chapter in considering it.

§ 2. In savage countries people marry very early, and the growth of population would be very rapid, if it were not restrained by infanticide and war, by pestilence and by famine. When men have left the savage state and live under settled government, they very often retain the habits of improvidence of the savage. In fact they almost always do, unless they are educated, and have some sort of ambition for themselves and their children. Not only the Chinese and other Asiatic races, but the agricultural labourers in Ireland and even in some parts of England marry recklessly without any thought of the morrow. For indeed their future is a matter neither of hope nor of fear to them; they have little hope of bettering their condition, and there is scarcely a lower level to which they can fall. As a result so many children are born that the resources of the family will not suffice to nourish and educate them : and though in Europe at least infanticide is rare, and children do not often die of actual starvation, yet the rate of mortality among the children of the very poor is terrible. Insufficient food and clothing, neglect, dirt, foul air and infectious diseases hurry off vast numbers of the children of the poorer labourers in town and country to an early grave. Skilled artizans are in a transitional state. We may hope that before long they will not marry without that sense of responsibility with regard to the education of their children which the middle classes feel now. This change may be described by saying that their Standard of Comfort is rising. For :—

> When any class of the population has obtained such habits of forethought as to be unwilling to marry without the expectation of being able to enjoy a certain given amount of the necessaries, comforts, and luxuries of life, then this amount is called the **Standard of Comfort** for that class of the population.

These necessaries, comforts, and luxuries are for a man's children as well as for himself; indeed the chief of them is a good physical, mental, and moral education for his children. Economic progress depends much on changes in the Standard of Comfort of the people, and therefore on the strength of their family affections.

§ 3. If there be a rise in the incomes of any class of the people, we may expect an increase in the number of marriages and births among this class. It is in fact well known that marriages are more frequent among all classes of the people in a period of commercial prosperity than in one of depression ; and the statistics published by the Registrar-General during the last thirty years prove that there have been as a rule more marriages in the years in which bread has been cheap, than in those in which it has been dear.

It may however happen that a rise in the incomes of any class is accompanied by a rise in their Standard of Comfort ;

which prevents any increase in the number of births among them. But a rise in the Standard of Comfort brings with it improved means of caring for and supporting infant life, so that out of every hundred children that are born, a larger number grow up to be efficient workers in the next generation if the Standard of Comfort is high than if it is low. We see then that the **Law of Population** is that :—

> A rise in the rate of wages causes either a rise in the Standard of Comfort of the people, or an increase in the number of marriages and births. A rise in the Standard of Comfort is almost sure to increase the percentage of children who grow up to be efficient workers. Therefore a rise in wages almost always increases, and a fall in wages almost always diminishes the rate of growth of population.

As a rapid growth of population has almost always followed on a rise of wages, Economists from the time of Locke have assumed that the wages of unskilled labour have never been much more than sufficient to enable them to continue the species. But Adam Smith's sagacity remarked that it is quite possible for the labouring classes to change their definition of necessaries. Shoes are necessaries in England, not in Scotland. Wheaten bread was a necessary in England before the reign of Henry VII.; after that the working classes ate a great deal of rye-bread; but again at the end of the seventeenth century wheaten bread became a necessary. At the present time the definition varies much from one country to another, and even from one part of the same country to another.

§ 4. Malthus published his famous Essay on Population in 1798. Perhaps no other book has been so much discussed by persons who have never read it as this Essay has. It may be worth while therefore to say something here about it and the circumstances under which it was written.

At the end of the last and during the early years of the present century, the English poor-law acted in such a way as to foster the growth of population upward indeed in point of quantity, but downward in point of quality. It put a premium on early and reckless marriages, at the same time that it discouraged not only every kind of thrift and forethought, but also all strength and manliness of character. " Under it the English peasant had a legal right to support in the shape of a poor-rate, doled out to him when his wages were judged insufficient. Children called for no self-denial on his part, the rate was doled out to him in proportion to their number. A labourer could not by deferring marriage earn a little portion to start with, or at least such a course would have required extreme self-denial; for while unmarried and childless, the payment of his service

was depressed to the sum just sufficient for his absolute necessity.   Like a slave or like a horse, he had his food nearly the
same at every time, and work as he might, was unable to reserve
a store for his needs[1]."

The consequences of these mistaken arrangements were
shewing themselves in wide-spread misery; and Malthus, a
kind-hearted clergyman, set himself to work to inquire whether
after all it was right thus to promote the increase in the
quantity of the population without caring for the quality.   The
conclusion at which he arrived is this:—The natural propensities
of man will cause population to increase as fast or faster than
the means of supporting them; therefore the efforts of the
legislator and of the moralist should be directed towards improving the character of the people; and towards discouraging
rather than encouraging a rapid increase of numbers.

Accordingly he urged "moral self-restraint" as a "Preventive
Check" to the excessive growth of population.   But what he has
said on this subject has been much misunderstood.   It has
been thought that he wished to impose great hardships on the
poor.   But in fact "he again and again explained to inquirers
that he wished to put no more restraint on the marriage of the
poor than such as every prudent parent in the middle classes
would wish to place on that of his children.   He advises delay
in marriage, and he argues that, without strong and lasting
attachments, the married state is generally more productive of
misery than of happiness, and that for the formation of such
attachments, time must be given to find out kindred disposi-
tions[1]."

Now it seems easy to object to Malthus, that the world has
gone along very well for thousands of years without men's
troubling themselves about his Preventive Checks to population;
and that therefore the world may be expected to go on well for
many more thousand years, even if men pay no attention to
Malthus.   This objection he anticipated and met by one of the
most crushing answers that patient and hard-working science has
ever given to the reckless assertions of its adversaries.   He
examined one after another the various countries of the world
in ancient, mediæval and modern times.   He found that in
some places Preventive Checks had been actually in operation
for many centuries; that in some parts of Switzerland, for
instance, large numbers of the population remain unmarried.
He found that in many other countries the hand of man had
habitually restrained population by infanticide and war; and
that in every country which had been inhabited for many
centuries, and in which man had not controlled population by

---

[1] F. W. Newman, *Malthusianism true and false*.

these means, the stern hand of nature had kept it down by what he called Positive Checks, that is, by want and famine, by infant mortality, and by terrible disease and pestilence. So that it is not a fact that the world has gone on very well hitherto: and Malthus argued that the faculties of thought and forethought were bestowed upon men to enable them to make the world go on better.

[He used the expression that population tends to increase indefinitely in a geometrical progression, and that under favourable circumstances it was found to double in 25 years, while food only increased in arithmetical proportion, and that therefore population must increase faster than food. The expression "arithmetical" is slovenly and no one defends it now, but he intended to express what is stated in the Law of Diminishing Return; viz. that if labour continued to increase at a great rate for a long time, the produce which it could obtain from land would not go on increasing at the same rate.]

§ 5. Malthus' statements with regard to the misery that has existed in past ages have been confirmed by more recent historians: but the practical conclusions that he deduced from them are more liable to be disputed. For he could not foresee the inventions and discoveries which were just about to be made when he wrote. He could not foresee how the growth of steam traffic would enable England, on the one hand to import food from countries where there was a scanty population; and on the other to send out her surplus population to cultivate new soils, and to spread the energy and genius of the English people over the earth.

There can be no doubt that this extension of the English race has been a benefit to the world. A check to the growth of population would do great harm if it affected only the more intelligent races, and particularly the more intelligent classes of these races. There does indeed appear some danger of this evil. For instance, if the lower classes of Englishmen multiply more rapidly than those which are morally and physically superior, not only will the population of England deteriorate, but also that part of the population of America and Australia which descends from Englishmen will be less intelligent than it otherwise would be. Again, if Englishmen multiply less rapidly than the Chinese, this spiritless race will overrun portions of the earth that otherwise would have been peopled by English vigour.

It must be remembered that the growth of population depends not on the number of those who are born, but on the number of those who grow up to maturity: that infant mortality is the natural consequence of improvident marriages; and that the character of the population of a country will be lowered if people marry early on insufficient means, and have families so large that, though they can just rear them, they cannot properly care for their physical, moral and mental education.

The best practical answer to the question which we have set ourselves to discuss in this chapter seems to be :—

> Just as a man who has borrowed money is bound to pay it back with interest, so a man is bound to give his children an education better and more thorough than he has himself received.

When people are in a position to do this they confer a benefit on the State by marrying. This practical principle measures equitably the same measure of public duty to rich and to poor. Its general adoption would cause the spectre of Malthusianism, which casts a gloom over economic speculation, to disappear, or at any rate to be no longer dreaded ; and would rid us of the competition for food which seems to dog the heels of progress.

§ 6. It will be convenient here to pause in our discussion of the Laws of increase of the three requisites of production and to make a short digression on the question which Malthus raised as to the proper administration of the Poor-law.

At present the management of the rates that are levied for the relief of the poor is entrusted to Guardians of the Poor. These Guardians, with the aid of paid officials, decide what aid from the rates is to be given in each case. This relief is either Indoor, that is within the doors of the Parish workhouse, or Outdoor. As Bastiat would say, the evils of Indoor relief are "seen"; those of Outdoor relief are often "not seen."

Indoor relief is unpopular ; it resembles imprisonment, and seems too hard a fate for those whose poverty is not the result of positive vice. When a man goes into the workhouse, his home is generally broken up, so that he cannot easily leave it and start in life afresh.

It seems therefore at first sight much better to give Outdoor relief to those who are not hopelessly infirm. Outdoor relief may be eked out by any little earnings of the man or his family, and perhaps by some assistance from relations or other friends. He rubs along in his old abode and with his own furniture : the cost of relieving him in his home is thus, even while it lasts, less than the cost of Indoor relief ; and, as soon as he is again able to earn considerable wages, the Outdoor relief can be stopped. Thus in its immediate result Outdoor relief is less burdensome to the rate-payer, as well as more agreeable to those who receive it, than Indoor relief is.

But Outdoor relief leads to great evils. If given in aid of wages, it is likely, as experience has shewn, to cause wages to be so low that labourers cannot live without support from the rates. And since 1834 it has been generally agreed that Outdoor relief should not be given to labourers who are in full health unless to enable them to tide over some passing emergency. But even with this restriction, Outdoor relief is often the booty of the idle, the dissipated, the crafty and the hypocritical ; for the Guardians, and Relieving officers employed by them, have not the time required for investigating properly the merits of each case ; and they have not as yet entered into systematic alliance with private distributors of charity. Thus while the honest poor suffer great hardships, those who are dishonest often receive Outdoor relief at the same time that their wants are abundantly provided for by private charity. And on the whole, it has been found that wherever Outdoor relief has been given freely, a large part of the population has become idle, thriftless, and base, in short " pauperised."

Yet Poor-law Guardians are under a great temptation to give Outdoor relief, because its evil results are distant, while the expense and the hardships of Indoor relief are present. It has therefore been thought right to offer an inducement to Guardians to apply "the Workhouse test"; that is, to offer only Indoor relief in ordinary cases, so that the inability of the applicants to provide for themselves might be tested by their willingness to submit to the restraints of the Workhouse. An Act was passed on Mr Goschen's motion in 1870, by which the expense of the Workhouses throughout the whole of London was borne by a Metropolitan rate. Each body of Guardians now knows that the whole of the Outdoor relief, but only a small portion of the Indoor relief which they grant, must come from the pockets of the rate-payers by whom they are elected. This Act, while it made the rich districts of London to contribute their due share to the support of the poor, diminished the pauperism of London, which till then had continually increased. It is to be hoped that the principle of this Act will be applied throughout England ; and that the expense of workhouses will be thrown upon counties, or other large areas, while each district bears the expense of its own Outdoor relief.

Whether this is done or not, it should be a rule that when a man applies for Outdoor relief, the burden of proving that he deserves it lies with him. It should be assumed that he does not deserve it unless he can shew either, that though he did not marry recklessly, it had never been possible for him to save ; or that he had made some effort to provide against the day of misfortune by subscribing to a provident society or by saving in some other way[1].

There are indeed some who think that every change in the poor-law should aim at the ultimate abolition of Outdoor relief.

---

[1] See Mr George Bartlett on *Thrift as a test of outdoor relief.*

But the deserving poor feel, and ought to feel, great anguish when they are forced into the workhouse. When a man has not undertaken the responsibilities of marriage without a fair chance of being able to provide for his children, when he has led a hard-working unselfish life and has saved to the utmost of his power, but has been weighed down by accumulated misfortunes ; every hardship, that is imposed on him needlessly, is an unjustifiable cruelty. It is true that the abuses of Outdoor relief are at present so great that it should be abolished if they could not be diminished. But it has not been proved that it is impossible to separate the deserving from the undeserving poor.

§ 7. It is indeed scarcely too much to say that the means by which alone the task could be accomplished have not yet been fairly tried. It seems clear that paid officials have not the time required for detecting the falsehoods of the unworthy. Still less have they time, even if they had the other qualities required for getting to the bottom of the sad tale which is unwillingly and shrinkingly told by those who have nobly struggled against misfortune. " If the poor are to be raised to a permanently better condition, they must be dealt with as individuals and by individuals ; for this hundreds of workers are necessary ; and this multitude of helpers is to be found amongst volunteers—whose aid, as we arrange things at present, is to a great extent lost. The problem to be solved, therefore, is how to collect our volunteers into a harmonious whole—the action of each being free, yet systematized ; and how thus to administer relief through the united agency of corporate bodies and private individuals ; how, in fact, to secure all the personal intercourse and friendliness, all the real sympathy, all the graciousness of individual effort, without losing the advantage of having relief voted by a central committee, and according to definite principles[1]."

There are in England a large and increasing number of people who are ready to take part in the work ; who have the leisure, the means, the education and the will required for it ; " on all sides we hear of people willing to give their time, if only they could be sure of doing good. They are dissatisfied, they say, with district visiting, which creates so much discontent and poverty, and does so little lasting good ; they want to know of some way in which their effort may fit in with more organized work....With our volunteers, home claims must and should come first ; and it is precisely those whose home claims are deepest, and whose family life is the noblest, who have the most precious influence in the homes of the poor. But if the work is to be valuable, we must find some way to bind together broken scraps of time, and thus give it continuity in spite of changes and breaks."

[1] *Homes of the London Poor*, by Miss Octavia Hill, p. 113.

It seems then that the case of every applicant for relief should be decided on by a committee, who may be the Poor-law Guardians, or a Volunteer Committee acting in harmony with them ; and who should receive three reports. The first should be from a paid officer, who should make it his study to learn all the guiles of the dishonest, and who, before reporting on the case, should have asked as a matter of business and without reserve all questions necessary for his purpose. The second should be a result of the organization of the various charitable societies in the neighbourhood, and should enable the Committee to know for certain what aid the applicant is already receiving. The third should come from a volunteer visitor who has gone into the applicant's history, and has drawn forth by sympathy whatever good there was in him.

The Committee might find that the case should be referred to some private charitable society ; or that relief could be given in some better form than a money grant. In many places there are so many charities that, if they were properly orga-nized, Outdoor relief would be rendered almost if not quite unnecessary. But if the Committee decided that the case of the applicant was not met by any existing charity ; that he had been prudent, self-denying and industrious ; and that he ought to receive Outdoor relief; then such relief might be given without fear that it would tend to pauperise the people. Very little Outdoor relief would be given under such a system ; but deserving people would not be forced into a workhouse, as they often are now, in consequence of their case being misunderstood[1]. Miss Octavia Hill has done much to shew the need and the feasibility of some such plan as this for diminishing the evils of pauperism, and has also thrown much light on the problem of preventing pauperism by improving the homes of the poor. She suggests the following rules for those who would share in this work:

" It is best to enforce fulfilment of all such duties as pay-ment of rent, etc.

" It is far better to give work than either money or goods.

" It is most helpful of all to strengthen by sympathy and counsel the energetic effort which shall bear fruit in time to come.

" It is essential to remember that each man has his own view of his life, and must be free to fulfil it ; that in many ways he is a far better judge of it than we, as he has lived through and felt what we have only seen. Our work is rather to bring him to the point of considering, and to the spirit of judging rightly, than to consider or judge for him.

" The poor of London (as of all large towns) need the develop-ment of every power which can open to them noble sources of joy."

---

[1] Portions of such a system are in work at Boston, and at Elberfeld.

CHAPTER VI.

GROWTH OF CAPITAL.

§ 1. WE have discussed the Laws of increase of two elements of production, viz. the Law of increase of production from land, and the Law of the increase of labour. The next step is to examine the Law of increase of the third element of production, that which supports and aids labour, viz. capital.

The growth of capital depends upon the *power* and the *will* to save.

The power of saving depends on the amount of wealth out of which saving can be made. Some countries, which have a large population and produce a great amount of wealth, have very little power of saving. The whole continent of Asia, for instance, has less power of saving than England has. The total produce indeed of its industry is larger than that of England; but the number of people among whom this is divided is so great that they are compelled to consume almost the whole of it in supporting life.

As Mill says, "the fund from which saving can be made is the surplus of the produce of labour after supplying the necessaries of life to all concerned in the production (including those employed in replacing the materials and keeping the Fixed Capital in repair); more than this surplus cannot be saved under any circumstances; as much as this, though it never is saved, always might be. This surplus is the fund from which the enjoyments as distinguished from the necessaries of the producers are provided; it is the fund from which all are subsisted who are not themselves engaged in production; and from which all additions are made to capital. It is the real Net Produce of the country."

Since the requisites of production are land, labour, and capital, the conditions on which the total produce of industry depends may therefore be classed as, firstly, fertility of the soil, richness of mines, abundance of watercourses, and an invigorating climate: secondly, the number and the average efficiency of the working population; this efficiency depending on moral as well as mental and physical qualities: thirdly, the abundance of the means which the industry of the past has accumulated and saved to help the industry of the present; that is, the abundance of roads and railroads, of canals and docks, of factories and warehouses, of engines and machines, of raw material, of food and of clothing; in short, the already accumulated capital of the nation.

The total produce of industry would be just as much increased by an addition to the quantity as by a proportionate improvement in the quality of labour. But it is otherwise with the net produce of industry; for in order to find it, we must deduct the necessaries of the labourers from the total produce; so that it would not be nearly as much increased by an addition to the quantity as by a proportionate improvement in the quality of labour. Therefore the power that a country has of accumulating capital is chiefly dependent on the efficiency of its labour. This efficiency, in so far as it depends upon the qualities of the individual worker, has already been discussed. But the efficiency of industry depends also on its organization; and the next chapters will shew how organization makes the most of the resources of a country by bringing labour and capital into those employments in which they will be most serviceable.

§ 2. Next as to the will to save.

The strength of the desire of accumulation depends on moral and social conditions which vary widely in different times and countries.

(a) The Intellect. The inclination to save arises from the hope of obtaining some future advantage, and this future advantage, if it is to afford motive for action, must be realised. Children and nations in an early state of civilisation are almost incapable of realising a distant advantage; the future is eclipsed by the present. For instance, some of the remnants of the Indian tribes in North America, though in possession of most fertile land, suffer great want merely from their apathy as regards the future. They are industrious when the reward to their toil is immediate; but they will not set anything aside for the future. They will not even do such work as fencing their fields, which offers great and speedy, though not quite immediate advantages. But when the child or the race grows up to maturity, it learns to exert itself for the sake of the future, as well as for the sake of the present.

Again the poor even in highly civilised countries are careless as to the future. They are too intent on satisfying their immediate needs to have time or inclination for forethought. And even those who are earning high wages seldom think of putting by, unless they are to some extent educated.

(*b*) The Sympathies. We saw in the last chapter one of the ways in which economic progress depends on family affection. And here it must be noticed that affection for others is one of the chief motives, if not the chief motive, of the accumulation of capital. There is probably more wealth saved for the sake of others than for the future enjoyment of those who save it. If people were swayed entirely by self-interest, they would invest in annuities for their own lives instead of leaving a provision for their families. Lavish expenditure generally indicates a selfish disposition that cares above all things for its own enjoyments. Those who are anxious for the well-being of others are more likely to save, than to spend all their incomes. Again the prevalence of intemperate habits in a country diminishes both the number of days in the week and the number of years in his life during which the bread-winner is earning full wages. Temperance increases a man's power, and generally increases his will to save for the benefit of his children, and also to bring them up well, and invest Personal capital in them.

(*c*) The hope of rising in the world. If people feel that they are bound down for ever by a sort of caste regulation to one station in life, they will not save in order to better their position; they will naturally have little motive to be frugal. "It is fixity rather than inequality of fortune which is to be dreaded, for wherever there is motion there is life."

(*d*) Whether the strength of the unselfish affections be great or small, the inducements to save will be powerful if great social advantages are to be obtained by the possession of wealth. The middle classes are much under the influence of this consideration and partly for this reason they save more than other classes. On the other hand, the love of display hinders saving. Accumulation of wealth is generally rapid in countries which are advancing from poverty to riches, because habits of thrift, which are formed when people are poor, remain when they become rich. The parsimony which our fathers learnt during the pressure caused by the great war, is doubtless one of the chief causes of the enormous growth of capital during the present generation.

(*e*) Political and commercial security.

A man who saves, hopes that he and his family may enjoy in security the fruits of his saving. This requires, firstly, that Government should protect his property from fraud and violence; secondly, that if he or those whom he leaves behind him are unwilling or unable to employ the capital in business themselves, they must be able to lend it out to others and to live in quiet on the interest of it. One cause of the rapid accumulation of capital in modern times is the fact that as soon as a man has saved a few pounds, he can buy a share in a railway or other public company which will yield him a small but safe income, without his troubling himself further about it. Saving banks, friendly and building societies collect and store up the savings of those who can only put by very small sums at a time. Commercial security and habits of confidence are a product of civilization, and grow with it. Political Security must be paid for; but the taxes which some Governments levy in money and in compulsory military service are a dear price for this security and materially diminish the countries' power of accumulating capital. Capital, as well as industry, requires to be protected *by* the Government and *from* the Government.

§ 3. The expense of fitting men for skilled work is defrayed by their parents; and it is chiefly drawn from wages; that is, from the income that is earned by labour whether manual or mental. This expense is an outlay of capital just as much as that which is involved in feeding and breaking in a young cart horse. We may say then, that wages are a chief source of the accumulation of Personal capital. The wages of manual labour have not hitherto contributed very much to the accumulation of Material capital; though there are some signs of a movement in that direction. A far more important source of accumulation is the wages of the professional classes.

In England at the present time the chief source is profit on capital. Some Economists have spoken as though all others might be neglected in comparison with it; but really it is only in a few countries and only for a short time that the accumulation made from profits has been at all considerable.

During the greater part of the world's history the rent of land has been the chief source of saving. A good deal is saved from rent in England now, and in the rest of the world probably more is saved from it than from profits on capital. There are two causes of the greater importance of the savings from rent in other countries. Firstly, the income that is derived from land is very great relatively to the income that is derived from capital. Secondly, while the greater part of the land in England is owned by a comparatively small number of men, the land on the continent and in new countries is divided among a very large number of the population. Now rich landowners are not a saving class; it seems to be certain that on the average they save less than those who derive an equal income from trade. But peasant proprietors are a saving class. In England poor men save much less in proportion to their income than rich men do; but in countries in which peasant proprietors abound, their savings are very large.

For the man who labours with his hands there is no savings-bank whose attractions can be compared with the land. "Give a man secure possession of a bleak rock, and he will turn it into a garden....The magic of property turns sand into gold[1]." The peasant proprietor can give every hour of labour, every penny of capital, that he has to spare, to his land, and be sure of having the fruits of his exertion and self-denial ever before him. He loves his land, and takes pride in it, his choicest amusement on a holiday is to walk round it and rejoice in it[2]. "With the wage labourer the case is different. If he would put any portion of his wages to a reproductive use, he must seek out some borrower, and the amount he has to lend being small, this borrower must be the savings-bank, which will lend the money out, he knows not when, he knows not where. This is a very cold-blooded affair compared with the application of earnings to the land by the proprietor thereof, who works over it and lives upon it, who feels that it is all his, and shall be his children's after him. Neither the imagination nor the affections are addressed very powerfully by the savings-bank. There is, besides, some delay involved in a deposit, which, however slight, defeats many a good resolution and brings many a half-consecrated sixpence to the grocery or the bar-room[3]."

The absence of peasant proprietors is thus a loss to England in many ways; but it were useless to repine at it. Modern machinery and modern methods of agriculture give, as we shall see, a great advantage to large farms in competition with small farms. In market gardening, indeed, and generally when each plant requires separate care, the peasant proprietor may hold his own; but not in the general work of the farm. An intelligent man, who owns a little land, can almost always get a larger income by selling his land and using the price of it in farming or some other trade, than he can by cultivating it himself[4]. The same spirit of commercial enterprise which causes capital to accumulate in England faster than in any other European country has prevented her from having a race of peasant proprietors.

All history shews however that the hope of purchasing a small piece of land or a cottage and garden, on which he may retire, in his old age, is one of the strongest inducements that a working man can have to lead an industrious, temperate and frugal life. Yet the English working man is practically debarred

---

[1] Arthur Young.

[2] For evidence of the intelligence of the peasant proprietor in some districts, and also of the vast amount of capital that he invests in the land, and the heavy crops he raises from it, see Mill, Bk. II. ch. vi. and vii. and Cliffe Leslie, *Land Systems of Various Countries*.

[3] Walker, *The Wages-Question*, ch. XVIII.

[4] See *The Agricultural Lockout of* 1874, by Clifford.

from this hope by the uncertainty and the heavy legal expenses, which he must incur in making such a purchase; for these expenses are much greater in proportion for a small piece of land than for a large one. A reform of England's land-laws would much increase her accumulation both of Material and Personal Capital.

§ 4. We may next inquire how far the accumulation of capital depends upon the rate of profits, and the rate of interest which the owner of capital can obtain by lending it to others[1].

A high rate of interest no doubt affords a liberal reward of abstinence, and stimulates the saving of all who are ambitious of earning social position by their wealth. Again, if a man is in doubt whether to save in order to make provision for himself or his family, the expectation of a high rate of interest may induce him to save; because the higher the rate of interest, the larger the amount of future enjoyment which can be obtained by sacrificing a given amount of present enjoyment.

But the history of the past and the observation of the present shew that it is a man's temperament, much more than the rate of interest to be got for his savings, which determines whether he makes provision for his old age and for his family, or not. Most of those who make such a provision would do so equally whether the rate of interest were low or high. And when a man has once determined to provide a certain annual income, he will find that he has to save more if the rate of interest is low than if it is high. Suppose, for instance, that a man wishes to provide an income of £400 a year on which he may retire from business, or to insure £400 a year for his wife and children after his death. If the current rate of interest is 5 per cent., he need only put by £8,000 or insure his life for £8,000; but if it is 4 per cent., he must save £10,000, or insure his life for £10,000.

Again, a high rate of interest is a great inducement to retire early from business, and live on the interest of what has already been accumulated. Sir Joshua Child indeed said two centuries ago, "we see that generally all merchants" in countries in which the rate of interest is high "when they have gotten great wealth, leave trading" and lend out their money at interest, "the gain thereof being so easy, certain and great; whereas in other countries where interest is at a lower rate, they continue merchants from generation to generation, and enrich themselves and the state." It is more true now than it was then, that many men retire from business when they are yet almost in the prime of life, and when their knowledge of men and things might

---

[1] The relation between interest and profits is explained in Book II. Much of this section is taken from Sargant's *Recent Political Economy*.

enable them to conduct their business more efficiently than ever. Thus a fall in the rate of interest would in some ways promote the production and the accumulation of wealth.

But it would diminish the *power* of saving from a given amount of capital, because the larger the income a man derives from his business the larger are the means he has of saving. Also it would promote the emigration of capital. As a rule however, a fall in the rate of interest is itself the result of a great accumulation of capital; and the income derived from a large amount of capital at a low rate of interest generally gives a greater total power of saving than the income derived from a small amount of capital at a high rate of interest.

On the whole it may be concluded that a fall in the rate of interest in a country is likely to check the growth of capital in some ways and to promote it in others; but that the latter effects are on a smaller scale than the former, so that a fall in the rate of interest will diminish the accumulation of capital to some extent, though often only to a small extent.

§ 5. We shall presently see that a fall in the rate of interest is to be expected in the distant if not in the immediate future of the world's history, in consequence of the operation of the law of Diminishing Return; and this will ultimately check the accumulation of capital. But the progress of invention is continually finding profitable employment for capital in new ways. Railways, factories and machinery absorb every year large amounts of capital, which are turned to good account and return a profit to their owners; so that there is no reason for fearing any great check, in the immediate present, to the growth of capital. And in fact while the population of England is increasing at the rate of about 1·3 per cent. per annum, the capital of England is increasing at an average rate of about 3 per cent. per annum[1].

It has already been pointed out that the operation of the Law of Diminishing Return may be prevented from becoming of very great importance as regards Agriculture, provided the increase of population be checked in time; but that even if population did not increase at all, the mere lapse of centuries would bring with it the exhaustion of the mineral riches of the earth.

---

[1] The total Material wealth of England increased from about £6,100,000,000 in 1865, to about £8,500,000,000 in 1875; i. e. at the rate of £240,000,000 a year. (See Mr Giffen in the *Journal of the Statistical Society* for March, 1878.)

CHAPTER VII.

ORGANIZATION OF INDUSTRY.

§ 1. THE last chapter finished the discussion of the three
requisites of the production of wealth,—natural agents, labour
and capital. Before proceeding to examine the modern methods
of production and exchange, it will be well to see how these
methods have gradually grown up.

In savage life there is no variety. Savage tribes are made
up of a number of persons all doing the same work. Every one
is as a rule warrior, hunter, fisherman, tool-maker and builder.
Every one provides for all his own wants ; and, except for
purposes of defence, might almost as well live apart from the
rest.

But even among savages men shew special aptitudes for
particular kinds of work. One man, for instance, is skilled in
making bows ; and others offer him in exchange for a bow more
food, or other things, than he could get for himself in the same
time as he can make a bow; so he settles down to bow making.
In this way there gradually arises that division of labour which
makes society a living whole. And in the earliest times we find
this much division : that the disagreeable work is done by
women and slaves, and the agreeable work by their lords and
masters.

" The first great advance beyond this state consists in the
domestication of the more useful animals ; giving rise to the
Pastoral or nomad state, in which mankind do not live on the
produce of hunting, but on milk and its products, and on the
annual increase of flocks and herds. This condition is not only
more desirable in itself, but more conducive to future progress ;
and a much more considerable amount of wealth is accumulated
under it. In this state inequalities of wealth have their origin ;
and encouraged by their security against present want, men
begin to turn their attention to domestic manufactures."

The next transition was to the Agricultural state, and in this the ownership of cultivated land formed a solid basis on which society could be built up.   Sometimes all the land was owned by the sovereign ; but more frequently the land round a village belonged to the whole village in common.

The Village Communities, as they are called, lived a settled monotonous life.   In this stage we find differences of employments ; but there is as yet nothing that can properly be called organization.   In some cases indeed a whole village devoted itself to one occupation, as to smith's work, or shoemaking. But more commonly each village was self-sufficing ; that is, it produced for itself almost everything that it consumed, and had scarcely any trade with its neighbours.   It often happened that each trade became hereditary in a family.   For instance, each village had its own blacksmith, who was the son of the last blacksmith, and whose son would be the next blacksmith.   Men had scarcely any freedom in the choice of their occupations.

The fixed customs which thus controlled men's lives have been especially powerful in the East.   In India the climate has caused a limp habit of body and mind, which has made people submit to the rule of despotic kings, and more despotic custom. No tyrant has ever attempted, or even wished, to control every action of his subjects' lives.   But Oriental custom decides the Caste or rank in society to which a man belongs ; it prevents him from having any social intercourse with members of any other caste ; it orders the most trifling details of his action in his work, in his amusement, and at his meals.   Custom also regulates the wage of each kind of service, and the price of every commodity with an inflexible rule.

Where there is a monopoly of anything, a fixed custom as to its price may indeed do more good than harm.   If a village is bound down by custom to buy its ploughs of one particular blacksmith, it is best that custom should also regulate the price at which he sells them ; for otherwise he might sometimes take advantage of the necessities of his neighbours, and charge an exorbitant price ; and anyhow there would be a great waste of time in higgling and bargaining between him and them.

§ 2.   The industrial system of the cities of Greece and Rome was based on slavery.   They took it as an axiom that nature had ordained slavery ; that without slaves the world could not progress ; no one would have time for culture, no one could discharge the duties of a citizen.   They deliberately accepted the belief that there were multitudes of men whom nature had consigned at their birth to weary toil for the benefit of others, and that it was a matter of no moment whether those men lived ignorant, debased lives or not.   The genial temper of the Athenians indeed led them to treat their slaves with kindness and even sympathy.   But history shews that every civilisation which is based on slavery, though it may have a precocious growth, is yet rotten at the core and speedily decays; for when a race has lived for several generations among the excitements of civilised life, but scorning work and despising those who work, it has become heartless and frivolous, and therefore weak.

The Teutonic races that peopled Western Europe seemed at one time to be in danger of being ruined, not indeed by slavery, but by a system of serfdom that was not very much better. But they had always a reverence for man as man, and this reverence was promoted by the Christian religion, and fostered by the popular character of the mediæval church. They did not deliberately treat it as a matter of indifference whether those who did hard work for them lived debased lives. They never got thoroughly to despise the worker or his work; so they have not become frivolous, apathetic or selfish; and their civilisation seems likely to endure.

The rigid customs which have weighed down the East in all ages, seem to have pressed severely, but much less severely, on our Anglo-Saxon forefathers. They lived in an invigorating climate, and were too energetic to endure much tyranny either from man or from custom. But ignorance is a tyrant to whose sway even energy submits. And while our forefathers were wholly ignorant, the only line of action that they could strike out for themselves was that of pillaging and plundering their neighbours. This way of living afforded a good deal of excitement, but very little comfort. Gradually knowledge and a taste for comfort grew up with the growth of towns, where men learnt to care very little for plundering others, and to dislike very much being plundered themselves. In the towns men defended themselves against oppression, and learnt the arts of civilisation. While the country was ravaged by the wars and the robberies of barons, while the country folk were generally serfs, the towns were the homes of order, of patient work, of intelligent and peaceful enterprise.

§ 3. The towns grew rapidly: and as their various forms of skilled industry made their appearance, there was Division of labour. A man would make only things of one kind, or perhaps only parts of things of one kind. His work would directly or indirectly do some service to a great number of his fellow-citizens; and the things which he consumed would be produced by the combined work of his neighbours.

This may be expressed shortly by saying that the industry of the towns had become highly organized. A body is said to be highly **organized** when each part has its own work to perform, when by performing this work it contributes to the well-being of the whole, so that any stopping of this work injures the whole; while, on the other hand, each part depends for its own well-being on the efficient working of the other parts.

So long as the towns were struggling against adversity, all the citizens worked together with public spirit and enterprise to secure their common welfare; but when a town had fully achieved its freedom, and begun to prosper, the oldest families of traders began to insist on their own privileges as the only proper full citizens, and as members of the Town-gild. The privileges of this Gild were attacked by younger trade associations, called Craft-gilds, which were formed by those who worked at the various crafts. This struggle between the handicraftsmen and the leading merchants continued for several generations : but time was on the side of the younger and more vigorous bodies. In one town after another the Craft-gilds, leaguing together, overthrew the Town-gild and obtained mastery of the town.

The Craft-gilds did good in very many ways; they helped to organize industry; they took care that each man understood his trade and did sound work; they took an interest in the moral conduct of the worker, and they secured him and his family from want. But after a time their rules as to the way in which work should be carried on became oppressive, so as to prevent a man from taking his capital or labour into whatever trade he liked; they hindered the free circulation of capital and labour. And in the course of time there came a reaction. When the Gilds had ceased to do more good than harm, their power began to diminish, and at last they lost it altogether. The freedom of circulation again increased until there remained few obstacles to a man's earning his living as he liked.

Meanwhile the banks were growing up. In the middle ages the usurers or money-lenders had lent chiefly to necessitous persons at high rates of interest. There was not indeed much opening for the profitable investment of capital in industry; but the experience that was thus obtained in the difficult art of passing capital from where it is not much wanted, to where it is much wanted, has been of great use to the world. It has prepared the way for that organization of capital which is effected by the banks and other agencies of the modern money market.

§ 4. Advancing to more modern times we find a continual growth of the specialisation or division of labour. The broadest division is that between agricultural and manufacturing labour. In mediæval times the country folk used in the intervals of agriculture to spin and weave, to make shoes and build houses. But as agriculture became systematized, as machinery came into use in manufacture, and as the skill of trained artisans increased, the farming population gradually made less and less for itself, and bought more and more from the towns. The agriculturists were of course scattered over the land, but manufacturers congregated in closely peopled districts.

In these districts a further division or specialisation has grown up, and separate trades have sought separate localities. The textile trades have separated themselves from other trades. Those that work in wool do not generally live among the Lancashire cotton workers, but are collected together in Yorkshire : and they themselves are divided into the " woollen trade" and the " worsted trade," and these again spread out into various branches, each of which has a favourite district of its own. This collection into the same locality of large numbers who are engaged in the same trade is called the **Localisation of industry**.

A manufacturing district offers many social advantages. Experience shews that skilled artisans are intelligent and self-reliant, even when their work is monotonous. They have escaped from the dominion of custom, and are apt to consider whether they cannot better their condition by moving from one place to another, and even from one occupation to another.

Thus in modern times a large number of social and economic changes have increased the extent to which the distribution of wealth is determined by free competition. Workmen compete with one another for the most advantageous employment ; and employers compete for the cheapest and most efficient labour, and vie with one another in the invention of new machinery and new modes of manufacture. For each new invention and each new adaptation of an old process leads to new ways of carrying on business; and every such change in a trade brings with it fresh openings through which new men, both employers and labourers, may edge their way into the trade. In fact the train, the steamship, the printing-press and the telegraph give inducements and facilities for competition in all directions ; a competition of which the earlier civilizations were wholly incapable.

These changes have brought with them another great change. Formerly production used to be chiefly in the hands of Small Masters ; that is of men each of whom produced goods for sale in his own neighbourhood, with the aid of one or two apprentices and hired workmen. But as we shall see in the next chapter, the progress of events has put these small masters at a continually increasing disadvantage in competition with the owners of large factories. And the machinery in these factories grows steadily. The amount which a manufacturer devotes to the purchase of machinery increases much faster than the amount which he spends on the hire of labour. In other words, Auxiliary capital is increasing at a greater rate than Remuneratory.

Large factories concentrated in one place send their goods to market all over the world. The manufacturer, the workman, and the shopkeeper of Manchester are dependent for their well-being not only on each other's conduct, but also on the course of events in other parts of England and in other countries. Thus "society has become the complex body of mutually dependent workers which we now see, by steps so small that year after year the industrial arrangements have seemed to men just what they were before, by changes as insensible as those through which a seed passes into a tree."

These changes have been more marked in England than in any other country. The adventurous races who peopled her shores brought with them a spirit of enterprise which has been transmitted to their descendants. Her seas and rivers have promoted commerce, and with it that flexibility of habits which is caused by free intercourse with distant places. Her climate has been singularly favourable to rapid changes in agriculture. Being entrenched by the sea she has escaped the devastating wars which have discouraged the accumulation of capital on the Continent. Her land laws, her poor laws, and her political and social arrangements generally have tended to draw a sharp line between the rich and the poor ; so that nearly her whole capital has been accumulated in comparatively few hands ; and her rich mines of coal and iron have given prominence to those industries in which, as we shall see, production on a large scale is at the greatest advantage, in which large capitals have the best chance of becoming larger, while small capitals are in great risk of becoming smaller.

§ 5. The growing intelligence of the labourer and the increasing facility of movement from one part of the country to another have caused a close communication and to some extent a free circulation of labour between the various centres of industry. Capital is every day obtaining freedom of circulation, and so are the skill and ability by which capital is managed ; profits tend to equality in different occupations and in different parts of the country.

It is not indeed true that a thousand pounds invested in one trade will bring in the same profits as a thousand pounds invested in any other ; for profits are exceptionally high in trades that are exceptionally difficult or disagreeable. The free circulation of capital cannot remove inequalities that are due to these causes. But it does cause the rate of interest at which a tradesman can borrow money, on good security, to be nearly the same in every town and every trade in the kingdom. Hence arises an important Law, the full meaning of which will appear further on, viz.

Profits tend continually to equality in all trades which involve equal risks, discomforts and exertions ; and which require equally rare natural abilities and an equally expensive training.

CHAPTER VIII.

DIVISION OF LABOUR.

§ 1. PLATO extolled the ancient Egyptians for having turned
to good account their knowledge of the fact that division of
labour gives increase of dexterity in every particular workman.
Use becomes second nature ; and there are many kinds of work
which can be done well only when they have been practised
from childhood. A carpenter, a blacksmith, or a coalminer is
seldom good at his trade unless he has been at it all his
life.

When the division of labour is carried very far a man's whole
attention is concentrated on one operation. A house carpenter
handles a great many tools one after another, and does many
different kinds of work ; but in a very large furniture manu-
factory a man will often work all the year round at making
some part of a table or a chair. In cloth factories many women
and children do scarcely anything all day but tie together
broken threads on the spinning jenny. Many workers in metal
factories do nothing but fit a piece of metal into a socket, and
pull down a handle so as to drill or punch or stamp the metal in
some particular way. Such operations are performed by men,
women, and even children, with a rapidity and an unerring
accuracy "which exceed what the human hand could, by
those who had never seen them, be supposed capable of
acquiring[1]."

[1] It is believed that in such cases there is a physical change in the
nerves by which the motions of the hands are directed, and that an intimate connexion thus gradually grows up between these nerves and the
nerves of sight, which enables them all to work in perfect harmony
with one another for the performance of this particular class of operations. When the operation was first performed, the "sensory" or feeling
nerves of the eye and hand sent up a message to the brain to acquaint it
with the exact state of things. The mind was thus set to consider the

There are many kinds of skill which are not, strictly speaking, manual, but which resemble manual skill in requiring practice from early childhood. Such for instance is the work of the wool sorter, who sorts a fleece of wool into eight or ten heaps of different qualities. He has gradually acquired a wonderful discernment by touch and sight of minute differences of quality.

§ 2. A second advantage of division of labour is the economy of skill and of other mental and physical excellencies, which is obtained by keeping a man always occupied on the highest class of work for which he is fitted.

Mr Babbage was the first to insist on this. He says, " The master manufacturer by dividing the work to be executed into different processes, each requiring different degrees of skill or of force, can purchase exactly that precise quantity of both which is necessary for each process ; whereas if the whole work were executed by one workman, that person must possess sufficient skill to perform the most difficult, and sufficient strength to execute the most laborious of the operations into which the work is divided." In any large factory we may see young children carrying light weights or picking up loose threads, older children and women moving heavier weights, or taking care of machines that can easily be managed, while the task of keeping the machines in working order is entrusted to skilled mechanics. Those who keep the machine in order are paid as high wages as the clerks who are occupied in keeping the accounts of the establishment ; but there would be a great waste of efficiency if the mechanics spent part of their time in keeping accounts, and the clerks part of theirs in repairing the machines.

case ; it determined by an act of the will what should be done next ; and sent down by the "efferent" nerves of the hand more or less clumsy orders, which were more or less clumsily executed. But there seems to grow up, after years of practice, a more direct connexion between the sensory and the efferent nerves, whose co-operation is required ; so that when the right time comes for the particular movement of a finger, the stimulus which prompts that movement is instigated at once by the "sensory" nerves that bring up to the brain the record of that movement. When the connexion has become well established, each part of the operation follows on the preceding *automatically*. That is to say, the mind is not called in at all in the case, no attention is required, the whole mental energy is at liberty for thinking about other things ; or it may lie idle and be stored up ready to come into full and fresh activity in the intervals of the man's work. In walking, writing, and playing the piano, we see actions which by continued practice from childhood can be performed almost automatically ; though even the simplest parts of them require the full attention of those who have not been trained to them.

The economy of inventions is best attained when it is the business of a certain set of people to study every new invention which bears on their particular trade. For each new leading idea with regard both to processes and machinery has many practical applications. Knowledge is acquired in working out one invention that is likely to be of use in seeking for others. If however the work of thinking is confined to a few, division of labour is carried too far. It is said that whatever superiority America has over England in mechanical inventions and improvements in manufacture, is largely due to the encouragement which American employers give to independent and originating thought among their workmen.

But undoubtedly the employer should be the master mind of the whole : his time should be occupied, not in doing work, but in deciding what work is to be done, how it is to be done, and who is to do it. As Bagehot says, " He settles what goods shall be made, and what not : what brought to market and what not. He is the general of the army ; he fixes on the plan of operations, organizes its means, and superintends its execution. If he does this well, the business succeeds and continues ; if he does it ill, the business fails and ceases. Everything depends on the correctness of the unseen decisions, on the secret sagacity of the determining mind."

§ 3. Next with regard to the economy of machinery.

Just as there is waste whenever a skilled man is engaged on work in which his skill is useless, so there is waste whenever a machine lies idle. A blacksmith could sometimes find use for a steam hammer, but there would be so much waste in keeping it idle the greater part of the day, that he cannot afford to have it.

Many things continue to be made by hand which would long ago have been made better and more cheaply by machinery, if there had been a large demand for them. For the trouble, expense and risk involved in inventing and patenting a new process, or a new machine, is the same whether the invention is to be applied to the production of many goods or few. But the profit to be derived from the invention depends on the extent of the manufacture to which it can be applied. The substitution of machinery for handwork has sometimes to wait for a brilliant invention by which a great practical difficulty can be overcome : but most new machines are really adaptations of old ones, which are sure to be made as soon as there is a demand for them.

In fact, the great advantage that the human hand has over machinery is that the hand can bring tools to work upon the material in almost any position : and many important mechanical inventions are merely new plans for copying the way in which the tools and the material are adjusted to one another by the hand.   This is sometimes done by giving new movements to the tools that are driven by a machine, but more often it consists in making some new fixed or moving socket for holding firmly the material exactly as it is wanted.

§ 4.   We have seen that the advantages of division of labour cannot be obtained in the production of any commodity unless it is one for which the demand is very great, so that it is produced in very large quantities.   We have next to inquire how far these advantages are dependent on the size of the factories in which the work is done.

This question is a very important one, because the hope of rising in the world is one of the chief inducements to energetic action, and to thrifty habits.   The prosperity of the nation depends greatly upon how far the upper classes are recruited by the best strength and ability that is born among the lower classes.   And one of the easiest and healthiest routes upwards which a working man can follow is that of first saving a little money while working as foreman or overlooker, and then starting a small establishment in that branch of his business of which he is a master.   We shall find that some of the advantages of division of labour can be obtained only in very large factories, but that many of them, more than at first sight appears, can be secured by small factories and workshops, provided there are a very great number of them in the same trade.

The manufacture of a commodity often consists of several distinct stages, to each of which a separate room in the factory is devoted.   But if the total amount of the commodity produced is very large, it may be profitable to devote separate small factories to each of these steps.

If there are many factories, large or small, all engaged in the same process, *Subsidiary Industries* will grow up to meet their special wants.

§ 5.   Firstly, there are the industries which make the special tools and machinery required for the process.   There are, for instance, large works in which the machinery wanted for the woollen trades, is made by a vast number of complex machines.

Secondly, there are the Subsidiary Industries which facilitate communication between various branches of a trade.   Their aid is important to all classes of factories, but especially to those which are devoted entirely to one stage of a process of manufacture.   Under this head come carriers, railway companies, and all classes of agents and intermediate traders, and again those who collect and spread information by trade newspapers, and in other ways.   Bankers also come under this head.   The payment for goods is facilitated by them as the transfer of goods is by the railways.   But further, they pass command over capital from hand to hand, and the help which they thus give to new men, who have but little capital of their own, is perhaps the most important of the forces which oppose the modern tendency towards the concentration of manufacture in the hands of a few large firms.

But small factories, whatever their numbers, will be at a great disadvantage relatively to large unless many of them are collected together in the same district. We may then consider the advantages of the *Localization of Industry*.

§ 6. The Localization of Industry promotes the education of skill and taste, and the diffusion of technical knowledge.

Where large masses of people are working at the same kind of trade, they educate one another. The skill and the taste required for their work are in the air, and children breathe them as they grow up. This is seen particularly in such manufactures as those of glass and pottery.

Again, each man profits by the ideas of his neighbours : he is stimulated by contact with those who are interested in his own pursuit to make new experiments ; and each successful invention, whether it be a new machine, a new process, or a new way of organizing the business, is likely when once started to spread and to be improved upon.

In a district in which an industry is localized a skilled workman is sure of finding work to suit him ; a master can easily fill a vacancy among his foremen ; and generally the economy of skill can be carried further than in an isolated factory however large. Thus both large and small factories are benefited by the localization of industry and by the assistance of subsidiary trades. · But these benefits are most important to the small factories, and free them from many of the disadvantages under which they would otherwise labour in competition with large factories.

§ 7. Still a large factory has many special advantages.

Firstly, greater economies can be attained by a large than by a small factory in such matters as the arrangement of buildings, steam engines, and other machinery ; and again in such work as that of clerks, doorkeepers, stokers, repairers of machines, &c. One high chimney can make a draught for a large furnace as well as for a small one ; one doorkeeper can admit five hundred men as easily as fifty.

Again, a large factory can often afford to have a machine to do work that is done by hand in a small factory. It is true that a small factory devoted to one short stage of the process of manufacture may have the best and most highly specialized machinery. But such a factory would not come into existence until the advantage of having special machinery for this stage had become well established. If there is a large demand for any kind of machine it may be worth a man's while to spend much money and trouble in trying to make it, with the intention of patenting it, and getting a royalty on each machine that is made.   But in fact a very small number of the improvements that are made are patented ; and a large manufacturer has greater inducements than a small one to make experiments which are not certain of success.   He can spend a large sum on trying a new process or a new kind of machine, without feeling the loss if the experiment fails.   If it succeeds, he is much more likely to get a good return on his outlay before others are able to take advantage of it than a smaller manufacturer would be.

But very often the most important advantages to large firms consist in their facilities for buying and selling.   The expense involved in buying a large quantity of goods is always smaller in proportion than that of buying a small quantity.   A large firm gains in the transport of goods ; particularly if it has a railway siding.   It gets prompt and trustworthy information from highly paid agents ; and thus learns when and from whom to buy, when and what to manufacture, when and to whom to sell, and lastly whom to trust and whom not to trust.   It can afford to advertise largely in print and by means of commercial travellers.   Something may also be allowed for the confidence which consumers feel that a large house will not descend to petty tricks and dishonesties ; it has too much to lose.

In some trades a large firm gains much by the variety of its wares.   A builder, who wants a great number of brass fittings, likes to order them of a firm which has a vast number of moulds and can fill up a large and various order from its own resources.   A large firm gains often in the matter of superintendence ; but not so much as at first sight appears.   It is true that in small works the master or manager looks after many things which in large works are left to the care of a foreman or overlooker ; but hired overlookers have not the same interest and energy in preventing waste through carelessness or dishonesty that the master himself has.   There are some trades, particularly those concerned with the more valuable metals, in which large firms are on the whole at a disadvantage as compared with small ones in the matter of superintendence.

§ 8.   There are many branches of trade in which the advantages of division of labour and specialization of machinery seem to have reached their limit.   In cotton spinning, for instance, a large factory contains many rooms which are exactly alike in all respects ; so that it resembles several smaller factories joined together.   It has then no great advantage over smaller factories in the work of production, but it has those general advantages in buying and selling and organizing which a large capital must always have over a small one. When the owner of such a factory wants to put more capital into his business, it may answer his purpose to put up looms for making his yarn into calico. He then has an advantage over those who only spin, because he has no trouble about finding a market for his yarns ; and he has an advantage over those who merely weave, because he has no trouble about bargaining for and testing the quality of the yarn that he uses. What used to be the work of several distinct trades is all done now under one roof.

This change is partly due to the modern facilities for the growth of firms which manage vast sums of capital. The number of very wealthy men has increased rapidly of late ; and the Limited Liabilities Acts[1] have enabled those who are not rich, and who perhaps have no time for business, to take shares in large trading concerns, without imperilling their whole fortunes. This has led to the formation of vast companies in almost every branch of business. Some of them undertake enterprises for which no private capital could suffice. The London and North Western Railway Company wields a capital greater than the whole accumulated wealth of many of the states whose names occupy a large place in history. There does not seem to be any limit to the amount of wealth which a single trading company can profitably manage in a business which can be managed by routine, and does not require the bold enterprise and prompt decision of a single mind.

But this great tendency to the concentration of capitals is opposed by the increasing variety in the number of things that have to be done, and in the modes of doing them. Industries subsidiary to the old established industries are springing up continually, and when they become well established, other industries subsidiary to these make their appearance. The growing variety of the wants of man, the growing resources of invention by which they are met, continually make openings by which new men edge their way into business. A glance at the Trade Directory of London or almost any other large manufacturing town will discover an astonishing variety of trades which are almost entirely in the hands of small masters.

§ 9. Whatever may be the result of the contest between large and small factories, it appears certain that the division of labour will continually increase. This increase is one of vital importance. It adds to men's power over nature, and furthers social progress by increasing wealth. Its effects are for the

---

[1] These Acts, passed in 1855—1862, enable a Company by writing "Limited" after its title to secure its shareholders against losing more than the amount of their shares by its failure.

most part good, but in some part evil. Division of labour is said to increase the *uncertainty* of industry. A man whose skill can be turned to account in only one trade is likely to suffer much when that trade is depressed, or his skill is displaced by machinery. On the other hand, division of labour accustoms producers to sell in widely distant markets, and it is not very likely that all of them will be depressed at the same time. Again the division of labour sometimes enables a man to pass easily between trades which used to be totally distinct. A country watchmaker could not easily become a gunmaker or vice versa : but many of the men in a large watch factory could easily find employment in a large rifle factory, and vice versa. When the late American war came to a close, a famous rifle factory devoted itself to making sewing machines. As we proceed further, we shall find other reasons for thinking that whatever tendency there is to a growing uncertainty of industry, is to be ascribed to other causes than the division of labour.

But division of labour does unquestionably cause some *monotony*. This is a very great evil in the case of work which involves continued muscular strain or long hours of work in a bad atmosphere. But when the work is light, and the hours of work not excessive, monotony is not very injurious. As Mr Nasmyth says[1], "If you call for the brute force of a man you will degrade the man. He goes to his house so physically exhausted that it is an utter absurdity to say to that man 'Read and improve yourself.' He would fall asleep immediately : he must go and take some excitement. But if you take the man who has been superintending some piece of machinery all day, in which there is very little or only a minimum of call for his brute force, you will find that that man's intellectual power, if he has any at all, will come forth, and he will be a reader and a self cultivated man. I have found that again and again. I think this is the result of machinery, that it takes away the necessity for brute labour, and very much elevates the intellectual and moral position of the working classes. The management of machinery requires much judgment and resource." The experience of Englishmen in backward countries shews that costly and delicate machinery cannot be worked profitably by a dull and ignorant people, however low may be the rate of wages which they are willing to take. The work of the mechanic, even where it is apparently monotonous, makes him shrewd, cautious and prompt.

Again even when division of labour makes the work of an individual monotonous and uniform, it makes the work of the country at large changeful and various. The worker in a town

---

[1] Tenth Report of Trades Union Commissioners, 1868, p. 65.

whose mental and physical energies are not strained by his work can hardly fail to be educated by the variety and excitement of the various work that is going on around him. His neighbours have interests in life sufficiently like his, and yet sufficiently different, to enable him to learn from them new ways of looking at things.

There is more division of labour in the town than in the country ; but the agricultural labourer lags behind the town workman in intelligence. The advances that have recently been made in agricultural science are chiefly due to the mental activity of towns-people.

§ 10. It will be useful to refer to the **Law of Division of Labour**, which may be stated thus :—

> When the demand for a commodity becomes very large, the process of making it is generally divided among several distinct classes of workers, each with its proper appliances, and each aided by Subsidiary industries ; for such a division diminishes the difficulty of making the commodity.

Anticipating a term which will be defined later on, we may say :—

The Cost of production of a manufactured commodity is diminished whenever an increase in the demand for it leads to an increased division of labour in making it.

The Law of Division of Labour implies that an increase in the amount of capital and labour which is applied to any process of manufacture is likely to cause a more than proportionately increased return. It is therefore sometimes called the **Law of Increasing Return**, so as to bring out the contrast in which it stands to the Law of Diminishing Return which applies to agriculture.

§ 11. The largest industry is that of agriculture ; but there is scarcely any other industry which is able to make so little use of the advantages of division of labour and of production on a large scale. For agricultural labourers cannot be grouped together in large masses ; they must be scattered over the country. And each season of the year has its special work: a man cannot spend his life in reaping. So that the work of agriculture cannot be broken up into a vast number of parts each of which is performed by a band of labourers who devote their lives to acquiring a special skill in this class of work.

Agriculture, however, seems to be following in the steps of manufacture. Field steam-engines are becoming common, and new machines to be worked by them or by horse power are appearing in rapid succession. The fields demand every day a smaller number of dull labourers and a greater number of intelligent mechanics.

This change is exercising an important influence in the competition between small and large farms. The small farmer cannot always afford to have a field steam-engine; he cannot afford to have a great number of machines for occasional use. Thus every year puts him at a greater disadvantage relatively to the large farmer. This disadvantage is diminished but not removed by the rapid growth of a subsidiary industry, which undertakes steam ploughing threshing, &c. for farmers. The growth of this industry is the most important step towards obtaining the advantages of division of labour that has ever been made by agriculture.

In comparison with a small farmer a large farmer gains something in economy of buildings, and in economy of materials. He is able to have a better rotation of crops; he can send a great many labourers into a field in which there is anything to be done quickly. He can, as a rule, borrow capital from the banks more easily than a small farmer can. Lastly, the large farmer is likely to have more knowledge and greater skill and enterprise than the small farmer. He probably received a better education at starting; and he can afford to leave to subordinates much work that the small farmer does himself, so that he has more time and opportunity for increasing his knowledge. And as farms change hands from time to time, the ablest farmers are likely to find their way to the largest farms. Thus the economy of skill is carried further under a system of large, than under one of small, farms. On the other hand the large farmer loses in the matter of superintendence. The small farmer works hard himself: he watches for every trifling gain and every small saving: and those who work under him have little opportunity of being idle or dishonest.

§ 12. These advantages enable spade husbandry to be as successful on small holdings as on large. A large market garden has few advantages over a small one except in buying and selling. An intelligent market gardener who cultivates a few acres by the labour of himself, his family, and perhaps one or two hired labourers, can pay a high rent for his garden, and yet earn very good wages for himself and very good profits on his capital. Similarly a well managed small vineyard in Southern Europe seems to be able to hold its own against the competition of larger vineyards. Each vine has its own history, the soil is seldom exactly of the same character for many consecutive yards; and the cultivator of a large vineyard could not carry in his head many of the trifling details that guide the action of him who devotes all his life to one little plot of ground.

But the greater part of the small holdings on the continent have generally the advantage of being owned by those who cultivate them. It has already been remarked[1] that the peasant proprietor has in land a constant source of pleasure and excitement and the safest and most convenient of savings-banks. He invests his capital and labour in his land, without requiring as high a profit on his capital as the wealthy farmer would, and without expecting as high wages for his toil as would be demanded by the hired labourer. He may through want of machinery, or of knowledge retain methods of cultivation that have been discarded as wasteful by the English farmer. But still he is content and happy. His produce is generally less in proportion to the amount of labour spent in raising it than is the case with an English farm. But his produce per acre is often large, and on the whole he contributes his full share to the agricultural wealth of the country.

[1] Chap. vi. § 3.

CHAPTER IX.

TENURE OF LAND.

§ 1. A GREAT deal has already been said incidentally about the tenure of land. In tracing the gradual organization of industry, we noticed how in very early times land was no man's property; how tribes of savages wandered over it and supported themselves by hunting; how, afterwards adopting a pastoral life, they drove half domesticated herds slowly from one pasture to another. We saw how, when agriculture appeared, land became the property of village communities. Recent historical research has shewn that in almost every part of Europe, in many parts of Asia, and probably in some other places, the land of each such village community was generally divided into three parts, or to use the Teutonic name, into three Marks.

The Town Mark contained the houses, which were the private property of the several families who lived in them. The Arable Mark was divided into three fields, one of which was left fallow each year, the other two being cultivated. Each family had for its use a lot in each field : so as always to have its proper share of land in cultivation. In most countries the lots were periodically redistributed.

The remainder of the land was the Common Mark. This was not cultivated, and each family had equal rights of pasture and of cutting wood in it.

The system of village communities somewhat modified prevails in Russia and India in the present day. It has some advantages; extreme misery is seldom found in it; men lead peaceful and contented, but monotonous lives. The community watches jealously to prevent any one from adopting methods of cultivation that are opposed to its interests, or even to its habits and prejudices. Thus grows up in the course of time a network of customary rules, which hampers the freedom and enterprise of individuals, and hitherto has been found to check and hinder agricultural improvement of every kind.

In Western Europe this system was transformed into the military system of Feudalism by the wars and conquest of the Middle Ages. In Feudalism the notions of ownership and government were so blended that the sovereign was regarded as having a kind of ownership of the land. His subjects held it from him on condition of rendering him military service when required. Gradually the rights of the Sovereign to land have fallen into abeyance, and private persons have now practically undisputed possession of it, but even to the present day bargains about land are not determined by free competition in quite the same way as bargains about other things. Each nation has special laws, customs, and sentiments with regard to the transfer and tenure of land.

§ 2. A large part of the Continent is owned by Peasant Proprietors. We have seen how the peasant loves his land as his friend, how gladly he invests his earnings in it ; how he gets to know the history of every square yard of it. He may not know of, or may be unable to afford the advanced methods of the rich English farmer. But in some kinds of cultivation he excels ; and even though he does not generally turn his labour to the best account, his untiring zeal often raises a large gross produce.

In some portions of Southern Europe the Metayer tenure prevails. The metayer has an hereditary right to cultivate a small piece of land on condition of giving a certain portion of the produce, generally one half, to the landlord. The landlord supplies the whole or a part, according to local custom, of the capital required for working the land[1]. The metayer resembles the peasant proprietor in having fixity of tenure. But in some other respects he resembles the members of a village community. For he is harassed and hampered by the rules which have grown up to secure the landlord's share of the produce ; and since he retains only a fixed portion of the fruits of his labour, he has not as strong an incentive to exertion as the peasant proprietor has.

The land of America is cultivated by those who own it[2].

---

[1] With regard to Metayers, Irish Cottiers and Peasant proprietors, the reader is referred to Mill, Bk. ii., and Cliffe Leslie's *System of Land Tenure*.

[2] "The American farmer is at least in nine hundred and ninety-five cases out of a thousand the owner of the land he cultivates." Mr Ruggles' report published by the New York Chamber of Commerce, 1874.

The ease with which men get land prevents the growth of any considerable class of agricultural labourers at present, so that the tenure of land in America resembles in many ways that of peasant proprietors. But the farms are not small, and the farmers are generally educated men, full of restless energy. They frequently sell their farms and move westwards to larger farms or richer soil; they are always on the look out for improved machinery and improved methods of cultivation. And in many other ways they present a striking contrast to the patient and unenterprising peasant proprietors of Europe, among whom the land and the method of cultivating it descend with little change from father to son.

The share of the produce that the metayer pays to the landlord is sometimes called "rent." But in this book the word will always mean that payment which the owner of land can obtain by free competition for lending out the use of it to others.

Rich land affords a larger return to the capital employed on it than could be obtained by applying the same amount of capital to the cultivation of poor land. In a populous country in which there is a great demand for food, and in which therefore some food has to be raised at great expense from poor land, the value of the produce raised from the rich land will be more than sufficient to pay the expenses of raising it. This surplus value the owner retains if he cultivates the land himself. But in England and some other countries there are always capitalists willing to cultivate the land with their own capital, and to pay this surplus to the landlord in the form of rent. This system has the great advantage of giving the management of the land to those who have capital, agricultural skill and liking for the work. We have already seen that the advantages of division of labour and of productions on a large scale are of less importance in agriculture than in manufacture: but their importance is increasing. The progress of the arts of agriculture brings with it a continually increasing demand for capital and for highly trained agricultural skill. And the progress of the nation in wealth and intelligence increases the number of able farmers who have a considerable command over capital. The combined action of all these causes is increasing the average size of farms, and raising the status of the farmer. In Scotland and some parts of England there prevails a system of long leases which secures to the farmer nearly the whole benefit of his skill and energy. If his lease is short he receives but scanty protection from the law. But custom so far shields him that he is seldom in great danger of losing all the benefits of the improvements he has made in his farm, through having his rent raised, or being ejected without compensation, by an unscrupulous landlord.

The Irish Cottier pays a rent for the use of his land and cultivates it at his own risk. But here his resemblance to the English farmer ends. The Irish Cottier is a poor and uneducated peasant who rents a small plot of land either directly from its owner or from a middleman who makes a living by subletting land. The ignorance and recklessness of the Irish peasant and his inherited thirst for land often induce him under the stress of competition to undertake to pay a rent higher than he can pay. Some of the smaller landowners and many of the middlemen grasp at such promises; and then the cottier finds idleness his best policy; thrift his worst. He has no Standard of Comfort, no inducement to prudence in marriage; and population is restrained chiefly by poverty, disease and famine. The misery of the cottiers cannot be removed without first removing the causes of their recklessness. This recklessness is to some extent—it is a matter of controversy to what extent — due to the bad legislation of our forefathers. There is good reason to believe that it is being diminished under the wise legislation of recent years.

The discussion of the question as to which is the best system of land tenure has been complicated by some uncertainty as to the meaning of the term "the best system." By the best system some mean that which gives the greatest gross produce, others mean that which gives the greatest net or surplus produce after deducting the necessaries of life for the labourers, while others again mean that which contributes most to man's general well-being. We have seen reason for thinking that the greatest net produce is on the average obtained under the system of large farms; and that the largest gross produce is obtained in some of those districts in which there is an intelligent and energetic race of peasant proprietors; for their untiring zeal keeps on applying more labour to the land long after the return from it has diminished so far that a capitalist farmer would have ceased from further cultivation.

Economists are not agreed as to what system best promotes general well-being. If a vote could be taken from all Economists throughout the world, it would probably be given in favour of the system under which the land is owned by its cultivator, whether in large farms as in new countries, or in small plots as in old, and this view is adopted now by many Englishmen. But nearly all English Economists of the past generation had a strong preference for the system of large farms. This is partly due to the same causes that have promoted the employment of large capitals in English manufactures[1], partly to the fact that

---

[1] See Book I. ch. vii. § 4.

England's position in the Great French war was largely owing to the vast *net* produce of her manufactures and agriculture[1].

§ 3.   Enough has been said now to shew that when land is let on the English system its rent is the surplus return which it gives to the farmer's capital after deducting what is necessary to replace his capital with profits.   It is easy to see that this rent will be increased by anything that enables the farmer to raise a greater produce with a given outlay, or by anything that gives him a better market for his produce.   But it is more difficult to analyse the various parts of his outlay; to measure the total value of his produce; and finally, by subtracting from this value enough to return him his outlay with profits, to determine the amount of his rent.   We shall be in a better position for doing this when we have examined the first principles of the theory of value.

[1] For instance Ricardo says, "Adam Smith constantly magnifies the advantages which a country derives from a large gross, rather than a large net income....Provided the net real income of a nation, its rent and profits be the same, it is of no importance whether it consists of ten or of twelve millions of inhabitants.   Its power of supporting fleets and armies, and all species of unproductive labour, must be in proportion to its net, and not in proportion to its gross income."

BOOK II.

NORMAL VALUE.

CHAPTER I.

DEFINITIONS. LAW OF DEMAND.

§ 1. IN the present Book we are to inquire into the influence that competition exerts upon wages profits and prices.
Of course competition is only one out of many causes by
which they are determined. In backward countries competition
exerts but little influence men do not forecast the future,
and deliberately shape their course by a calculation of distant
advantages. They rather drift along under the influence of
custom, doing the same work in the same way, and for the
same remuneration as their fathers did it. But in advanced
countries, particularly in Western Europe, Northern America
and Australia, competition is far the most important of all
the influences that affect wages profits and prices. And it
will therefore be our best plan to begin our examination of
wages profits and prices by inquiring how they would be determined if free competition were the only influence acting
upon them. In Book III., when we are discussing Market
values, our attention will be directed chiefly to other influences. But in this Second Book we have to shut our eyes
to those other influences as far as we can, and think only of
the effects which would be produced in the long run by free
competition, if every one were quick to seek out and follow

his own economic interests. We have in this Book to examine *Normal Values.* For :—

    That condition of a thing which would be brought about by the undisturbed action of free competition is called its **Normal Condition.**

§ 2. [That which is according to the laws or precepts made by authority is legal: That which is according to the Laws of nature in their ordinary operation is normal. Of course everything in nature happens, in one sense, according to the Laws of nature. But very often we have in view some particular set of Laws ; and when it is understood that special reference is made to these Laws, we may say that that condition of a thing which is brought about by their undisturbed action, is its normal condition. Every tree grows according to the Laws of nature, but if a tree is planted in such a position that it cannot grow "naturally," that is according to the laws of its own nature, its shape is said to be abnormal. So it is in one sense according to the Laws of nature that the branches of a tree are swayed by the wind. Yet we say that they are in their normal position only when the wind is still. This is the position which they adopt, and in which they rest when not disturbed. When we speak of Normal values, or Normal prices, or Normal wages, or Normal profits, the particular set of Laws which we have in view are those Laws of human nature and human conduct which are brought into play when competition is perfectly free. It is true that when man is influenced by custom or prejudice, or when he is prevented by ignorance or apathy from competing freely, his action is according to the Laws of his nature, and is in one sense natural. But it is not according to those Laws of his nature which we have specially in view when discussing the economic condition of highly civilised countries. We therefore do not call his action Normal in the special or technical sense in which the word is used here.

If the wind blew equally from all quarters the *mean* or average position of a branch would be the same as its normal position. But if the wind blew more towards the east than towards the west, the mean position of the branch would be to the east of its normal position. And in the same way with regard to value : if competition were perfectly free, the average value of a thing would be the same as its Normal value. But since in fact competition is not perfectly free, the average value of a thing may differ from its Normal value; although the two seldom differ much.

Adam Smith and the older Economists spoke of the " Natural" rates of wages profits and prices. They used the word Natural to mean that which is according to man's nature when competition is free. But it has been found best to use

"Normal" for this purpose, because the word "Natural" has been used loosely: men often call an arrangement "Natural" merely because they approve it, and without taking the trouble to examine whether the Laws of Nature actually tend to bring it about.]

§ 3. Before entering upon the theory of Normal value it will be well to define some words which will be used in it.

The growth of the spirit of competition causes men to look about them to see where they can buy cheapest, and where they can sell dearest. A man may not trouble himself much about small retail purchases: he may give half a crown for a packet of paper in one shop which he could have got for two shillings in another. But it is otherwise with wholesale prices. A manufacturer cannot sell a ream of paper for six shillings while his neighbour is selling it at five. For those whose business it is to deal in paper know almost exactly the lowest price at which it can be bought, and will not pay more than this. The manufacturer has to sell at about the market price, that is at about the price at which other manufacturers are selling at the same time. When the competition among dealers is perfect, there can be but one price in the same market : so that we may say

> A **Market** for a ware is a place where there is such competition among buyers, and also among sellers, that the ware cannot have two different prices at the same time.

"Originally," says Mr Jevons, "a market was a public place in a town where provisions and other objects were exposed for sale ; but the word has been generalized, so as to mean any body of persons who are in intimate business relations and carry on extensive transactions in any commodity. A great city may contain as many markets as there are important branches of trade, and these markets may or may not be localized. The central point of a market is the public exchange, mart or auction rooms, where the traders agree to meet and transact business. In London, the Stock Market, the Corn Market, the Coal Market, the Sugar Market, and many others are distinctly localized ; in Manchester the Cotton Market, the Cotton Waste Market, and others. But this distinction of locality is not necessary. The traders may be spread over a whole town, or region of country, and yet make a market, if they are, by means of fairs, meetings, published price lists, the post office or otherwise, in close communication with each other." That is, they will all pay the same price for the same thing in the same place. When it is said that the price is the same for all the dealers in a market that extends over a large district, each buyer is supposed to pay extra the expense of its being delivered to him.

5—2

§ 4.   There are two ways in which a person may regard anything that he has.   He may consider its use to himself, or he may consider what he can obtain in exchange for it.   From the one point of view he looks at what Adam Smith calls its value in use, from the other at its value in exchange.

> The **value in use** or utility of a thing to a person is the amount of pleasure or satisfaction which he derives from possessing it.
>
> The **value in exchange** or exchange value of a thing is the power of purchasing other goods which its possession conveys.

"Value" standing alone always means value in exchange, and never value in use.

Value implies a relation between commodities.   For instance, the value of a pound of beef may be its power of purchasing three pounds of sugar or five grains of gold.   If sugar were to become scarce or gold were to become more plentiful, the value of a pound of beef might become the power of purchasing two pounds of sugar or six grains of gold.   Such a change would not justify us in saying that the value of beef had fallen or risen, but only that it had fallen relatively to sugar, and risen relatively to gold.   But if we found that a pound of beef would exchange for a greater quantity of almost every other commodity than before, we might then say that its value had risen.   Its value would have risen relatively to commodities in general; it would have obtained a greater purchasing power over commodities in general.

In every civilised country some commodity is chosen as a medium of exchange and a measure of the value, or general purchasing power, of other things.   This commodity is generally one of the precious metals, gold and silver; coins of fixed weight are made of these metals and stamped by Government, and are the money of the country.   The number of them for which a pound of beef can be exchanged represents its value and is called its *price*.   If beef becomes scarce, and rises in price, while the prices of all other things remain unchanged, there is a rise in the general purchasing power or value of beef.

Of course the value of money itself may have fallen; that is, each coin may purchase less of all other commodities than before.   In that case, though the price of beef has risen, its value or general purchasing power may have remained stationary; the greater price for which it is sold may only give the power of purchasing the same amount of other commodities as before.

In a later chapter[1] something will be said of the changes that may occur in the purchasing power of money.   But while

[1] Book III. chap. I.

examining the theory of Normal value we shall, for convenience, assume that the purchasing power of money remains un-changed. So that a rise or fall in the price of a thing will always mean a rise or fall in its general purchasing power or exchange value.

§ 5.   If things were exchanged for one another without the use of money there would be no distinction between buyers and sellers; but this distinction makes its appearance as soon as money comes into use to represent general purchasing power.

> A **buyer** is one who wishes to obtain a particular com-modity and offers in exchange for it a certain amount of money, that is, of command over commodities in general.

> A **seller** is one who is willing to part with a particular commodity that he has in his possession, and demands in exchange for it a certain amount of money, that is, of command over commodities in general.

The price of any commodity in a market is determined by the eagerness of buyers on the one hand, and the eagerness of sellers on the other. The remainder of the chapter will be occu-pied in explaining the Law of the eagerness of buyers, or the *Law of Demand*.

§ 6.   It is a matter of common experience that the larger the stock which sellers determine to sell, the lower will be the price at which it can be got rid of. *Vice versâ*, the lower the price at which anything is offered for sale, the greater is the amount of it which can be sold off. Examples occur to us every day. In a good apple year, the price of apples is low ; in a bad year it is high. At the end of the season a fashion-able shop sells off at a great reduction, and so gets many customers.

These facts shew how the Utility of anything to a man, its power of satisfying his wants, depends partly upon the quantity of things of the same kind that he has already. The more he has of it the less will be the utility of more of it to him. Suppose he wants to buy some flannel. If he could not get it for less than five shillings a yard he might be willing to buy a single yard at this price: that is, the Value in Use or utility of a yard to him may be greater than the satisfaction that he could obtain by spending the five shillings in any other way. But we may suppose that he is able to get flannel at one shilling a yard, and that at this price he buys twenty yards. This shews that the utility to him of the twentieth yard is not less than the satisfaction he could get by spending the shilling in other ways ; but that the utility of a twenty-first yard would be less than this satisfaction. In other words a shilling just *measures* the utility of the twentieth yard, the final yard which he buys. To use Mr Jevons' happy phrase, the *Final Utility* of a yard of flannel to him is measured by one shilling.

In speaking of the utility of a commodity we must always have in our minds some particular amount of that commodity and the particular person to whom it is useful.

The utility of a commodity to any one depends on the amount of it he has at the time, and the opportunity he has or expects to have of getting it, or other things that will serve as substitutes for it. But further, the price which he is willing to pay for a thing depends not only on its utility to him but also on *his means;* that is, the amount of money or general purchasing power at his disposal. A greater utility will be required to induce him to buy it if he is poor than if he is rich. A shilling is the measure of less pleasure to a rich man, than to a poor one. A rich man in doubt whether to spend a shilling on a single cigar, is weighing against one another smaller pleasures than a poor man, who is doubting whether to spend a shilling on a supply of tobacco that will last him for a month. The clerk with £100 a year will walk into business in a much heavier rain than the clerk with £300 ·a year; for a sixpenny omnibus fare measures a greater utility to the poorer man than to the richer. If the poorer man spends the money, he will suffer more from the want of it afterwards than the richer would. The utility, or satisfaction, or value in use that is measured in the poorer man's mind by sixpence is greater than that measured by it in the richer man's mind. If the richer man rides a hundred times in the year and the poorer man twenty times, then the utility of the hundredth ride which the richer man is only just induced to take is measured to him by sixpence ; and the utility of the twentieth ride which the poorer man is only just induced to take is measured ·to him by sixpence. For each of them the Final Utility is measured by sixpence ; but this Final Utility is greater in the case of the poorer man than in that of the richer.

§ 7.   The lower the price that a man has to pay for a thing, the more of it is he likely to buy. A fall in price will not indeed make every purchaser increase his purchases. It might in the case of sugar ; it would not in the case of carpets. But a fall in the price of carpets would induce some of the householders in a large market to buy new carpets ; just as an unhealthy autumn increases the mortality of a large town, though many persons are uninjured by it. For in a large market there must be some who are doubting whether to re-place an old carpet by a new one ; and their decision will be affected by a fall in the price of carpets. There will not be any exact relation between the fall in price and the increase of demand. A fall of one-tenth in the price may increase the sales by a twentieth or by a quarter, or it may double them. But in a large market every fall in price will cause an increase of demand. The **Law of Demand** then is :—

> The amount of a commodity which finds purchasers in a market in a given time depends on the price at which it is offered for sale ; and varies so that the amount demanded is increased by a fall in price and diminished by a rise in price. Its price measures its Final Utility to each purchaser, that is, the value in use to him of that portion of it which it is only just worth his while to buy.

CHAPTER II.

LAW OF SUPPLY.

§ 1. IT was said in the last chapter that the exchange value or the price of a commodity is determined by the eagerness of buyers on the one hand, and the eagerness of sellers on the other. The Law of Demand is a general statement of the action of buyers. *The Law of Supply*, to which we now turn has to do with the action of sellers.

The Laws concerning the action of sellers fall into two distinct classes, according as the commodities which are sold can be produced freely by anyone, or are monopolized. Deferring the consideration of the latter, we may at present confine our attention to things the production of which is free to all, those which anyone may produce.

We have to inquire how a man calculates the price which will remunerate him for producing a commodity. The inquiry is difficult; and therefore it will be best to consider first the simple case of a producer who makes things with his own hands.

Let us suppose then that a carpenter is doubting whether it is worth his while to make boxes for sale. In calculating the price which will remunerate him, he must allow for wear and tear of tools, for the price of material, for interest on the capital he has invested in tools and materials, and for rent of his workshop. Next he must allow for his own wages. Of course he does not pay himself wages. But he calculates the wages he could earn by other work that is as much to his taste and not more fatiguing. It will not be worth his while to produce the box unless its price will repay him the first mentioned expenses, and afford him such remuneration for his labour as shall not be less than these wages. This fact may be expressed by saying that it will not be worth his while to produce it, if its price is less than its *Expenses of Production*. We must carefully examine the meaning of this term.

§ 2. The production of a commodity requires the use of tools, machinery, workshops, etc.; it also consumes raw material and labour. Thus it requires capital and labour; and capital, as we have seen, is the result of labour and abstinence. Now there are two ways of estimating these various elements.

Firstly, we may regard them as so much labour and abstinence. The carpenter's work in making the box involved muscular exertion and fatigue; and abstinence from immediate consumption was necessary in order to provide the tools with which he worked. Next with regard to the wood of which the box was made. It may have been grown on land that paid rent; but in order to avoid considering rent at present, we may suppose that it was got from some of the wild forests of South America. In this case there was clearly no rent paid for it; but we must reckon the labour of those who cut the tree down, and of those who brought it to the carpenter. And so on.

Then again there is another set of efforts and abstinences of which account must be taken. The efficiency of the carpenter's work in making the box depends not only on the exertion which he undergoes at the time of making it, but also upon his skill in carpentering. And to acquire this skill, he and his teachers had to exert themselves; and his parents had to use self-denial to pay the expenses of his education. In fact his skill is Personal Capital, which owes its existence to labour and abstinence. Thus then the production of the box is the result of a great number of efforts and abstinences undergone by different people at different times.

It will be convenient to have a collective name for all these efforts and abstinences reckoned together. This is found in the term "Cost of Production."

The **Cost of Production** of a thing then consists of the efforts and abstinences required for producing it.

The carpenter, however, in deciding whether to make the box or not, would not care to examine all these efforts and sacrifices; he would decide in a much easier way. He would calculate what it is proposed to call its Expenses of production. He would, as we have seen, want to know what prices the various efforts and sacrifices in question would command in the open market; he would want to know what price he would have to pay for his material, what wages he could obtain for his own labour, what was the rate of interest at which he could borrow such capital as he wanted, and so on. These various sums of money when taken together may be called the *Expenses of Production* of the box. It has already been seen that the work of man in production consists really in moving things and rearranging them; so that the work of taking a box to market is as much productive as that of making it. The Expenses of production of a box when offered for sale in any market include therefore the expense of carrying it to that market. We may then say:—

> The **Expenses of Production** of a thing in a market are the sum of the prices of the efforts and sacrifices which are required for its production there: or, in other words, the sum of the expenses which would have to be incurred by a person who should purchase them at their market prices.

§ 3.   The carpenter would decide to make boxes if the price which he could obtain for them exceeded their Expenses of production; and other carpenters in similar circumstances would do the same.   Thus the supply of boxes would be increased; and the increased competition of sellers would lower the price of boxes towards their Expenses of production.   If many carpenters thought that the demand for boxes would continue to be large relatively to the supply, and that therefore the price of a box would long remain greater than its Expenses of production; then they would not only keep to the box-making trade themselves, but also bring up their sons to the work.   By so doing they would increase the supply of boxes, and then perhaps the increase might be so great as to force down the price below the Expenses of production.

If the price falls below the Expenses of production, carpenters will seek every convenient opportunity of turning to some other occupation.   Those who were specially skilful in box-making would indeed lose the benefits of this skill if they sought another employment.   But some would gradually leave the trade, and carpenters would not bring up their sons to it.   So the supply of boxes would be lessened; the competition of sellers would diminish and that of buyers would increase until the price was again brought up to the Expenses of production.

§ 4.   The carpenter then working with his own tools, raw material, etc., calculates the Expenses of production of a box, including his own remuneration among them, that is, including what he could earn in other ways by labour that was equally difficult and equally attractive to him.   If now we look at an employer who has men to make boxes, we find that he will calculate the Expenses of producing a box very nearly as the carpenter would.   He would have to arrange for making payments not only for his raw material, etc., but also for the wages of those whom he employed.   And he would have to allow for the remuneration of his own labour in managing the business —his own *Earnings of Management*[1], as we may say—just as the carpenter had to allow for the remuneration of his own work.

---

[1] These are sometimes called "Wages of Superintendence."

At a later stage we shall see that there is a market for business ability very much as there is a market for carpenters' work ; that an employer gets to know the value of his own time, the Earnings of Management which he may fairly expect to get, almost as exactly as a carpenter knows what wages he may expect. He generally reckons these Earnings together with the interest on his capital ; he calls the two together "profits ;" and expects to make a certain rate of profits in his business. He expects to have returned to him with profits all his Circulating capital, such as raw material, which is consumed in a single use, and the wages which he pays away. And he expects to receive profits, together with an allowance for *Depreciation*, on his Fixed capital[1]. Depreciation includes the wear and tear of his buildings, machinery, etc., and their tendency to become obsolete through the progress of invention, and the changes of trade.

The interest which he expects to receive, depends not only on the amount of capital invested, and the annual rate of interest ; but also on the time which elapses between his making each outlay on the production of goods and his receiving the price of these goods. Let the rate of interest be five per cent. a year. If then he spends £100 in the production of a thing one year before it is ready for sale, there will be a corresponding sum of £5 to be reckoned under the head of interest in its Expenses of production. But if he has to spend the £100 two years before the thing is ready for sale, the corresponding sum to be reckoned under interest would be £10 ; or, at compound interest, something over £10.

In deciding for instance whether to make some boxes, the manufacturer calculates the price that he will get for them, and he calculates their Expenses of production. He makes a definite allowance for the remuneration of his own labour just as the carpenter does for his. He reckons in these expenses not only the outlay of money that he will make, but interest on this outlay together with his own Earnings of Management, or more strictly, profits. If he sees his way to getting a price that will cover these Expenses of production, and therefore give him adequate profits, he is content and continues his production. If he sees his way to getting a still higher price, one which will afford him exceptionally high profits, he strains every nerve and borrows more capital in order to extend his business and increase his supply. But if he expects that the price will be less than these Expenses of production and therefore not afford him adequate profits he checks his supply, and perhaps begins to think about directing his capital and his energies to some other branch of production.

---

[1] See Book I. ch. III. § 7.

§ 5.   Thus we see that the interest of every producer of a commodity is always to calculate the amount of it that is being produced for market.   If this amount seems likely to be small so that its price will rise above its Expenses of production, he will produce as much as he can, so as to derive as much benefit as possible from the high price which he anticipates.   If, on the other hand, the amount brought to market seems likely to be so great that its price will fall below its Expenses of production, then he will check his own production so far as he conveniently can.   So that if the price of a commodity is likely to be higher than its Expenses of production, it is the interest of each producer to do what he can to increase the supply; and the effect of this is to lower the price towards its Expenses of production.   And if its price is likely to be lower than its Expenses of production, it is the interest of each producer to do what he can to check the supply; and the effect of this is to raise the price towards the Expenses of production.   That is to say :—

> Every producer of a commodity calculates the price at which he will be able to sell it, and the Expenses of producing it.   He thus determines whether to increase or diminish his production.   If there is free competition, that is, if he is not acting in combination with other producers, he increases or diminishes his supply according as the price of the commodity seems likely to be greater or less than its Expenses of production.   Thus he is led by his own interests to act in the same way as he would if his only object were to regulate the amount produced so that it could just be sold off at a price equal to its Expenses of production.

This Law of Supply may be called the **Law of Normal Supply,** because it refers to the results that are in the long run brought about by free competition.   Of course all the Expenses of production of a thing are themselves liable to variation.   Wages may rise and fall, the rate of interest may rise and fall ; and so on.   But we shall presently find that with some exceptions these Expenses are themselves governed in the long run by Economic Laws ; and we shall presently get to understand what is meant by the Normal wages, the Normal rate of interest and so on.   The Expenses of production with which we are here concerned are these Normal Expenses.

§ 6.   In the above illustration it was assumed that if the trade of box-making became exceptionally profitable, a great many people would begin to make boxes, or would make more boxes than before: that is, it was supposed that the box-making trade is open to free competition.

We might have supposed that the boxes were of a peculiar

kind and patented, so that only one person had the right of making them: or that all the box-makers combined together, and not only kept new comers out of the trade, but also agreed among themselves as to how many boxes they would make. In these cases the supply would not be governed by the Law of Normal Supply. The supply might be small, and the price very much above the Expenses of production, and yet producers might not increase, but rather diminish the supply so as to raise the price still further. This could not happen if competition were free, because then any one who checked his production when prices were exceptionally high, would lose by so doing. For others would go on producing fast, and before long the price would fall, and his opportunity of making boxes and selling them at a high price would have passed away. Every one must make hay while the sun shines, because he cannot make it shine when he wants to. Under free competition a single producer cannot control prices; and therefore each one tries to get as much profit as he can out of the time of high prices; he makes and sends to market as many goods as he can whenever their price is above their Expenses of production.

§ 7. The Law which regulates Normal value follows at once from the Law of Normal Supply. Whenever the price is above the Expenses of production, there are forces at work tending to bring it down; whenever the price is below the Expenses of production, there are forces at work tending to raise it. Just as when a weight is suspended by a string, if the weight is disturbed towards the left from its position of equilibrium, or rest, the force of gravity at once tends to make it swing back. Soon it does swing back to its position of rest; but it does not stop there; it moves on to the right, and then the force of gravity makes it swing back to the left, and so on. If frequently disturbed, it will hardly ever remain in its position of equilibrium, but will always oscillate about it.

The Normal price, or as Adam Smith says, "the natural price is as it were the central price to which the price of every commodity is continually gravitating. Different accidents may sometimes keep them suspended a good deal above it, and sometimes force them down even somewhat below it. But whatever may be the obstacles which hinder them from settling in this centre of repose and continuance, they are constantly tending towards it." And the **Law of Normal Value** is :—

> The Normal value of a thing in any market, or, that value which would on the average, be brought about by the undisturbed action of free competition among its producers, is equal to its Expenses of production there. Whenever the value is below this level, forces are brought into play which tend to raise it; whenever it is

above this level, forces are brought into play which tend to lower it. The value of a commodity is in equilibrium and has no tendency either to rise or to fall when the amount produced can just be sold at a price equal to its Expenses of production.

But this law is not complete because it takes no account of the fact that the Expenses of production are not fixed, but depend upon the amount produced. To this point we shall return[1].

It follows from this Law that things whose Expenses of production in any market are equal, tend to have the same exchange value ; and to exchange for one another in that market. For the sake of brevity it is usual to omit all mention of the place in which the exchange is supposed to be made; but whenever we speak of the relative exchange values of two commodities we must have in our minds some one particular place in which we suppose them to be exchanged. If the value of salt is compared with that of tin, it makes a great difference whether the market to which reference is made is near the Cheshire salt mines or the Cornish tin mines.

§ 8. So far nothing has been said of the way in which Insurance against risk enters into Expenses of production. Insurance against the destruction and the depreciation of capital may perhaps best be included under the head of wear and tear of buildings, machinery, etc. Prudent manufacturers generally insure their premises against fire by paying to an Insurance Company a premium which they count as one of the necessary Expenses of their business : and they make a yearly allowance for the depreciation of their machinery through the constant tendency of invention to render obsolete that which is old. A prudent shipowner, if he does not pay a premium to underwriters to insure his ship on each voyage, puts by a fixed sum annually to form an insurance fund of his own.

Secondly, there is the risk of having to sell the produce at a loss. For instance, iron and other things have often to be sold for less than their Expenses of production when trade is suddenly depressed ; and a change of fashion may have the same effect on articles of dress. But the Law of Normal Value makes allowance for this risk once, and if Insurance against it is made under a separate head, it is really counted twice over; for the chance that the price of the commodity may fall below the Expenses of production is of the same kind as the chance that the price may rise very high. When the average price at which it is sold is computed, the low prices are reckoned in together with the high prices. The trade is therefore a remunerative one if this average price

---

[1] See Book II. chap. v. § 3.

covers the Expenses of production, without any separate allow-ance being made for the insurance against the risk of a fall in price.

§ 9.   It is important to remember that there is no necessary connection between the selling price of any individual thing and its Expenses of production; the connection is between the Expenses of carrying on a certain process of production and the total sum that is received by selling the products.   There is no connection between the Expenses of a fishing boat on any excursion and the price which is got for its haul.   The haul may be bad, and the price got for it much below its Expenses of production, or the haul may be good and the price much above these Expenses.   What the Law of Normal Value states is that the total price got for the fish must in the long run, taking good and bad hauls together, cover the Expenses of the boat.

The price of every individual thing is, as we saw in the last chapter, limited by its value in use to the purchaser.   If a boat brings back only a few fish, only a small price can be got for the catch.   So again, the value in use of a bell with a flaw in it is very little; it can be used only as old metal and therefore its price is only that of the old metal in it.   When it was being cast the same trouble and expense were incurred for it as for other bells which turned out sound.   Its Expenses of production were the same as those of sound bells : but they have great value in use and are therefore sold at a high price.   The price of each particular bell is limited by its value in use : what the Law of Normal Value states is that the price of cracked bells and sound bells together must in the long run cover the expenses of making bells.

§ 10.   [The main outline of the Law of Normal Value was worked out by Adam Smith and Ricardo.   They were careful to guard against implying that the price of each individual thing is equal to its Expenses of production ; but still this mistake has been made.   This mistake has indeed led some people to approve a proposal made by Mr Carey, to say that the Value of a thing is equal to its Expenses (or, as he says, Cost) of *reproduction.*

It is quite true, as Mr Carey says, that when a new invention has very much diminished the difficulty of making, say, a steel rail, no one will pay for an old steel rail a price equal to the expenses which were incurred in making it by the old method. He seems to think that they will always pay for it a price equal to the Expenses of its reproduction, that is of producing a similar rail by the new method.   But this is not the case.   If trade has become suddenly bad, and iron-masters have many steel rails on hand, no one will pay for a steel rail a price equal to its Expenses of reproduction ; because rails are being sold for less.

Again, no one will pay for a bell with a flaw in it, or for a dress that has gone out of fashion, the Expenses of its reproduction. When fashion is displacing broad ribbons by narrow, broad ribbons sell for less, and narrow ribbons sell for more than their Expenses of reproduction. Gunpowder in time of war and quinine in time of fever often fetch more than their Expenses of reproduction.

If the phrase "Expenses of reproduction" were substituted for the phrase "Expenses of production" in our Law of Normal Value, the meaning of the Law would not be altered by the change. For the Expenses of reproduction of a thing are in the long run the same as its Expenses of production. The statements that value must be equal to Expenses of production, and that it must be equal to Expenses of reproduction, are equally false when they refer to the market value of any individual thing, and equally true when they refer to the Normal Value about which the market value oscillates. The advantages of the two phrases are so far about equally balanced : but the phrase Expenses of production has this very great advantage over its rival, that it calls attention to the way in which the difficulty of producing a thing determines supply in the first instance, and value in the second. Producers debating whether to increase their supply of a commodity do not inquire whether the price they get for it will cover its Expenses of reproduction, but whether the price will cover its Expenses of production.]

CHAPTER III.

RENT.

§ I.   IT remains to inquire how the Expenses of production
of a commodity may be affected by the payment of rent for the
land on which it is produced; but before doing this it will be
well to take up our account of the rent of land where we left it
at the end of the first book.   Rent was then defined as that payment for the use of land which the owner can obtain by free
competition for lending out the use of it to others.   We have
now to inquire how the amount of this rent is determined in any
particular case.

Suppose a farmer to have £500 which he is thinking of
applying in extra cultivation of his farm ; and to have calculated
that it will only just answer his purpose to do so.   He has
calculated, that is, that if he applies this extra £500 he will,
after paying for labour, seed, taxes, &c., get an extra net produce
of the value of about say £40 ; i. e. at the rate of 8 per cent. on
the extra outlay.   This is, we suppose, just sufficient to remunerate him : so that if he expected to get less, the chance of
the improvement turning out unsuccessful and the prospect of
additional trouble in working it, would induce him to invest the
money in railway stocks or some other securities.

He hears at this time that a small adjacent farm of 50 acres
is to be let, and he is asked what rent he would be willing to pay
for it.   His £500 would just be enough for working this farm,
and he could work it with the same trouble that it would give
him to apply the extra £500 to the farm he already has.   He
calculates that taking one year with another he may expect to
get from it £100 worth of net produce after paying for labour,
seed, taxes, &c.

So he will pay just £60 rent for the use of this land.   If he
can get the land for this he will take it : but he will not give
any more for it ; and it will not be likely to be worth any one
else's while to offer more.   So the landlord cannot get more than
this for it.   If he puts up the farm to competition and plays off

one farmer against another, he may just get £60; and this is then the competition rent, or as it is sometimes called the Economic rent of the farm. Many disturbing circumstances such as custom, the absence of an active spirit of competition on the part of the farmers, generosity or sluggishness on the part of the landlord, may cause the actual rent to be less than this. But £60 is the rent that will be obtained, if there is a perfectly good market for the hire of land : that is, if on the one hand the landlord exerts himself to get the best rent he can for the land, and on the other hand there are competent men in the neighbourhood who are ready to rent farms.

§ 2.   This illustration shews us that

    (i)   The Economic rent of a piece of land is found by subtracting from the value of its annual produce an amount sufficient to return the farmer's outlay with profits.

Of course allowance must be made for the risk of bad harvests : this is done by assuming that the harvest is an average one. It must also be supposed that the farmer has neither more nor less skill and enterprise than most others in his neighbourhood, or as we may say, that he is an average farmer[1]. The rent then is the surplus return which the land gives in an average harvest, after repaying the average farmer's outlay with profits, provided he has applied so much capital to it as to make this surplus return as large as he can. If he has applied less than this amount of capital some one else who intends to apply more than he has done, and thus obtain a larger surplus return, may offer to pay a higher rent.

Further the above illustration shews that :

    (ii)   The amount of produce which a farmer must retain in order to be remunerated for his outlay, can be discovered by observing what amount of additional return is just sufficient to induce him, or another farmer in the same neighbourhood, to apply extra capital to his land[2].

---

[1] A farmer of more than ordinary ability ought in justice to retain for himself that portion of the net produce of the land which is due to his exceptional qualities. Such a farmer is almost certain to improve his land, and invest capital in it in various ways. His landlord has the power of raising his rent above that which the land could have paid, if it had remained in the hands of an ordinary farmer, by the threat of ejecting him without compensation for his improvements. But this is very seldom done in England.

[2] The first part of the theory was known to Economists before Adam Smith's time. It is commonly, though perhaps erroneously, supposed that he had no knowledge of this second part. Ricardo did more towards working out the second part than any one else : but he did not invent it, and the form in which he stated it is open to some exceptions.

That is, it can be discovered by observing the Return to his last Dose of capital. The return to this dose remunerates him, but only just remunerates him ; therefore if he retains for himself as many times this return as he applied doses, he will just be remunerated for applying them. Therefore to find his rent, this return must be multiplied by the number of doses he applies, and then subtracted from his total produce. The **Law of Rent** then is :—

> If a farmer applies as much capital to his land as he profitably can, his rent is what remains after deducting from his total produce the return to his last dose multiplied by the number of doses he applies[1].

[1] In Book I. Chap. iv. § 3 it was shewn that if the doses of capital which a farmer applies to a given piece of land are measured along the line Ox, the returns due to the several doses can be represented by the figure $OPQM$. It was also shewn that, on account of the Law of Diminishing Return, when a certain number of doses have been applied to the land, the returns to these doses must diminish ; that is the line PQ must gradually approach Ox.

This diagram may be used to represent the theory of rent. After the farmer has applied a considerable number of doses to the land, the

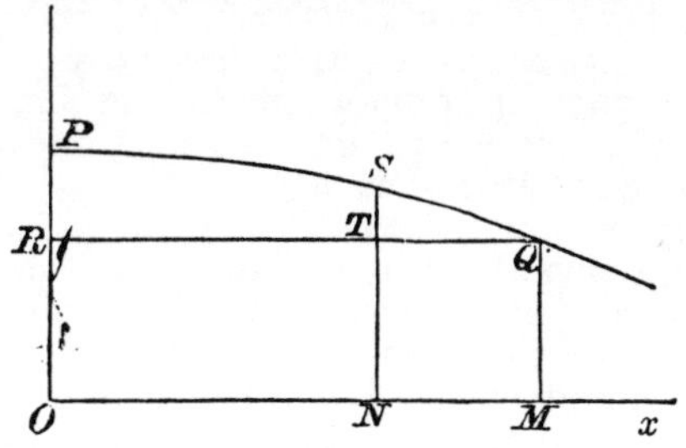

returns will begin to diminish. A point will be reached at which the return due to the last dose only just repays the farmer for applying it. At this point he will stop. Let each dose be £10, and let the last dose which it is worth his while to apply, be the fortieth. Suppose that this fortieth dose is represented on the figure by the point M; so that MQ, the return due to it, is just sufficient to repay the farmer for applying a dose of £10.

Since the return to this dose just remunerates the farmer, the returns to the other doses must more than remunerate him. For instance, SN being the return to the dose at N, draw QTR parallel to Ox cutting SN in T and OP in R, then NT is equal to QM, and therefore NT is that portion of the return due to the Nth dose which is required to remunerate the farmer for applying that dose ; TS is surplus produce which the landlord can claim as rent. So if we draw vertical lines from other points in Ox, the portions of them that lie between Ox and RQ will be those

§ 3. It may happen that there is in the neighbourhood waste land for which no rent can be obtained. The return to the capital applied to this land remunerates, but only just remunerates, the farmer.   So that in this case we may say that

> The amount of produce which a farmer must retain in order to be remunerated for his outlay, is equal to the produce that could be raised by the same amount of capital from an adjacent piece of land that pays no rent.

The Law of Rent may therefore be stated thus :—

> The rent of a piece of land is the excess of its produce over the produce of an adjacent piece of land which is cultivated with an equal amount of capital, and which would not be cultivated at all if rent were demanded for it.

Land that is cultivated, but is so poor as not to be able to pay any rent, is often spoken of as *on the Margin of cultivation.*

[§ 4. Whenever the increased demand for food causes a rise in the value of agricultural produce, it causes a twofold rise in the rent of land. As the value of food rises, the amount of it which is necessary to remunerate the farmer for his outlay diminishes: and therefore the surplus portion of the produce, which the landlord can claim as rent, increases in amount. And as each part of this surplus rises in value the value of the rent is raised twice, once in proportion to the increase in the amount of the produce which goes as rent, and once in proportion to the rise in value of each part of it.

In a country in which there is any uncultivated land, an increase in the demand for food causes an extension of the Margin of cultivation, at the same time that it causes a rise in the rent of land. In such cases it is sometimes said that the rise in rent is caused by the extension of the Margin of cultivation. But this is incorrect : the two changes are the effects of the same cause : viz. the increase in the demand for food.

On the other hand when a diminution of the demand for food, or increased facilities for its importation cause a fall in its value, there is a twofold fall in rent. For the amount of agricultural produce which is necessary to remunerate the farmer for his

portions of the returns to the corresponding doses of capital that are required to remunerate the farmer. And those portions which lie between RQ and PQ will be surplus portions which the landlord can claim as rent.

If now we suppose, as we did before, that these vertical lines are thick lines, so that altogether they fill up the space $POMQ$; then $POMQ$ represents the total produce of the land. In the same way $ROMQ$ represents the farmer's share of the produce ; and PRQ *represents the surplus portion of the produce which the farmer has to pay to the landlord as rent.*

outlay increases; and therefore the surplus portion which the landlord can claim as rent diminishes. And as each part of this surplus falls in value, the value of the rent is lowered twice, once in proportion to the diminution in the amount of the produce which goes as rent, and once in proportion to the fall in value of each part of it.

But the effect of increased facilities for the importation of food in lowering rents can only be temporary. The ease with which it enables labourers to obtain an ample supply of food increases the growth of population and wealth; so that before long the farmers will find the demand for milk, vegetables, hay, straw and other produce, which cannot easily be imported from distant countries, much greater than it would otherwise have been; and the demand for other kinds of their produce not much less. After the repeal of the Corn-laws in 1848, it was expected that the free importation of corn would make rents fall; but their repeal has caused an enormous increase in England's wealth, and rents are very much higher than they were then. At the present time however, the great development of wheat fields and railways in the north-west of America, and the newly discovered methods of importing fresh meat, are lowering the prices of corn and meat; and threatening to cause a fall of rents. It is difficult to estimate the effect of these permanent causes of depression because they are much overlaid by three temporary causes :—firstly a succession of bad harvests in England ; second-ly "railway-wars" in America leading to extremely low rates of freight ; and thirdly a great falling off in the demand for meat, especially on the part of the working classes, occasioned by the present commercial depression.

In a country which imports a great deal of food, an increase in its production at home will not much affect its price ; and therefore an improvement in the arts of production will make but little change in the amount of the produce which is required to return the farmer's outlay with profits ; nearly the whole of the increase will go to the landlord in the form of higher rents.

In a country which produces its own food, the immediate effect of a sudden improvement in the arts of cultivation would be to lower the price of agricultural produce, to make it unprofitable to apply so much capital as before to good land, and to throw some land out of cultivation. It can be shewn that if the fall in price did not at once lead to an increased demand for food, the part of the produce which goes to the landlords — their "corn-rents" — would probably fall[1] ; and that

---

[1] Mill, after Ricardo, says they would certainly fall. He assumes that the cultivated part of a country consists of three qualities of land, yielding at an equal expense 60, 80, and 100 bushels ; and he then shews that an improvement which increased the return to each dose of

their rents measured in money would certainly fall. After a time however the growth of population would cause such a demand for food that its value would rise to its old level : no more corn than before would be required to return with profits each dose of the farmer's capital, more capital would be applied in cultivation than before the improvement, and there would be a very great increase of rents.]

[§ 5. It has already been seen that the Law of Diminishing Return does not apply to mineral produce in the same way as it does to agricultural. For this reason the theory of the rent of land cannot be applied directly to mines. It is true that the rent of a mine is the excess of the value of its produce over that amount which is required to return with profits the capital of those who rent the mine ; and we can determine what this amount is by discovering how much produce could be obtained by this capital if it were applied to a mine which is being worked but for which no rent is paid. (Just before a mine is abandoned it passes, as a rule, through the stage of being worked, but yielding no surplus from which rent can be paid.)

But it is not true of a mine as it is of a farm that this rent is a fixed annual payment. There is a certain maximum net surplus which can be got from a farm by applying just the right amount of capital to it, and the rent is fixed so as to be equal to the value of this surplus in an average harvest. It is the business of the tenant to apply the capital requisite for obtaining this net surplus ; the landlord has no further concern in the matter, than to see that the tenant does not leave the land in a worse condition than he finds it in. And farming contracts are all subject to a general condition that the land is not to be impoverished by the tenant.

But contracts for the rent of mines cannot be subject to this condition, because a mine is impoverished whenever ore is taken from it. The owner must therefore take care that those to whom he leases it do not work it so as to raise a very large amount annually without paying him a rent equivalent to the deterioration of his property. This deterioration may be regarded as the diminution of the power that the mine has of returning to capital surplus profits over and above the ordinary trade profits : and corresponds therefore to the surplus profits which the lessees

capital by one-third, would lower corn-rents in the ratio of 60 to $53\frac{1}{3}$. But the distribution of fertility in a country might be such that we should rather suppose it to consist of three qualities yielding at an equal expense 60, 65, and 115 bushels ; and in that case the improvement would raise corn-rents in the ratio 60 to $66\frac{2}{3}$. Problems of this kind cannot be properly treated by numerical illustrations; they can be solved easily and completely by the aid of mathematics or of diagrams like that given in the present chapter.

can make by working the mine, that is to the rent which the owner can obtain from them. It is an extremely difficult problem to calculate what bargain should be made in the case of any particular mine. It should secure the interests of the owner and yet leave the lessees proper freedom to decide for themselves how much capital they will apply in any year to the working of the mine, and therefore how much produce they will raise from it. In practice this is roughly done by his demanding a *royalty* of so much a ton on the gross produce raised, in addition to a fixed annual payment.]

CHAPTER IV.

§ 1. WE may now consider the relation of rent to Expenses of production and to value.

We have seen that the Normal value of a thing, or that value which would on the average and in the long run be brought about by the undisturbed action of free competition among its producers, is equal to its Expenses of production. But this Law requires further explanation, because it often happens that different portions of the same commodity have different Expenses of production. We shall find that its price is then regulated by the Expenses of production of that portion which is raised under the most unfavourable existing circumstances.

Suppose for instance that, with an average harvest, ten million quarters of corn are raised in England, and that the Expenses of production of the last million quarters are at the rate of 50s. a quarter. If the farmers had expected to get less than 50s. a quarter they would not have raised these last quarters. And since they find it worth their while to raise the whole ten million, we know that they get 50s. for each of the last million. And in the same market there can only be one price for one and the same commodity. Therefore the average price of all the corn in the market must be 50s.

The Expenses of production of some of the corn may have been only 30s. a quarter. The 50s. got for a quarter of this corn is divided into 30s. which goes to the farmer, and 20s. which, as we have seen, goes to the landlord as rent. And if a person looks at this corn he may argue that its whole Expenses of production were 30s. to cover the farmer's outlay and 20s. to pay his rent, and that therefore rent enters into the Expenses of production of this corn. He would be right if he meant

only that the Expenses of production of this particular quarter
of corn cannot be found by merely reckoning up the wages and
profits of the labour and capital that were spent in raising it.
But he would be wrong if he meant that the selling price of
corn was governed by the rent that has to be paid for the use
of land.   He would then be mistaking cause for effect, and
effect for cause.   Rent is not the cause of a high price of corn,
but its effect.   The price of corn must be on the average just
high enough to cover the Expenses of production of that portion
of it which is raised under the most unfavourable conditions.
The amount that is raised, and the price at which it is sold,
are thus governed by the numbers of the population which
demands corn on the one hand, and by the amount of fertile
land, which is the source of supply, on the other.   The price
is determined by the Expenses of production of that which
is raised under the most unfavourable conditions and which pays
no rent.   The rent is governed by the excess of this price over
the Expenses of production of the other produce that the
farmer raises more easily.   Ricardo taught that Rent does
not enter into Expenses of production.   By this he meant that:—

> The Normal value of a commodity is equal to the
> Expenses of production of that portion of it which is
> raised under the most unfavourable existing circum-
> stances, and which pays no rent.   Rent does not
> determine the Normal value of produce; but is
> determined by it.

[§ 2. It has often been said that the doctrine, Rent does not
enter into Expenses of production, applies to raw produce but
not to manufactured.   This statement requires to be interpreted
carefully.   For it is as true of manufactured as of agricultural
produce that its price must equal the Expenses of production of
that portion of it which is raised under the most unfavourable
existing circumstances, and pays no rent.   It may be said that
every manufacturer in England pays ground-rent.   But it is no
less true that every hop-grower in England pays rent.   The
price of hops must be equal to the Expenses of production of
that portion of his crop which is due to his last doses of capital—
those doses which he is only just induced to apply to the
land,—and though other portions of his crop pay rent, this
portion does not.   As the hop-grower reckons how much
capital it will answer his purpose to expend on an acre of land,
so a man building a woollen factory reckons how much capital it
will answer his purpose to expend on a yard of building ground.
If he is building a new factory, he will weigh against one
another the advantages of building it (say) three or four stories
high.   He may think that the advantages and disadvantages of
the fourth story are nearly balanced.   That is, he may think the

extra cloth that he will obtain by having a fourth story, will on the whole just cover its Expenses of production including profits on the capital invested in building the fourth story, but not including any ground-rent.   He must pay the ground-rent whether he has three stories or four; so that if he decides on having the fourth story, the extra cloth due to it will be cloth which he has only just been induced to produce, cloth produced under the most unfavourable existing circumstances, cloth which pays no ground-rent.

It is true that a manufacturer when making up the profit and loss account of his business would count his rent among his expenses.   If the ground-rent in, say, Leeds rises, a manufacturer finding his Expenses of production increased may move into the country, leaving the land on which he used to work to be built over with shops and warehouses, for which a town situation is more valuable than it is for factories[1].   For he may think that the saving in ground-rent that he will make by moving into the country, together with other advantages of the change, will more than counterbalance its disadvantages.   In a discussion as to whether it was worth his while to do so, the ground-rent of his factory would be reckoned among the Expenses of production of his cloth.

This is true.   But it is no less true that in making up the profit and loss account of the cultivation of land, the farmer's rent must be reckoned among his Expenses.   A hop-grower, for instance, may find that on account of the high rent which he pays for his land, the price of his hops will not cover their Expenses of production where he is; and may abandon hop-growing, or seek other land for it; while the land that he leaves may perhaps be let to a market-gardener.   After a while again the demand for land in the neighbourhood may become so great that the price which the market-gardener obtains for his produce will not pay its Expenses of production, including rent; and so he in his turn makes room for, say, a building company.]

[1] This process is actually going on.   When steam came into use some industries that had been scattered throughout the country wherever water-power was to be had, were brought together into a few large towns.   Now there is a change in the opposite direction, and many of these towns are becoming the commercial centres of manufacturing districts.

CHAPTER V.

INFLUENCE OF DEMAND ON VALUE.

§ 1. A CHANGE which affects the Expenses of production of all commodities in like proportion does not alter the purchasing power of one thing relatively to another; it does not alter values. For instance if interest on capital were an equally important element in the Expenses of production of all commodities, a rise or fall in interest would not affect values. But in fact interest is a very large element in the Expenses of production of some things, and a very small element in those of others. It is a large element in cases in which a great deal of Fixed capital is used, particularly if, as happens in some kinds of mining, much of it has to be sunk a long time before any return can be got for it[1]. Again the manufacture of lace by machinery requires much Fixed capital, and interest enters as a very important element into its Expenses of production. On the other hand the Expenses of production of hand-made lace consist almost exclusively of wages; interest enters into them to a very insignificant extent. A fall in the rate of interest would then lower the value of machine-made relatively to hand-made lace. Another cause which may alter the Expenses of production, and therefore the Normal value of a thing, is the discovery of an improved method of making it. Another is a change in the Normal rate of wages of some class of workmen who are engaged in making it. Another is a change in the difficulty of producing it, occasioned by a change in the amount of it that is produced. The effects of this last cause will be examined in the present chapter.

§ 2. We have already seen that some commodities obey the Law of Increasing, and others that of Diminishing Return. For instance, the more capital and labour are applied to watch-making, the smaller will be the difficulty of producing a watch.

[1] Book II. ch. ii. § 4.

A temporary increase in the demand for watches will no doubt raise their price, thus raising the wages of labour and the profits on capital in the trade above their Normal level.   But a slow and gradual increase in the demand will bring with it a corresponding supply of labour and capital in the trade, so that wages and profits will remain at about their Normal level.   And meanwhile advantage will be taken of those various economies which arise, as we have seen, from increased division of labour and production on a larger scale. Thus a gradual growth of the demand for watches will diminish their Expenses of production and therefore their Normal value.

On the other hand an increased supply of raw produce, however gradually it may be called forth, is almost sure to obey the Law of Diminishing Return.   It may indeed happen that the new demand leads to openings up of fresh sources of supply, and to improvements in the arts of production ; but the general progress of knowledge would in any case have done much towards bringing about such changes.   And on the whole, an increase of demand for raw produce seems almost always to increase the difficulty of producing it, and therefore to increase its Normal Expenses of production, and therefore its Normal value.

Adam Smith pointed out that in an uncivilised country wood and meat and leather and milk are of low value relatively not only to manufactures, but also to corn.   For where there is an unlimited supply of land, trees can be cut down and animals can be reared without the steady work, so abhorrent to uncivilised races, that is required for the cultivation of corn.   Gradually, as civilisation progresses, the increasing scarcity of land, and the increase of capital and patient industry causes the Normal value of wood and animal produce to rise relatively to that of corn, at the same time that the Normal value of corn rises relatively to that of manufactured commodities.   Among some savage races and occasionally where there is a sparse civilised population, a pound of meat exchanges for less than a pound of corn.   But in England even before the repeal of the Corn Laws a pound of meat was worth two or three pounds of wheat.   And now that the artificial obstacles to the importation of corn are removed, while the natural hindrances to the importation of fresh animal food are not yet surmounted, the difficulty of obtaining wheat has fallen still further relatively to that of obtaining meat ; so that now a pound of good meat will purchase about seven pounds of wheat.

§ 3.   We are now in a position to see what is the nature of the influence which Demand exercises on Value.   There is one exceptional case in which value is determined entirely by demand.   This is the case of a commodity which is fixed in amount, as for instance Raphael's pictures. Their price depends on the desire that people have for such pictures, and the means at their disposal for purchasing them. According to the Law of Demand the price of a commodity "measures its Final utility to each purchaser, that is, the value in use to him of that portion of it, which it is only just worth his while to buy." The greater the number of pictures, the less will be the competition among purchasers for them, the less will be the price which measures their value in use to those who are only just induced to purchase them. In this exceptional case in which the supply is fixed, the price is determined solely by the utility of the thing; Demand is the sole regulator of value.

The opposite extreme case very rarely occurs; it is that in which the Normal Expenses of production are fixed ; that is, are the same whatever be the amount produced. In this case Normal value is determined by Expenses of production alone. The part which Demand plays here is to determine the amount produced. If no one will pay for the thing a price equal to its fixed Expenses of production, the thing will not be made; so that even in this exceptional case Demand is a condition of value. And if there are any who will give this price, the amount produced is determined by the condition that its value in use to those purchasers who are only just induced to buy it, is measured by this price.

But in the case of most commodities it is not true either that the amount produced is fixed, or that the Expenses of pro-duction are fixed ; and therefore as a rule, Demand is one, but only one of the causes that determine value. An increase of Demand increases the amount produced, and this alters the Expenses of production ; so that value depends partly on Demand, because Normal value is equal to Normal Expenses of production, and Demand is one of the determining causes of these Expenses.   The Law of Normal Value[1] requires then to be supplemented by the statement that:—

> The Normal supply of a commodity is such that its Normal Expenses of production equal the price which will call forth a demand for this amount ; and the price so determined is the Normal price.

The Normal price of a commodity is therefore not fixed, but may rise or fall slowly. And we shall presently see how meanwhile the Market price oscillates with comparative rapidity up and down on either side of the Normal price ; just as a cork floating on the surface of the water oscillates quickly up and down with every passing wave on either side of the mean level of the water, while that mean level itself is rising or falling slowly with the flowing or ebbing tide.

[1] Book II. ch. ii. § 7.

CHAPTER VI.

DISTRIBUTION.

§ 1. WE have seen that the Expenses of production of a commodity may be reckoned in such a way that rent does not enter into them. The remaining Expenses may be classed as wages, profits, the expense of raw material, and other Circulating capital, the wear and tear of Fixed capital, and taxes. For instance, the Expenses of making a box, putting aside rent and taxes, may be classed as firstly the wages of the carpenters who made it and the profits of the manufacturers by whom they were employed ; secondly the price of the wood, hinges, lock and other Circulating capital that was used up in making it ; and thirdly the wear and tear of the buildings, machinery and other Fixed capital employed.

But all these may, as a rule, be classed as wages and profits. For the repairs of Fixed capital and the outlay of Circulating capital may be divided into wages, profits, the repairs of Fixed and the outlay of Circulating capital ; and these Expenses can again be analysed in the same way ; and so on.

For instance, the price of the lock, or the expenses of repairing the planing machine used in making the box, may be resolved into the wages and profits of those who made the lock or repaired the machine, the price of the Circulating capital they used up, and the wear and tear of the Fixed capital they employed, and so on.

It is true that some of the expenses incurred may be monopoly prices of certain things ; as for instance the price of the lock if it is patent : while others may be taxes ; and these cannot be analysed into wages and profits. But though such exceptions must not be overlooked, and though in a few cases they are of great importance, we may yet say that the Expenses of production of a thing can generally be divided into wages and profits. These wages and profits include between them the remuneration of the efforts and abstinences required for producing it. We have now to consider how these efforts and abstinences are measured by their several remunerations ; that is how the Cost of production of a thing is measured by its Expenses of production. We shall thus see what is the influence that Cost of production exerts on value—not directly indeed, but indirectly—Cost of production affecting Expenses of production, and Expenses of production affecting value.

§ 2. That part of the net income of a country which is derived from a farm is not the whole value of the crops, but only what remains after deducting the value of the seed sown in it, of the food of the horses who ploughed it, of the wear and tear of the plough, and so on. So the whole net annual income of a country consists of all those commodities and conveniences of life, which are produced during the year, after making allowance for replacing the Auxiliary capital that is consumed or worn out during the year. This net annual income is divided into :—firstly *earnings* of all kinds of work including business management, secondly *interest* on capital, thirdly *rent* obtained for the use of land or any other property that is naturally or artificially limited, fourthly *taxes* paid to the state. And a corresponding classification may be made of those among whom the income is divided : they may be classed as firstly those who earn an income by work, secondly capitalists, thirdly landlords, fourthly the State. Of course the same person may appear in two or more of these classes ; employers generally appear in the first two classes, and landlords who farm their own land in the first three. Again, the State is generally a landlord and a capitalist.

In the first Book we have inquired into the *Production* of wealth ; and have seen how the real net annual income of the country is determined. We have seen how that share of it which the landlord can claim as rent, is fixed by definite economic laws; and as the share which the State assumes to itself as taxes depends on causes which cannot be examined here, we must take it for granted. We may then regard the amount which remains after deducting rent and taxes from the net annual income of the country, as a given Fund, and call it the Wages-and-profits Fund[1]. The problem of *Distribution* with which we shall be chiefly occupied during the rest of the present volume consists of an inquiry into the way in which this Fund is divided up.

§ 3. The term "labourer" has been used by Economists to include all kinds of workers, and not merely unskilled labourers, to whom the term is confined in trade usage. And the term "wages" has been used to include the earnings of all kinds of work except that of business management.

---

[1] The way of looking at the source from which wages are paid is not quite the same as that adopted in what has been called "the Wages-Fund theory." This will be discussed at a later stage ; see Book III. ch. VI.

The Earnings of Management are generally classed with interest by Economists as well as by men of business. And this is doubtless the best classification in many social and some economic inquiries; because those who get the Earnings of Management are to some extent a separate class from those who get earnings of other kinds. Account will be taken of this fact when we come to discuss Market values, but in the theory of Normal values we are seeking for fundamental economic laws. And it is a universal rule of science that in seeking these fundamental laws, we should class together things that are similar in nature, and may be expected to obey similar laws. And therefore we shall find it best to class Earnings of Management with the earnings of other kinds of work; because they are similar in nature to other earnings, and are in the long run governed by the same laws. The earnings of a business man are uncertain, but so are those of a fisherman; they are got by mental work, but so are those of the barrister and the physician, whose incomes have been classed by all Economists with the wages of skilled labour. And if instead of classing Earnings of Management with other earnings, we were to class them with interest under the head of profits, we should be classing together two things entirely different in nature and governed by wholly dissimilar laws. For though in the passing vicissitudes of trade it is sometimes difficult to draw a clear line between the interest on a business man's capital and his Earnings of Management, yet we shall find that there is little in common between those fundamental laws which determine in the long run the Normal rate of interest, and those which determine the Normal Earnings of Management. It seems therefore best to class Earnings of Management with wages under the head of *Earnings;* to regard the net income of the country, after deducting rent and taxes, as divided not into wages and profits, but into interest and earnings; and to call it the *Earnings-and-interest Fund.* We have then to seek for the laws which determine in the long run that remuneration of abstinence which is called interest, and those various remunerations of industry which are called earnings.

This inquiry has two sides, that of Supply and that of Demand. The Law of Supply of capital has been already discussed; and a general account has been given of the increase of population. But some account must be given of the Laws of Supply of unskilled labour, of skilled labour and of business power. Afterwards we shall consider the relations in which Normal Supply and Demand stand to one another, and the Laws which determine Normal Interest and Normal Earnings.

[§ 4. But before going further it will be well to guard against some misunderstandings.

Firstly, some confusion has arisen from the use of the term "Cost of production" in two senses. It has been used to indicate what are here called the "Expenses," as well as what is here called the "Cost of production[1]." Thus the Law of (Normal) value has been stated to be that value tends to equal cost of production ; this of course does not mean that the value of a thing tends to equal what is called in this book its Cost of production, *i.e.* the efforts and abstinences that have been required for making it. What is meant is that the value of the thing tends to equal the sum of those values which measure the efforts and abstinences required for making it ; that is, Cost of production is used to denote what we have expressed by the term Expenses of production. For an exchange value or price, though it may be equal to a set of exchange values or prices, cannot be equal to a set of things unlike in kind to it. There cannot even be any direct comparison between one set of efforts and abstinences and another. We cannot subtract the labour of a carpenter in making a box from the labour of a watchmaker in making a watch. But we can subtract the exchange measure or price of the work of a carpenter in making a box from the price of the work of a watchmaker in making a watch. It may happen that an hour's work by a business manager, or two days' work by a watchmaker, or three days' work by a carpenter, or ten days' work by an agricultural labourer, may all have the same exchange measure, say, a guinea. A guinea may also be the exchange measure of the abstinence or sacrifice involved in the loan of 20 guineas for a year. These various efforts and abstinences, these elements of Cost of production, are certainly not equal to one another. But they would all exert an equal influence upon value ; because their Economic measures, **the expenses which would have to be incurred by anyone who would purchase them** are all equal.]

[§ 5. Again it is sometimes implied that besides the four classes who get respectively earnings, interest, rent and taxes, there is another distinct class of "consumers" who may bear the burden or reap the benefit of economic changes. But there is no such class. Of course the consumers of any particular commodity will suffer as a body if anything should raise its price. If for instance the wages of the producers rise, there will be a gain to this branch of industry at the expense of the consumers ; that is, probably of some landlords, and some

---

[1] Mill used the phrase in these two senses ; he himself distinguished clearly between them ; and a careful examination of the context will show which sense he meant in each place. But the want of a formal distinction between them has confused many of his readers. See the *Fortnightly Review* for April, 1876.

capitalists, and some labourers and the State. But there is no separate class of consumers of things in general, on whom the burden or the gain of any economic change can be thrown. Every such burden and every such gain must be distributed among the receivers of earnings, capitalists, landlords, and the State. There is of course a class of dependents—children, invalids, paupers and others—but what they consume is portioned out to them by the will of others who have an independent income ; and not according to economic laws. The consumption of those who depend on the support of another, is really a part of his consumption.]

[§ 6. Again there are some intricate questions connected with the interpretation of the term "the net annual income of a country." They have but little bearing on the main argument of the book, but they cannot be entirely ignored. This net income is found by deducting from the total produce of land and capital and labour, whatever is required to replace the Auxiliary capital consumed or worn out in the year. But it must be remembered that this total produce includes all results of man's work, which have market value, whether the work be manual or mental, whether it produces material wealth or not. It includes the benefit derived from the advice of a physician, the pleasure got from hearing a professional singer, and the enjoyment of all other services which one person may be hired to perform for another. It includes the services rendered not only by the omnibus driver, but also by the coachman who drives a private carriage. It includes the services of the domestic servant who makes or mends or cleans a carpet or a dress, as well as the results of the work of the upholsterer, the milliner, and the dyer.

We must however be careful not to count the same thing twice. If we have counted a carpet at its full value, we have already counted the values of the yarn and the labour that were used in making it ; and these must not be counted again. But if the carpet is cleaned by domestic servants or at steam scouring works, the value of the labour spent in cleaning it must be counted in separately ; for otherwise the results of this labour would be altogether omitted from the inventory of those newly-produced commodities and conveniences which constitute the real income of the country.

Again, suppose a landowner with an annual income of £10,000 hires a private secretary at a salary of £500, who hires a servant at wages of £50. It may seem that if the incomes of all these three persons are counted in as part of the net income of the country, some of it will be counted twice over and some three times. But this is not the case. The landlord transfers to his secretary, in return for his assistance, part of the purchasing power derived from the produce of land ; and the secretary again transfers part of this to his servant in return for his assistance. The farm produce the value of which goes as rent to the landlord, the assistance which the landlord derives from the work of the secretary, and that which the secretary derives from the work of the servant are independent parts of the real net income of the country ; and therefore the £10,000 and the £500 and the £50 which are their money measures, must all be counted in when we are estimating the income of the country.

The benefit which a man gets from living in a hired house must be reckoned in the total produce of the country's land, labour and capital ; for the rent that he pays, after deductions have been made for Depreciation, is the interest on the capital of the owner of the house ; and the Earnings-and-interest Fund must therefore include the benefit which is got from living in it.

If a man lives in his own house, the benefit he derives from it, after making deduction for Depreciation and repairs, is part of the real income of the country ; and the same may be said of the benefit he gets from the use of furniture, clothes, and other things which are not in ordinary usage reckoned among capital. This shows that our account of the Earnings-and-interest Fund requires a slight correction. We ought strictly to regard it as found by deducting from the net produce of the country, not only for rent and taxes, but also for the benefits that are derived from the use of furniture and other commodities which we do not call capital, because they are in the hands of consumers. In estimating these benefits, allowance must of course be made for Depreciation and repairs.

It may be noticed that if we had adopted the plan which Mr Jevons has advocated, of calling all commodities in the hands of consumers, capital[1]; that is of using the word capital as synonymous with Material wealth, this last difficulty would not have arisen, for we should have included the benefits derived from the use of these commodities as part of the Earnings-and-interest Fund, and regarded the owner of them as paying interest to himself ; just as in reckoning up the rents of a country we suppose a landowner who farms his own land to pay rent to himself. But Mr Jevons' plan, though it would be convenient in some ways, is so opposed to ordinary usage, that it seems best to adhere to the old use of the word. In this sense it includes carriage horses that are let out on hire, and farm horses whoever owns them. It includes a doctor's horses and

---

[1] *Theory of Political Economy*, pp. 245—253. Mr Giffen includes all material wealth under the £8,500,000,000 at which he estimates "the capital" of the country.

carriage if he hires them, in which case the revenue from them enters into the Earnings-and-interest Fund; but if they are his own, and used partly for his own enjoyment, partly as a source of revenue, it is difficult to say how much of their value should be regarded as capital[1].]

[1] See Book I. ch. iii. § 1.

CHAPTER VII.

SUPPLY OF UNSKILLED LABOUR.

§ 1. "THE **Real wages** of labour may be said to consist in the quantity of the necessaries and conveniences of life that are given for it; its **Nominal wages** in the quantity of money... The labourer is rich or poor, is well or ill rewarded, in proportion to the real, not to the nominal, wages of his labour[1]."

This distinction is very important; but in the present book we have agreed to neglect variations in the purchasing power of money. And so long as we do this, a rise or fall in the Nominal or money wages of labour means just the same as a rise or fall in the general purchasing power of these money wages, and therefore just the same as a rise or fall of Real wages.

There is another distinction which turns upon the difference between two ways in which wages may be measured.

> The wages that a man earns in a day may be called his **Time wages**: the wages that are paid to him for doing a given amount of work of a given quality (whether the bargain made with him is by the day or by the piece) may be called his **Task wages**.

For instance, if a man is hired at 15*s.* a week and a boy at 5*s.* a week, and the man does three times as much work on the average as the boy, their Task wages are equal though their Time wages are unequal. The full importance of this distinction will be seen further on. The wages of which we speak in this chapter are *Real Time wages*.

We have already seen that according to the Law of Population "a rise in the rate of wages causes either a rise in the Standard of Comfort of the people, or an increase in the number of marriages and births. A rise in the Standard of Comfort is almost sure to increase the percentage of children who grow up to be efficient workers. Therefore a rise in wages almost always promotes, and a fall in wages almost always checks, the growth of population."

---

[1] *Wealth of Nations,* Book I. ch. v.

It is true that when the labourer's wife and children can earn good wages, he may be able to bring up his family in comfort even when his own wages are low. But this correction is of much less importance than at first sight appears. For if the mother were not working for wages, she would be doing work at home that would promote the health, and the moral, if not the intellectual education of her children. While she is earning wages, some of this work will be neglected, and she will have to spend part of her wages on hiring others to do the rest of it. The wages of the children themselves are perhaps a more important means of providing them with food and clothing; but those children who are set to earn wages at an early age are often unhealthy as well as ignorant. So that we shall not go very far wrong if, in considering the effect of wages on the growth of population, we confine our attention to those earned by the labourer himself. Perhaps the chief exception to this rule is the case of agricultural families in new countries, who work together so that the family life is not broken up, and the physical, mental and moral well-being of the children is well cared for.

§ 2. The Standard of Comfort which young people are prudent enough to secure for themselves before they marry, varies from place to place and from time to time. When a high Standard of Comfort sets in, social opinion requires parents to provide wholesome rooms, nourishing food and a good education for their children. The next generation of workers is then healthy, intelligent and skilful, and of great value to employers, who by competing with one another keep up the rate of wages : the produce raised by them is so great that their share increases without diminishing the rate of profits. It is true that a rise in wages may lead to dissipation and extravagance, and fail to benefit the rising generation; but such cases are rare except in districts in which men, and, what is perhaps more important, women have been rendered hard, coarse and reckless by the nature of their occupations.

When a rise in wages results in an improvement in the homes, the food, education and therefore in the working efficiency of the people, it may elevate them permanently. And so if wages are already very low, a further fall may cause a *degradation of labour.* "With less food, which is the fuel of the human machine, less force will be generated ; with less clothing more force will be wasted by cold ; with scantier and meaner quarters, a fouler air and diminished access to the light will prevent the food from being duly digested in the stomach, and the blood from being duly oxydised in the lungs; will lower the tone of the system, and expose the subject increasingly to the ravages of disease. Now in all these ways the labourer becomes less efficient simply through the reduction of his wages[1]." The produce of his labour is less: the portion that he receives as his share is smaller, but the portion that capital receives as its share is not greater. "What is taken from wages no man gains; it is lost to the labourer and to the world."

§ 3.   So far we have been considering the causes that determine the supply of unskilled labour generally; but the supply of unskilled labour in any particular trade is determined by other things besides the rate of wages.   If equal wages were offered in ships going to the Mediterranean and the North Sea, the former would be full and the latter empty; so higher wages are offered on the latter ships to counterbalance the disadvantage of the ungenial climate to which they sail.   Carters who work underground in mines are paid more than carters who work above ground; and again, a night porter gets higher wages than a day porter.   If a trade has any disadvantage, such as unhealthiness, dirtiness, &c., higher wages will be necessary to induce men to seek the trade than would have been required in the absence of the disadvantage; and the necessary addition to wages may be called the money value of this disadvantage. In the same way if a trade offers any exceptional personal advantage, such as a good social position, lower wages will attract men to it than would be necessary in a trade similar in other respects, but without the advantage: and this difference of wages is the measure or money value of the advantage.

> If the wages and the money equivalents of the other special advantages of a trade be added together into one sum, and the money values of its special disadvantages be subtracted from the sum, the balance that remains may be called the **Net Advantages** of the trade.

If any unskilled occupation offers higher Net Advantages than other occupations in the same place, additional supplies of labour will as a rule speedily drift into it and will force down its wages.   To this general rule there are important exceptions: but they will be best discussed at a later stage.

[1] Walker *On Wages*, ch. IV.

CHAPTER VIII.

SUPPLY OF SKILLED LABOUR.

§ 1. WE have seen that the supply of unskilled labour depends chiefly on the food, clothing and other necessaries of life which labourers have been able to afford their children in preceding generations. The natural instincts which are common to all ranks of human life, and even among the lower animals, induce parents to exert themselves to provide food and shelter for their offspring. But it is otherwise with the special requirements of the skilled labourer; for his education demands an investment of capital, the fruits of which will appear in after time in his wages.

Adam Smith says: "When any expensive machine is erected, the extraordinary work to be performed by it before it is worn out, it must be expected, will replace the capital laid out upon it, with at least the ordinary profits. A man educated at the expense of much labour and time to any of those employments which require extraordinary dexterity and skill, may be compared to one of those expensive machines. The work which he learns to perform, it must be expected, over and above the usual wages of common labour, will replace to him the whole expense of his education, with at least the ordinary profits of an equally valuable capital. It must do this too in a reasonable time, regard being had to the very uncertain duration of human life, in the same manner as to the more certain duration of the machine."

Thus Adam Smith seems to imply that the Laws which determine the investment of capital in the education of the labourer are similar to those which govern the investment of capital in any vendible commodity. If this were the case, the Normal price or wage of skilled labour would be determined simply by its Expenses of production, just as the price of a commodity is determined. Take for instance the supply of cart-horses. There is some price which on an average just repays the expenses of rearing and breaking in horses of various kinds; and such a number of each kind are reared as will sell for prices which will cover their respective Expenses of production. The calculations of horse dealers may fail through their having incomplete knowledge of the circumstances of the market, or because of sudden changes in the demand for horses. Still if we take long periods, the average supply of horses of various kinds is such, that the prices at which they can be sold are equal to the Expenses of rearing and preparing them for their several kinds of work.

Again, the skill of a slave is vendible, and therefore the Law of Normal Supply applies to it. A slave-owner who rears slaves for hire in different employments, calculates the expenses of each kind of training, and the probable future demand for each kind of work. He estimates the rate of hire and the length of time during which it can be earned. He allows for inconstancy of employment and for uncertainty of success, but not necessarily for any discomforts except those which are likely to injure the health and shorten the life of the slave. He allows for the fact that the expenses of education will be incurred soon, and that the wages will not be received for many years; after having made these calculations he can tell whether it will be worth his while to bring up the slave as an unskilled or as a skilled labourer. He will know whether the higher wages which the slave can earn for him will be worth more to him than the extra expenses involved in giving him the higher training. Suppose for instance he finds that by incurring an extra expense of £100 for the slave's education, he can secure, after allowing for the chance that the slave may die early, an increased receipt in wages which will only be equal to £100 spread over the rest of the slave's life time; he will then certainly not give him the education. He would not give it if this increased value would be £200. If it were £300 he might be in doubt, but if it were £400 he would probably give it [1].

Thus slave-owners adjust the supply of any kind of skilled slave labour to the demand for it, so that the pecuniary gain which is derived from a slave's work in any occupation corresponds to the trouble and expense of bringing him up to it [2].

§ 2. But parents when selecting trades for their children differ from slave-owners when choosing occupations for their slaves in four important respects. Firstly, parents in estimating

[1] Calculations of this kind are worked out in Engel's *Der Preis der Arbeit*.

[2] For this reason the population of a slave country might be better educated than the children of poor labourers in a free country; but their masters generally fear that education might lead them to rebel; and a slave, because he is a slave, is almost always limp and apathetic in character: and the attempt to educate him for difficult work, or for responsibility, is like trying to put a polish on soft wood. But in ancient

the Net Advantages of a trade for their son take account of everything that will add to his comfort and happiness, while the slave-owner may take account of such things only so far as they affect the slave's efficiency.

Secondly, parents who give their son an expensive education expect that he, not they, will reap its chief fruits ; but the slave's skill is the property of his owner. Parents resemble the slave-owner in having to estimate on the one hand the Net Advantages of each occupation, and on the other the trouble and expense of preparing for it. But even when they have made these estimates they cannot decide on their course by a mere arithmetical calculation, as he can. For they must also decide this moral question : To what extent are we ready to sacrifice ourselves for our son's benefit ? What is the value to us of an advantage that will be enjoyed by him ?

Thirdly, few parents are capitalists ; most of them cannot borrow money on anything like the same terms as a capitalist can. To take an extreme case : some unskilled labourers, even with the help of the wages that their children bring in, cannot purchase as much food and clothing and house-room as the health of the family requires ; and it would be useless to ask one of them to calculate the advantage which his son might derive if £50 were spent in preparing him for a skilled occupation. It is likely that these ·advantages may include wages for his son when grown up at the rate of £30 a year more than those of an unskilled labourer. If he worked out this sum he would find that, allowing the market-rate of interest, the present value of these extra wages would be several hundred pounds. In such a case a slave-owner would make the outlay on business principles. The father does not because he cannot.

Fourthly, in assuming that the slave-owner is a capitalist, we supposed him to manage his affairs as capable business men do. We supposed that he is always on the look out, as business men are, for profitable investments of his capital ; that he watches the variations of supply and demand with regard to each particular kind of slave's skill ; and that he is continually making out the profit and loss accounts of various modes of educating his slaves.

But parents do not generally carry on their inquiries in this business-like way : a poor and ignorant parent is not likely to think of obtaining for his son a lot in life very different from his

Greece and Rome, when the moral sense of the world had not outgrown slavery, and slaves worked without a feeling of degradation, masters used often to give a high literary or artistic education to their slaves as a matter of business.

own. A man brought up with narrow surroundings is apt to
acquiesce in them.   His own start in life was a poor one, and it
seems to him quite reasonable that he should make what he can
out of the labour of his son; his wages almost imply that the
world expects him to do it, and his neighbours do it; so he
allows a small present gain to himself to outweigh a great
future advantage for his son.   The poor are moved as much as
any other parents by the sight of the sufferings of their children,
but they are careless about the distant future both of their children and of themselves; for they have not a vivid imagination;
they are ruled by custom and not by the deliberate use of their
reason.   The lower we go in the social scale the less do parents
seem to see the benefits that they may confer on their sons by
investing trouble and money in their education ; and the smaller
is their power of making such sacrifices.   The rate of interest
at which parents discount future advantages to their children
increases with the narrowness of their education and the
pressure of immediate want.

§ 3.   Mill was so much impressed by the difficulties that
beset a parent in the attempt to bring up his son to an occupation widely different in character from his own, that he said :—
"So complete, indeed, has hitherto been the separation, so
strongly marked the line of demarcation, between the different
grades of labourers, as to be almost equivalent to an hereditary
distinction of caste ; each employment being chiefly recruited
from the children of those already employed in it, or in employments of the same rank with it in social estimation, or from the
children of persons who, if originally of a lower rank, have
succeeded in raising themselves by their exertions.   The
liberal professions are mostly supplied by the sons of either the
professional or idle classes : the more highly skilled manual
employments are filled up from the sons of skilled artizans, or
the class of tradesmen who rank with them : the lower classes of
skilled employments are in a similar case ; and unskilled
labourers, with occasional exceptions, remain from father to son
in their pristine condition.   Consequently the wages of each
class have hitherto been regulated by the increase of its own
population rather than that of the general population of the
country."

But he goes on, "The changes now so rapidly taking place
in usages and ideas are undermining all these distinctions ; the habits or disabilities which chained people to their
hereditary condition are fast wearing away, and every class is
exposed to increased and increasing competition from at least
the class immediately below it [1]."

[1] *Political Economy*, Book II. ch. xiv. § 2.

This movement has continued since he wrote, and the divisions between the various grades of English society are not so clearly marked in this generation as they were in the last. Each of Mill's four grades is subdivided into a number of lesser grades, rising one above the other like the steps of a long staircase that is arranged in four flights, with a short landing at the end of each of them.

Parents generally bring up their children to an occupation in the same social grade as their own. But when the supply of labour in one grade is such that its Net Advantages are much greater than those in the grade next below, the more thoughtful and self-denying parents in the grade below push their sons into that grade. Thus the Law of Supply, though its action is more slow with regard to labour of different grades than with regard to different kinds of commodities, yet acts in the same way in the two cases. When the Net Advantages of a trade rise above what is required to compensate for the trouble and expense of preparing for it, *i.e.* are abnormally high, forces are brought into play which tend to increase the supply of labour in that trade. The increase will come first and chiefly from other trades in the same grade, unless the Net Advantages of other trades in the same grade are also abnormally high. In that case the increase of supply will come chiefly from the grade immediately below, and will come more slowly. In any case the increase will be chiefly due to the action of parents in selecting an occupation for their children, but will be to some extent caused by a change of occupation on the part of adults. On the other hand, when the Net Advantages in a trade fall below what is required to compensate the trouble and expense of preparing for it, forces will be brought into play which tend to diminish the supply of labour. For the most versatile men in the trade, and those who have the least taste and the least Specialised skill for the work, will begin to seek other occupations ; and parents will avoid bringing up their sons to it.

To complete our account of the causes which determine the supply of different kinds of skilled labour we must examine the various advantages and disadvantages that attract men to or repel them from different trades, and the various industrial qualities that may be required in a trade.

§ 4. Firstly, with regard to the various advantages and disadvantages of which account must be taken in estimating the Net Advantages of a trade.

Under this head must obviously be reckoned the *constancy or inconstancy of employment* in a trade, and the *chances of success or failure* in it. To allow for these inequalities we must, when we are estimating the wages of a trade, look for the wages earned not in a day but in a year, or even in several years, by those who have an average success in it. We cannot measure the wages of a fisherman by the price for which he can sell his fish when he returns with a boat full, without taking account of the many days when he returns having taken nothing. We cannot reckon the wages of a dock porter as those which are to be had when the docks are full of ships eag er tobe unloaded, without taking account of the fact that sometimes the harbour is nearly empty and most of the porters waiting in enforced idleness. In comparing the wages of a bricklayer, a carpenter and a railway guard, we must re-member that the railway guard's employment is secure at all times, that the carpenter may be thrown out of work by dulness of trade, and that bricklayer's work may be interrupted by dulness of trade and by unfavourable weather. In estimating the earnings of barristers we must take account of the many who fail as well as of the few who succeed.

But independently of considerations such as these, which properly enter into our estimate of the average wages to be earned in a trade, there are other advantages and disadvantages which must be reckoned separately. These may be classed under the heads of *healthiness, comfort* and *social position.* Danger may be regarded as a kind of unhealthiness. Dirtiness, physical and mental strain, anxiety and monotony are the chief discomforts to be considered. Adam Smith points out that the aversion which men have for the work of a butcher, and to some extent for the butcher himself, raises the earnings of butchers above those of bakers. If earnings were equal in the two trades the number of bakers would increase, and that of butchers would diminish, until the wages of butchers had risen above those of bakers enough to compensate for the disagree-ableness and the social disadvantages of the butcher's work. Again, the wages of domestic servants, including their board and lodging, are much higher than are those of women who do work of equal difficulty in factories or in their own homes. For the servant must always submit to some loss of freedom, and if she happens to fall under the control of an ill-mannered mistress, to some loss of dignity.

When the disagreeableness of work takes the form of dirtiness it generally has the further disadvantage of involving a loss of social position; the most disagreeable of all work is chiefly done by those who cannot get any other employment; and its wages are therefore low, in consequence of the in-competence of those who do it, and in spite of its repulsive character. But personal discomfort which arises from a sense of danger, often does not repel men. As Adam Smith says: "The dangers and hairbreadth escapes of a life of adventures, instead of disheartening young people seem frequently to recommend a trade to them...the distant prospect of hazards from which we can hope to extricate ourselves by courage and address is not disagreeable to us, and does not raise the wages of labour in any employment. It is otherwise with those in which courage and address can be of no avail. In trades which are known to be very unwholesome, the wages of labour are always remarkably high."

The fact that an occupation offers some very high prizes, attracts men into it in two ways. Firstly, young men form, fortunately for the world, high estimates of their own chances of attaining excellence, and thus are more attracted by the prospects of a great success than they are deterred by the fear of failure; and secondly, the social rank of an occupation depends more on the highest dignity and the best position which can be attained through it, than on the average good fortune of those engaged in it. The learned professions offer such high attractions independently of the earnings to be got in them, that their average earnings are much lower than what could be earned by an equal amount of trained ability and industry in other occupations.

§ 5. Next, to consider the various industrial qualities, physical, mental and moral, that may be wanted in a trade. A man's physical and moral qualities depend chiefly upon the character of his home in youth. If he was well fed and housed, if his father, and what is perhaps more important, if his mother had energy and kindness and honesty, he is pretty sure to have those physical and moral qualities which are a necessary condition of industrial efficiency. That part of a man's wages which he owes to his education may be regarded as a kind of *profit* on the capital invested in it: that part which he owes to exceptional natural qualities may be regarded as a kind of *rent;* that is, it is the income derived from an agent of production the supply of which is determined by natural causes, and not by the deliberate outlay of human effort for the sake of future advantage.

The wages in a trade that requires only physical strength, when they are paid by the day, are generally very low; but when they are paid by the piece, as in the case of navvies, an exceptionally strong man can sometimes earn high wages. Much work that requires great strength is also to some extent dirty and disagreeable; and when it requires specially trained skill, and that intelligence and judgment which find a good market in any trade, it receives very high wages. For instance many of those engaged in iron and glass works must have great natural intelligence and a long special training. They are often thrown out of employment by depressions of trade, and their skill would be useless to them if for any reason they had to leave the trade. Their work is dirty and disagreeable, and it requires great physical strength, and a power, which many strong men have not, of enduring great and sudden variations of heat and cold. So it is not to be wondered at that in times of prosperity the best iron heaters and glass-blowers, working piece work, can earn wages many times as high as those of some to whom custom has given a higher social position.

Many kinds of office work require a rare combination of high mental and moral qualities; but almost any one can be easily taught to do the work of a copying clerk, and probably there will soon be few men or women in England who cannot write fairly well. When all can write, the work of copying, which used to earn higher wages than almost any kind of manual labour, will rank among unskilled trades. In fact the better kinds of artisan work educate a man more, and will be better paid than those kinds of clerk's work which call for neither judgment nor responsibility. The best thing that an artisan can do for his son is to bring him up to do thoroughly the work that lies at his hand, so that he may understand the mechanical, chemical or other scientific principles that bear upon it ; and may enter into the spirit of any new improvement that may be made in it. If his son should prove to have good natural abilities, he is far more likely to rise to a high position in the world from the bench of an artisan than from the desk of a clerk.

§ 6. Next, if we compare those industrial qualities which are Non-specialised, and can be turned to account in many trades, with those which are Specialised to one trade, we shall find that the former are rising in importance relatively to the latter.

It has already been remarked that the division of labour sometimes enables a man to pass easily between trades which used to be totally distinct[1]. This remark may be extended. The great tendency of the growth of machinery is to supplant manual work which requires only physical strength, or skill that is got by the constant practice of one set of movements. Machinery can make uniform movements more accurately and effectively than man can ; and most of the work which was done by those who were specially skilful with their fingers a few generations ago, is now done by machinery; and since machinery does not incroach much on that manual work which requires judgment, while the management of machinery generally does require judgment, there is a much greater demand now than formerly for intelligence and resource. Those qualities which enable men to decide rightly and quickly in new and

---

[1] Book I. ch. viii. § 9.

difficult cases, are the common property of the better class of workmen in almost every trade; and a person who has acquired them in one trade can easily transfer them to another. They are Non-Specialised. It is however true that there is much technical trade knowledge with regard to processes and the quality of materials, which is of little use save in the trade in which it was acquired; and the progress of industry tends to increase the amount of the Specialised knowledge which is needed by the better class of workmen in almost every trade.

§ 7. We have seen that the supply of skilled labour is not adjusted to the demand for it as easily as the supply of a vendible commodity is adjusted to the demand for it. For a capitalist can devote his capital to producing any commodity which is in great demand, and obtain his reward in the high price that he gets for it. But if a capitalist goes to the expense of increasing the supply of skilled labourers in any trade, the skill when acquired will belong, not to him, but to those whom he has educated. The only partial exception to this rule is met with in the system of apprenticeships. This system does enable capitalists to invest some capital profitably to themselves in the education of the sons of the poorer classes. In some cases the employer pays a lad considerable wages for several years during which he is learning the trade; but during the last two or three years of his apprenticeship, the lad's work is worth much more than the wages for which he is bound to serve by the terms of the apprenticeship; and thus repays with interest the expense which his master incurred for him, both in paying him wages and in loss from his spoiling material and his clumsy use of tools. But the system labours under some disadvantages. The spirit of the age in England, and to an even greater extent in new countries, renders lads unwilling to be bound to a master for a long period of years. Moreover in Adam Smith's time it was complained that masters often neglected to give proper instruction to their apprentices, and this evil is greater now than it was then. For the lad used to be taught by the master, who had a direct interest in teaching him well; while now he is taught by a hired workman who generally has no such interest. But if the workman is the apprentice's father he will take pains with the lad; and therefore employers like to have as apprentices the sons of those already in their employ; and fathers like to have their sons apprenticed under them. Something like a trade caste has grown up in this way in glass blowing and some other trades.

As we have seen, the rate of interest at which parents discount future advantages to their sons increases with the narrowness of their education and the pressure of immediate want. This fact affords a strong argument in favour of any public or private action which may aid the poorer classes of parents in giving an improved education to their children. In this matter Government will find a direct pecuniary gain in doing what a private individual will not do unless from a sense of duty. A Government which can borrow money, as ours can, at a little over three per cent. interest, may make a good investment by spending money on education, and thus advancing the capital which the poor man has no means of borrowing at any tolerable rate of interest. About a tenth of the total income of the country is paid to Government in Imperial and Local taxes; so that with the present rate of taxes Government will gain about a tenth of whatever increase in the national wealth comes from an improved system of education. And it is probable that this tenth would be sufficient to repay with interest any outlay that Government may make on that general and technical education, which is required to enable Englishmen to hold their own in competition with those who have been taught in the admirable schools, that are to be found in some foreign countries.

CHAPTER IX.

SUPPLY OF BUSINESS POWER.

§ 1.   LET us next inquire what are the causes which determine the supply of business power of different kinds; and how the rate of Earnings of Management in a trade affects the supply of business power in it.

The successful barrister or physician may obtain earnings equal to those of three hundred unskilled labourers; but on the whole the most highly paid work is that of business management.   It is only within the last few generations that this work has taken its present shape: it is only quite recently, and only in a few countries, that much intellect of the highest order has been required for, and given to, the task of conducting manufacturing and commercial enterprises.

In old times there was little variation in the character of the things that were made, or in the manner of making them. Inventions came slowly; in some trades new processes were scarce discovered once in a century; and after they had been once discovered, a generation or more might elapse before they came into general use.   The business man of former times required industry, sound judgment, and the power of dealing with men; but he could very often get on without much faculty for originating new schemes.   But now the manufacturer or merchant who controls a large capital cannot be sure even of holding his own unless he is quick to take advantage of new inventions, and has some power of striking out new lines for himself.   The difficulty of this work of pioneering is increasing in many ways.   For fashion and taste change more rapidly than they used to do; and these changes affect the great masses of the population, and not only the upper classes as in the olden times.   And again every change in the manner of carrying on any trade alters the character of the things that it wants to buy from other trades, and each trade buys from and sells to many more trades now than formerly. A manufacturer has to watch the progress of the trades to which he sells, as well as of his own.

Again, those nations which had no manufactures were content till lately to buy any of the ordinary English goods that would at all serve their purpose. But now the English manufacturer meets the competition of Americans and others, who make a special study of the needs of each backward country. To hold his own, he must vary the machines and implements and other things which he offers to other countries so as to suit various climates and various soils; he must meet the special requirements of races of different temperaments and habits, and in different phases of civilization. This requires wide knowledge and a constant activity of intellect.

Much of the work of business is then so difficult, and requires so much special training and such a rare combination of natural qualities, that the Earnings of Management got by it may be very high, without there being many men who can do the work and get these high earnings.

§ 2. We have already seen that the faculties required by the skilled workman,—his Personal capital—may be classed as Specialised and Non-specialised. The skill and knowledge which are of little use save in the trade in which they have been acquired are Specialised capital; the general ability and resource, the energy and strength of character, the honesty and steadiness, which can be easily transferred from one trade to another, are Non-specialised capital. And we have seen that the progress of invention tends to diminish the importance of mere manual skill, and of the knowledge of the rules of thumb that have been handed down from earlier generations, and that therefore in many, though not in all trades, the importance of the workman's Specialised qualities has diminished relatively to his Non-specialised.

The same change is going on with greater rapidity in the case of the employer. The employer who was "master of his men" in this sense that, if any of them were doing their work badly, he could shew them how to do it better, is becoming rare in many trades; and much work that used to be done by the head of a business is now done by foremen, overlookers, and sub-contractors. This change is to be regretted; it tends to impair the thoroughness of work, and it causes estrangement between the employer and the employed by lessening his personal influence over them. But evil as the change is in some respects, it has the advantage of leaving the whole time and energy of the head of the business free for what has become, in this modern phase of the division of labour, his chief work.

Bagehot compares him to the military commander of modern times who, instead of mixing in the fray himself, sits at the far end of a telegraph-wire with his head over some papers, and directs and organizes from a distance. It is his work to study changes in the markets in which he buys, and in those in which he sells; to be on the alert for new wants and new inventions, and to devise new modes of getting over new difficulties. And most of the qualities that are required for this work are Non-specialised. They depend partly on early training, partly on the education of business; but if educated in one trade they can be transferred to another.

It is true that a man who is not well acquainted with the technical details of the trade in which he is engaged, is at some disadvantage, however great be his general or Non-specialised business power. But, as Bagehot points out, the disadvantage need not be very great if he has a competent staff of subordinates who possess the requisite detailed knowledge. So that the head or managing mind of a business may lose less than those who work under him would by changing his trade. A minister of state may move from the Indian Office to the Foreign Office, or from the Poor Law Board to the Admiralty, without any great loss of efficiency. He obtains information on technical details from the permanent Secretaries and clerks under him. His judgment and sagacity are as useful in one office as in another, while much of the technical knowledge of his subordinates is of little value save in that office in which it has been acquired. It is true that "Little good for the most part comes of people who have been brought up on one side of the business world going quite to the other side, of farmers' sons going to cotton spinning, or of lacemakers' sons going into shipping. Each sort of trade has a tradition of its own, which is never written, probably could not be written, which can only be learnt in fragments, and which is best taken in early life, before the mind is shaped and the ideas fixed. But each trade in modern commerce is surrounded by subsidiary and kindred trades, which familiarise the imagination with it, and make its state known[1]." And when high profits are being made in that trade, business power comes into it from the surrounding trades.

§ 3. We have seen that the supply of skilled workers in any trade depends on the estimate that men form for themselves, and parents form for their children, of its Net Advantages on the one hand, and of the difficulties of preparing for and entering it on the other. We saw that if they made their calculations correctly, and if there were no natural or artificial barriers against entering a trade, the supply would be so adjusted to the

---

[1] In *Fortnightly Review*, vol. XIX.

demand that the Net Advantages of being in that trade would correspond to the trouble and expense of preparing for it. And we have now seen how the supply of business power in a trade is increased by a rise in the Earnings of Management that can be got in it. But the case of business power differs from that of skilled labour in several respects.

Firstly, the average Earnings of Management cannot be easily ascertained. It is comparatively easy to find out the wages of bricklayers or puddlers by striking an average between the wages that are earned by men of various degrees of efficiency, and allowing for the inconstancy of their employment. But the Earnings of Management which a man is getting, can only be found after making up a careful account of the net profits of his business, and deducting interest on his capital. The exact state of his affairs is often not known by himself ; and it can seldom be guessed at all accurately even by those who are in the same trade with himself. It is not true even in a little village at the present day that every one knows all his neighbour's affairs. " The village innkeeper, publican or shopkeeper, who is making a small fortune does not invite competition by telling his neighbours of his profits, and the man who is not doing well does not alarm his creditors by exposing the state of his affairs[1]." But what we are now discussing are the causes that determine the supply of business power in each trade *in the long run;* and the average rate of profits in a trade cannot rise or fall much without general attention being attracted to the change before long. And though it is a more difficult task for a business man than for a skilled labourer to find out whether he could improve his prospects by changing his trade, yet the business man has great opportunities for discovering whatever can be found out about the present and future of other trades ; if he wishes to change his trade, he can, as we have seen, generally do so more easily than the skilled workman can ; and he can choose any trade for his son.

Secondly, the supply of business power in a trade differs from the supply of skilled labour in being partly dependent on the supply of capital necessary to give it scope. But this difference again is less important than it appears. We cannot properly examine here the banking and other modern agencies by which capital is transferred from where it is not wanted to where it is wanted. For our present purpose it is sufficient to assume that " A very great many of the strongest heads in England spend their minds on little else than thinking whether other people will pay their debts. And the combined aggregate of these persons is a prepared machine ready to carry capital in

---

[1] Cliffe Leslie in *Fortnightly Review*, vol. XXV.

any direction. The moment any set of traders want capital, the best of them, those whose promises are known to be good, get it in a minute, because it is lying ready in the hands of those who know, and who live by knowing, that they are fit to have it [1]." A man who has business power and a little capital can get more capital. If he turns this to good account his improved position will enable him to borrow still more ; and thus before long he may wield a capital so large that his profits leave him a rich income after paying interest on what he has borrowed. Again, a man without capital may be taken into private partnership by others ; or he may become the manager of a joint-stock company. " It is no longer true that a man becomes an employer because he is a capitalist. Men command capital because they have the qualifications to profitably employ labour. To these captains of industry (or organizers of industry) capital and labour alike resort for the opportunity to perform their several functions [2]."

We may conclude then that though there are several differences between the case of business power and that of skilled labour, yet these differences do not prevent the supply of business power in a trade from being determined in all essential respects in the same way as the supply of skilled labour. We shall however see further on that the Earnings of Management of a man working with borrowed capital fall short of the income of a man of equal ability working with his own capital by more than the mere interest on it.

[1] Bagehot, l. c.
[2] Walker *on Wages*, ch. XIV.

CHAPTER X.

INTEREST.

§ 1.   THE Laws of Normal Supply of capital and of different kinds of industry have now been examined.   Our next step is to investigate the relation between Normal Supply and Demand, and the way in which the Normal interest on capital, and the Normal earnings of each kind of industry, are determined.

We have seen[1] that the total net annual produce of a country's capital and industry, after rent and taxes have been deducted from it, consists of interest on capital, and the earnings of different kinds of industry ; and we have called it the *Earnings-and-interest Fund.* The share which capital obtains of this Fund depends firstly upon the amount of the Fund, and secondly on the manner in which it is divided.

Firstly, with regard to the amount of the Earnings-and-interest Fund that is obtained by a given amount of capital and labour. This depends on the extent and the richness of the natural sources of agricultural and mineral wealth, on the progress that has been made in the arts of agriculture, mining, and manufacture, and on the means that nature and art have provided for conveying men, goods and news rapidly and inexpensively from one place to another. A country which has abundant and easy communication with distant places can often obtain a very high return to her capital and labour even though her own soil be poor ; for the concentration of her industry may give her such advantages in manufacture and in the carrying trade that she can purchase much of her food and raw material from abroad at a moderate cost. But the highest returns of all are obtained in new countries where the arts of civilization are used in turning to account the rich resources of Nature ; this condition however cannot be fully satisfied unless the population is sufficiently dense to enable them to organize easy means of communication with one another and avail themselves of the Division of labour.

[1] Book II. ch. vi. § 2.

Such then are the causes which determine the amount of the Earnings-and-interest Fund which Nature returns to a given amount of capital and industry. Our next step is to inquire how this Fund is divided into the share which capital takes as interest, and that which industry takes as earnings. Afterwards we shall have to inquire how the share which goes to industry is divided among the various ranks of unskilled and skilled labour, and business power.

When a capitalist employs his own capital in business, he must be reckoned both among those who supply the capital which aids industry in production, and among those whose industry forms the demand for the aid of capital. The interest which he gets for his capital is not clearly marked off in practice from the Earnings of Management which he gets by his work ; the two are reckoned together under the name of profits. But for the purposes of theory we must distinguish between the two : we must regard as interest that part of his income which he could get by lending his capital to be used by others ; just as, if a man cultivates his own land, we must regard as rent that portion of his income which he could get by letting the land to others.

§ 2. The rate of interest which results from the division of the Earnings-and-interest Fund into the shares of capital and industry will be found to depend upon the urgency of the demand of industry for the aid of capital.

In a civilized state all production requires both capital and industry ; each of these demands the aid of the other, but not to the same extent at different times and places. If in any place there is an abundant supply of industry and a scarce supply of capital, while such methods of production are used as to give those who are working with much Auxiliary capital a great advantage over those who are working with little ; then the demand of industry for the aid of capital will be urgent. That is to say, a given amount of capital employed in production will be able to get a large share of the produce which it aids industry in raising ; because industry is in urgent need of the assistance of a great deal of capital, and the scarcity of capital enables the owners of it to hold out for very advantageous terms without running any risk of its being left unemployed.

Conversely, the demand of industry for the aid of capital will not be urgent if there is a large supply of capital in proportion to the population, and the methods of production are such that no great gain would arise from an increase in the amount of Auxiliary capital used. Industry will not then be compelled to resign to capital enough of the produce to afford a high rate of interest.

Thus we see that, other things being equal, an increase of

capital will diminish the competition of industry for the aid of capital; and will tend to raise earnings at the expense of interest. In just the same way, other things being equal, an increase of population, capital being stationary, will increase the competition of industry for the aid of capital, and will raise interest at the expense of earnings.

But other things do not generally remain equal. The progress of civilization increases the demand of industry for the aid of capital independently of any increase in the population of the country. For it causes a continual increase in the amount and expensiveness of the machinery and other things which men use as means to the attainment of their ends. Let us look at some instances of this change.

Formerly men pumped up by hand, or brought in buckets whatever water they wanted. Now water-companies erect expensive works, and the water flows where it is wanted. Every such water-supply represents effort economised by being capitalised. So all the modern contrivances for lighting and draining towns, for carrying men and goods by railways and canals, and for carrying news by telegraph, enable men to attain their ends with much less total effort than they otherwise could, on condition that they capitalise a large part of their effort; that is on condition that they make a great outlay at starting in the expectation of being rewarded by the benefits they will derive from it in the course of years. Again, the more durable the Fixed capital that is used, the larger the total amount of the capital that can be employed. For instance the amount of capital which can profitably be invested in the buildings of a country increases rapidly when massive stone buildings begin to displace wooden fabrics that are quickly built and that quickly perish. This change is now going on in America.

Almost every important invention leads to an increase of the scope for the profitable employment of capital. Whenever a machine is made to do work that used to be done by hand, the scope for the employment of capital is increased. The **Net Return** of a machine may be defined as the value of the work that it does after allowing for Depreciation and the expenses of working it, including the Earnings of Management. Machines are often invented which cannot be used because their Net Return would not afford the market rate of interest on the capital invested in them. In course of time, when the machine is improved so that its Net Return would afford this interest, it is brought into use, and offers a fresh field for capital. Thus every increase in the advantages that can be obtained by the use of expensive machinery increases the scope for the profitable employment of capital, and thus raises the rate of interest.

We see then that an increase in the durability of Fixed

capital, and an extended use of machinery and other Auxiliary capital, increase the amount of capital which is required to assist and give employment to industry; conversely every such change diminishes the amount of industry which is required to assist and give employment to capital. Every such change increases the demand of industry for the aid of capital.

§ 3. Next, the amount of capital, of which the aid in production is demanded by a given population in a given state of the arts of production, depends on the rate of interest at which they can obtain its aid.

To fix the ideas, let us take some particular trade, say that of hatmaking, and inquire what determines the amount of capital which it absorbs. Suppose that the rate of interest is 4 per cent. per annum on perfectly good security ; and that the hatmaking trade absorbs a capital of one million pounds. This implies that there is a million pounds worth of capital which the hatmaking trade can turn to so good account that they would pay 4 per cent. per annum *net* for the use of it rather than go without it : net, that is exclusive of all allowances for Trade and Personal Risks and Depreciation. Some things are necessary to them ; they must have not only some food, clothing, and houseroom, but also some Circulating capital such as raw material and some Fixed capital such as tools and perhaps a little machinery.

Of course competition prevents anything more than the ordinary trade profit being got by the use of this capital; but the loss of it would be so injurious that those in the trade would have been willing to pay 50 per cent. on the capital, if they could not have got the use of it on easier terms. There may be other machinery which the trade would have refused to dispense with if the rate of interest had been 20 per cent. per annum, but not if it had been higher. If the rate had been 10 per cent., still more would have been used ; if it had been 7 per cent., still more ; if 5 per cent., still more ; and finally the rate being 4 per cent. they use more still. When they have this amount the Final Utility, as we may say, of the machinery, i.e. the utility of that machinery which it is only just worth their while to employ, is measured by 4 per cent. A rise in the rate of interest would check their use of machinery ; for they would avoid the use of all that did not give a net annual surplus of more than 4 per cent. on its value. And a fall in the rate of interest would lead them to demand the aid of more capital, and to introduce machinery which gave a net annual surplus of something less than 4 per cent. on its value. Again, the lower the rate of interest the more substantial will be the style of building used for the hatmaking factories and the homes of the hatmakers. And a fall in the rate of interest will lead to the employment of more capital in the hatmaking trade in the form of larger stocks of raw material and of the finished commodity in the hands of retail dealers.

A fall in the rate of interest would increase the demand for capital on the part of some trades more than of others. A century ago it would have had little effect upon agriculture ; but now it would much promote the use of farming machinery and of improvements the return to which is expected to be spread over a long period of years. In cotton manufacture, again, it would have but little effect, because the work of that trade is of so uniform a character, and on so large a scale, as to give continuous employment to almost any machine that can be invented for it ; though even in that trade an increased command over capital will quicken the adoption of improvements in machinery. But in the wood and iron manufacturing trades there are a great many machines which it would be economical to use if they could be kept continually at work ; but for which small factories can only find occasional employment. The use of such machinery would be increased by a fall in the rate of interest.

Of course there are some years of depression of trade in which the Net Return of a good deal of machinery is nothing at all ; and again some machinery is made which never gives any Net Return. But if we look at average results, we find that the Net annual Return of the machinery and other capital in use in a country just affords interest on its value at the rate current there. If for instance we supposed, what is about the fact, that the rate of interest in England is 4 per cent., and that all the various trades of England employ between them in different ways a capital of £4,000,000,000 ; this would show that £4,000,000,000 is just that amount of capital which can be employed in England at the present time without the use of any which is thought likely, after allowing for risks, to give an annual Net Return of less than 4 per cent. on its value.

§ 4. Thus the Demand for the loan of capital obeys a law similar to that which holds for the sale of commodities. Just as there is a certain amount of a commodity which can find purchasers at any given price, and when the price rises the amount that can be sold diminishes, so it is with regard to the use of capital. In any given state of the arts of production in a country, there is a certain amount of capital which it would be worth while for the various trades to employ in industry if they have to allow capital's share of the year's Earnings-and-interest Fund to be 7 per cent. on the capital ; or, as we may say, if they have to pay 7 per cent. per annum for the use of capital. If they have to pay 6 per cent. for its use, it will be worth their while to employ a larger amount ; if 5 per cent. a larger amount still; if 4 per cent. a larger amount still; and so on. And the **Law of Demand for capital** is :—

> The Demand for capital increases with every increase in the numbers of the population, the natural resources of the country, the efficiency of the arts of production, the scope that these arts afford for the employment of Auxiliary capital, and the durability of Fixed capital. The rate of interest at which capital can find employment in a country with any given industrial population in any given state of the arts of production, depends on the amount of the capital offered for loan. It rises with a diminution and falls with an increase of this amount. Conversely, the amount of capital for which occupation can be found, increases with a fall and diminishes with a rise in the rate of interest at which capital is offered on loan. The current rate of interest measures the Final Utility of capital to each borrower; that is the advantage to him of the use of that capital which he is only just induced to employ.

§ 5. The rate of interest is in equilibrium when it is just that at which the whole supply of capital can find employment.

The annual addition to the capital of a country is seldom any considerable part of the whole, so that if we consider only short periods of time we may, without any great error, regard the supply as fixed during that time. On this supposition, the Law of the rate of interest becomes similar to that of the value of a commodity, the amount of which cannot be increased: Demand is the sole regulator of value. The rate of interest is then simply determined as just that which will call forth a demand for the existing capital.

§ 6. But when we are considering long periods of time we cannot neglect the influence which the rate of interest exercises on the increase of capital : and the problem becomes difficult. To simplify it, let us begin by making the opposite assumption to that which we made when we supposed the supply of capital to be fixed independently of the rate of interest. Let us now suppose that the rate of interest,—the price that can be obtained for the use of capital—exercises an overwhelming influence on the accumulation of capital.

Let us imagine for instance that people would save rapidly if they could obtain 5 per cent. per annum interest for their capital; but that if they could not obtain as high a rate as this, many of them would cease to save and begin to consume their capital. In this case the Normal rate of interest for secure investments would be fixed at 5 per cent. For so long as the rate of interest was more than 5 per cent., capital would accumulate rapidly. The growth of capital would make the division of the produce more favourable to industry and less favourable to capital ; earnings would rise and interest would fall. If it fell below 5 per cent., the accumulation of capital would be checked, and many would consume their capital. The demand of industry for the aid of capital would thus be increased, the division of the produce would become more favourable to capital ; earnings would fall, and the rate of interest would rise again to 5 per cent., and so on. Thus a rate of interest of 5 per cent. per annum would be the Centre or Normal value toward which the remuneration of abstinence continually gravitated, and any deviation from which would be but a temporary irregularity, which the moment it exists, sets forces in motion tending to correct it.

On this assumption the Normal rate of interest would be fixed at 5 per cent. independently of all changes in the field for the employment of capital ; such as the opening up of rich new countries, or inventions that gave room for vast extensions of Fixed capital. Of course such a change might raise the rate of interest temporarily ; but since this rise would, on our present hypothesis, call rapidly into existence a vast increase of capital, interest would not remain for any considerable time higher than 5 per cent. On this supposition the Normal rate of interest would be rigidly fixed in the same way as is the Normal value of a commodity, the Expenses of production of which are independent of the amount produced[1].

§ 7. But in fact the influence which the rate of interest exerts on the accumulation of capital is much weaker than we have supposed it to be in this imaginary case. The motives which men have for saving are various, and their characters differ widely ; some will be improvident however high be the rate of interest ; and however low it be, others will save for their families and for their own old age. On the whole a fall in the rate of interest in a country is likely to check the growth of capital in some ways, and to promote it in others, but the latter effects are on a smaller scale than the former, so that a fall in the rate of interest will diminish the rate of accumulation of capital to some extent, though often only to a small extent[2].

The Law of Supply of capital is then that :—

> The natural resources, and the numbers of the industrial population of a country, and the state of the arts of production in it, constitute the field of employment for capital, and determine the rate of interest at which any given amount of capital can be employed in

---

[1] See Book II. ch. v. § 3.   [2] Book I. ch. vi. § 4.

> it. The rate is in equilibrium when it is just that at which the whole supply of capital can find employment. The supply depends upon the slow operation of many causes, one of which is the rate of interest.

Combining this with the Law of Demand we get the **Law of the Normal Rate of Interest,** which is :—

> When the economic conditions of a country have been nearly uniform for a long period of time, the supply of capital is such, that the rate of interest which can be obtained for it is that which has been required to cause this supply to be forthcoming; and the rate thus determined is the Normal rate.

§ 8. The greater part of the capital in England has been accumulated since the country entered on the economic phase in which it is now; and the Normal rate here is about four per cent. a year on good security. In the case of England the influence which foreign markets exert on the rate of interest is of primary importance. If the rate were to rise much above four per cent., a great deal of capital that is now sent abroad for investment would be retained at home. More capital would be employed here; the demand of capital for the aid of industry would rise; and this would make wages rise at the expense of interest. On the other hand, if the rate were to fall much below four per cent., the amount of capital seeking investment here would diminish; there would be less competition on the part of capital for the aid of industry; the division of the produce of capital and industry would be more favourable to capital ; and the rate of interest would rise.

The Normal rate of interest in England does not seem likely to deviate much from four per cent. for some time to come ; but it may be slowly altered by changes in the field of employment, while the market rate of interest is oscillating rapidly up and down on either side of the Normal rate as a centre.

§ 9. Before the invention of the steam-engine it seemed likely that the Normal rate of interest in Western Europe would soon become lower than it is now. The changes that have come over the face of modern industry have given room for the profitable employment of a vast amount of Auxiliary capital of which £700,000,000 have been invested in English railways. Successive inventions together with the development of foreign commerce have enabled capital to increase much faster than population, without causing any fall in the rate of interest. And history records several other periods during which the wealth and capital of a nation increased very rapidly, while at the same time the opening out of new fields for the employment of capital was causing a rise in the rate of interest.

In new countries the return which nature gives to man's

work is often so rich that, though the wages of labour are high, ten per cent. or more can be got for the use of capital. But capital rushes in from older countries; and before a district has been occupied for many generations, the richest natural sources of wealth become private property for which a high rent is demanded. And then the produce which remains to be divided between capital and labour, the Earnings-and-interest Fund, obeys the Law of Diminishing Return and does not increase as fast as the capital increases: so that it no longer affords a very much higher rate of interest than that which can be had in older countries. A rate of eight per cent. on sound investments has spread like a wave steadily over the greater part of the North American Continent; and this is being followed by waves of seven and of six and even five per cent. interest that have already started on their way westward and southward from the Northern Atlantic States.

§ 10. It is difficult to forecast the distant future of the rate of interest. Hitherto the progress of civilization has increased the willingness to save at a low rate. In old countries, in which men are accustomed to work patiently for small gains and to value highly the possession of a secure income, a low rate of interest seems to have little effect in checking the accumulation of capital. In England for instance, in spite of the low rate of interest, the capital of the country is increasing at the average rate of about £200,000,000 annually, that is by a little more than a thirtieth of its total amount. If this rate of increase were sustained for four hundred years, the capital owned by Englishmen would be multiplied a million fold, and in eight hundred years a billion fold. But however high the hopes we may have of the future progress of the arts of production, we cannot suppose that there will ever be a field for the profitable employment of as much capital as this. Sooner or later the rapid growth of capital must increase the competition of capital for the aid of labour, and diminish the competition of labour for the aid of capital; so that capital's share of the total net produce will cease to be proportionately as large as before. And, at the same time, the total net produce that can be obtained by a given amount of capital and labour will diminish according to the Law of Diminishing Return. So that ultimately the Normal rate of interest will fall.

There is no reason to think that it will fall rapidly down to a *minimum* and then remain stationary. Rather should we expect that, with some slight oscillations, the Normal rate of interest will keep on falling, but that the rate of its fall will become continually slower and slower. It is thus likely never to attain but always to be approaching its *mininum*. But we have no means of guessing what that *minimum* will be.

CHAPTER XI.

WAGES.

§ 1. WE have seen how the produce of land, capital and industry, exclusive of rent and taxes, is divided into Interest and Earnings; into the share which remunerates abstinence, and the share which remunerates work whether bodily or mental. Let us now look at the way in which this latter part is Normally subdivided among unskilled labour and the different kinds of skilled labour and of business power.

We are not now concerned with the advantages which custom or social opportunities or trade organizations give to the various ranks of industry in bargaining for their several shares of the Earnings-and-interest Fund; but when we come to discuss the theory of Market wages in the next Book, we shall see how such advantages may cause the wages of a trade to diverge for a considerable time from their Normal level.

Let us first inquire what constitutes the Normal demand for the work of each trade. This demand depends partly upon the desire of consumers to obtain the things which that trade produces or helps to produce, and partly upon the extent to which its aid is wanted by other industrial classes and the owners of capital who take part in making these things. Thus the demand for the work of a trade may be said to depend on the *competition for its aid* in production. The meaning of this term may be made more clear by an illustration.

The recent advance in England's wealth has caused a great demand for building; and those who produce other things have had to give more of them than before for the purchase or hire of a house. There has been an increased competition for the aid of the building trades, which has raised their wages and enabled them to obtain a larger share of the wealth of the country than before. Now suppose that during such a rise in the price of houses, there is a sudden check to the supply of (say) house carpenters. The rest of the building trades will then find it difficult to obtain the aid of carpenters to supply roofs, floors,

&c. And since the work of masons, plasterers, and master builders will be of little use without such aid from the carpenters, the competition of the other building trades for the aid of carpenters will force up the wages of carpenters, and enable each of them to obtain an exceptionally large share of the Earnings-and-interest Fund.

This competition will not act directly; the masons will not ask the carpenters to assist them in their work. It will act indirectly through the master builders; for, as we shall see presently more fully, in all conflicts between the different industrial classes the employers of labour act as buffers, which absorb part of the force of a blow, but pass on most of it to others. The scarcity of carpenters will compel employers to offer them higher and higher wages; the consequent rise in the price of houses will check the demand for them; the employers will have an over-abundant supply of masons and other labourers, and will lower their wages. Meanwhile the check to the building trade will increase the competition among master builders, and so diminish their own Earnings of Management. Thus the increased competition for the aid of carpenters will raise their wages, and this rise will be obtained partly at the cost of those who require houses, partly at the cost of the rest of the building trades including the master builders.

§ 2. The demand for unskilled labour depends on the competition there is for its aid, whether in producing things or in ministering directly to people's wants. It is increased firstly by every increase in the amount of capital that is ready to support and assist industry, and secondly by every increase in the amount of business power and of skilled labour of various kinds, that are competing for the aid of unskilled labour in the work of production.

When the wages of unskilled labourers exceed that amount which enables them to maintain the Standard of Comfort to which they are accustomed, population increases fast; but when they are less, the growth of population is checked. For instance, the daily wages of unskilled labourers in England have seldom been less than what would purchase half a peck of wheat; and they have seldom risen above what would purchase two pecks; they have oscillated up and down between these two limits. If it were a fact that whenever the day wages of unskilled labour were less than a peck of wheat, population diminished, and that whenever they were greater than a peck of wheat, population increased rapidly; then a peck of wheat would be the Normal day wages of unskilled labour. For when a high rate of wages caused a rapid growth of unskilled labour, it would increase the competition of unskilled labour for the aid of capital and of other classes of industry; and this would lead to a fall of wages : conversely when a low rate of wages checked the supply of unskilled labour, it would lead to an increase in the competition on the part of capital and other classes of industry for the aid of unskilled labour; and this would lead to a rise of its wages. Thus a peck of wheat would be the centre or Normal value towards which the remuneration of unskilled labour constantly gravitated, and any deviation from which would be a temporary irregularity, which, the moment it exists, sets forces in action tending to correct it.

The Standard of Comfort is not in fact rigidly fixed. But yet it is, at any place and time, so nearly fixed, and does exercise so great an influence on the growth of population, that the wages which afford the means of maintaining this Standard may fairly be called the Normal wages of unskilled labour there and then. When wages are at this level they are in equilibrium, unless there happens to be at the time a great change in the field of employment for labour. This is the Normal or Centre value about which fluctuations of Supply and fluctuations of Demand cause the wages of unskilled labour to oscillate. But the Normal value itself varies from place to place and from time to time with changes in the Standard of Comfort of the people. A rise of wages caused by an increased demand for labour will be temporary, unless it lead to a rise in the Standard of Comfort; in which case it will be permanent, and Normal wages will be raised.

§ 3.   Next with regard to various kinds of skilled labour. The demand for each class of skilled labour depends on the competition there is for its aid. It is increased firstly by every increase in the capital that is ready to support and assist industry, and secondly by every increase in the unskilled labour, in the skilled labour of other classes, and in the business power that are competing for the aid of labour of this class.

The causes which determine the supply of skill of any kind in one generation are, as we have seen, chiefly to be sought in the opportunities and the habits of the previous generations. The trouble and expense which parents will undergo in preparing their son for his work depend on their means, their habits of forethought and self-denial, and their knowledge of and access to various trades. The poorer and the more ignorant parents are, the higher is the rate at which they are likely to discount the wages which their son will receive at a future time. The lower parents are in the social scale, the greater must be the advantages which they can procure for their son by a given outlay on his education in order that they may be induced to make it.

Parents generally bring up their sons in the same industrial grade as their own ; there is so much freedom of intercourse between different trades of the same grade in the same place that their wages (or more strictly their Net Advantages) seldom differ much for any long period together. Any increase in the inducements to parents to bring up their children to a trade, or to adults to enter it, increases the supply of labour in it; the chief part of this supply being drawn from trades in the same grade with it.

Thus we are brought to the **Law of Normal Wages,** which is :—

> The amount of the Earnings-and-interest Fund, and the way in which it is divided into the shares of interest and earnings being already known, the wages of each trade depend on the way in which this latter share is sub-divided. The Normal wages of a trade are therefore determined by the relation in which its wages (or more strictly, its Net Advantages), must stand to those of other trades in order that the supply of labour in it may be kept up, and this depends on the difficulty of the work to be done in it, on the expensiveness of the general and special education, and on the natural qualities, physical, mental and moral, required in it.

> Trades in the same industrial grade generally require an equally difficult and expensive education, and have equal wages. The lower the grade of a skilled occupation, the higher is the ratio which its wages bear to the expenses of preparing for it.

When a rise in the wages of a trade above the Normal value causes a rapid increase of the numbers in it, its members find a diminished competition on the part of others for their aid; they are at a disadvantage in bargaining for their share of the produce of land, capital and industry, and their wages fall. Conversely when a fall in the wages of this grade below the Normal value checks the increase of the numbers in it, the competition on the part of capital and the other classes of industry for the aid of this trade is increased, and its wages rise. But when the wages are at the Normal value they are *in equilibrium;* the growth of numbers is neither so fast as to lower them, nor so slow as to raise them. Toward this value the wages of the trade continually gravitate, and any deviation from this rate is a temporary irregularity, which, the moment it exists, sets in motion forces tending to correct it.

But these forces often act very slowly because of the friction of various social and economic obstacles that hinder men's passing from one trade to another, especially if they are in different grades; and the "temporary irregularities" may extend over very long periods of time. Fluctuations of supply and demand cause the wages of each trade to oscillate above and below their Normal value; just as a floating cork oscillates with each passing wave, above and below the surface of the sea. The

Normal wages of skill of various grades rise or fall slowly, as the tides rise or fall.   They change with those slow changes in the social condition of various ranks of the people which work themselves out in the course of many generations.

The effect of progress is as a rule to increase the supply of intelligence and ability, so that if the difficulty of the work to be done did not increase, the wages of skilled labour would be likely to fall.   And in fact the Task-wages, that is the wages that are paid for skilled labour of a given efficiency, are falling in many branches of manufacture; though they are on the whole rising in some trades which are under specially favourable circumstances, as for instance the building trades.   But the difficulty of the work to be done, and the intelligence required for doing it are increasing, and the average earnings of the workers —their Time-wages—are generally rising, even where their Task-wages are falling.

§ 4.   A rise in the Time-wages of any trade tends to diminish profits.   But if the wages that are paid for work vary according to its efficiency—if Task-wages are unaltered—the share of the produce of industry that is left for others will be the same whether Time-wages are high or low.   It is only where the rise in Time-wages is not accompanied by a corresponding increase in efficiency, and therefore Task-wages rise, that the change is injurious to capital.   In fact when a labourer has to be supplied with costly machinery, a rise in Time-wages is a great benefit to capital, if it lead to such an increase of efficiency as to keep Task-wages unchanged.   Of course the machine itself some-times "sets the pace," and an indifferent worker may be able to do all that is required.   But such cases are much more rare than is generally thought.   Of two weavers or two turners working side by side at similar looms or similar lathes driven by the same machinery, one will often do twenty per cent. more in a day than the other; and it would be to the advantage of the employer to secure the energetic man by paying him more than twenty per cent. more Time-wages, that is, by paying him Task-wages at a little higher rate than he pays the inefficient man. For in this way he will turn his machinery and the space in his factory to the best account.

Even in the case of unskilled labour it is to the advantage of capital that Time wages should rise, provided Task wages do not rise too.   If two labourers at 18s. a week will do as much work as three at 12s., the former are in the long run cheaper. For they are likely to remain longer in full health and strength and to have healthier and stronger children than the others ; and a much heavier burden will be imposed on capital through the poor rates by three low-waged than by two high-waged labourers.

There is however a limit beyond which a rise in the Time-wages of unskilled labourers will not cause a proportionate increase of their efficiency, and when this limit is passed any further rise in Time-wages will raise Task-wages too ; but even then the rise of Task-wages will be slower than that of Time-wages. The growth of capital and the progress of the arts of manufacture will, if wars can be kept down, make the world rich enough to afford high wages for that little unskilled labour which cannot be supplanted by machinery. This increase of wealth will not indeed raise the wages of unskilled labourers if their Standard of Comfort remains low and they marry imprudently. But a time may come when the Standard of Comfort of un-skilled labourers will be such as to keep them from rapidly increasing their numbers, even though their wages have become as high in old countries as they are now in new countries.

[§ 5. The influence which demand exerts on wages is some-times expressed by saying that under a system of free competi-tion every man's wages tend to be equal to the *discounted value* of the produce of his labour.

Let us for instance imagine a thing to be made by unskilled labour alone without any superintendence, and without the aid of any capital except that which was advanced in the payment of wages. Suppose that this capital has been advanced gradually, some of it a short time, some a long time, on the average half-a-year before the thing is ready for sale. Let the rate of interest for six months, allowing for risk, be five per cent. Then if the thing can be sold for £105, the Discounted value of this half-a-year beforehand will be £100. And competition will tend to make the wages of those who made it equal to this Discounted value of £100.

But a case as simple as this never occurs in practice. The earnings of many different kinds of industry, one of which is almost always that of Superintendence or Management, enter into the Expenses of production, and therefore into the price of almost everything that is sold. And in order to deduce from the price the earnings of one of these kinds, we must find out not only the interest on the capital employed but also the earnings of the other kinds of industry, and deduct them all from the value of the produce raised. We cannot then speak of the Discounted value of the work of any one of these classes. But we may still speak of the "Net Return" of that labour. The Net Return of a machine was defined as the value of the work that it does after allowing for Depreciation and the Expenses of working it, including the Earnings of Management. The **Net Return** of a man's labour is the value of the produce which he takes part in producing after deducting all the other Expenses of producing it [1].

[1] A statement of this kind has been mistaken by some writers for a

This phrase is very useful when we are examining the part which Demand takes in determining wages. For instance, if the demand for houses is rising, the Net Return of the labour of some or all of the various building trades must be increasing. There may be signs of a greater scarcity of labour in one of the building trades, as for instance that of the carpenters, than in others; and if we believe that the earnings of other branches of the building trades (including the Earnings of Management of the master builders) are not likely to rise, we may say that the competition for the aid of carpenters' labour will increase, that the Net Return of their labour will rise in value, that they therefore will get an increased share of the Earnings-and-interest Fund ; and that their wages will rise.

Again the phrase Net Return of labour can be usefully applied in explaining the influence of Demand in equalising Task-wages in the same occupation. This influence may be described by saying that under a system of free competition every man's wages, or more generally every man's earnings, tend to equal the Net Return of his industry.]

theory of wages. But really it is only the Law:—"Value tends to equal Expenses of production"—written in a new form.

CHAPTER XII.

EARNINGS OF MANAGEMENT.

§ 1. We have seen that the supply of business power is determined in all essential respects in the same way as the supply of skilled labour ; we have now to examine the Laws that govern the Normal Earnings of Management. These Laws appear at first sight to differ much, and they really do differ a little from those which govern the Normal wages of skilled labour; the chief difference arising from the fact that the Earnings of Management can be obtained only by those who have the control of capital. Let us then begin by comparing the Earnings of Management of two men carrying on similar business, the one with his own capital, the other with borrowed.

The man who works with his own capital considers that his Earnings of Management are the whole net profits of his business after deducting the interest that he could obtain by letting out his money on good security. But interest at a much higher rate than this must be paid by a man who borrows capital for his business, at all events unless his own property is sufficient to give good security for it; and interest at this high rate must be deducted from the profits of his business in order to find his Earnings of Management. The rate of interest which he has to pay is high, because in his case a new set of risks is introduced in addition to those unavoidable risks which exist in every business.

> Those risks which arise from such causes as the chance of destruction or depreciation in value of the capital employed, or of the goods produced in it, are inseparable from business, and may be called **Trade Risks**. Those further risks which are introduced when the capital of one man is under the control of another, may be called **Personal Risks**. These are due to the mistakes that the lender may make with regard to the borrower's business ability, and honesty.

A man trading with his own capital has every motive for exerting himself to discover whether he is carrying on his business at a loss. But the man working with borrowed capital has not such strong motives.   If his moral sense is not very active he may, without intending any deliberate fraud, carry on a losing business so long as to cause heavy losses to his creditors. If he has not a strict sense of honour, and finds himself in difficulty, he may plunge into rash speculations : for if they succeed, the gain will be his ; and he may not care whether he fails for a large or a small sum.

. One way in which the lender can insure himself against these various risks is by charging a high rate of interest for his loans.   But a very high rate would be required to cover the risk of loans made for a long period of time ; and therefore such loans are generally made for short periods.   The shorter these periods are the less is the risk which the lender runs, and the sooner can he recover the use of his capital for himself, if the course of his own trade should make him wish to do so.   Thus Bankers and others are willing to lend money for a few months[1] at a rate of interest sometimes not exceeding three or four per cent. a year, even when the best security that the borrower can offer would not induce them to lend him capital for a long period of time at any moderate rate.

But a man who is much dependent on such short loans labours under great disadvantages.   For if any misfortune should injure his credit, or if a disturbance of the money market should cause a temporary scarcity of loanable capital, he may be quickly brought into great straits.   He may not be able to obtain a renewal of the loans on moderate terms, or even on any terms, and may thus be cut short in his most hopeful enterprises.   One of the chief symptoms of an impending commercial crisis is a rapid succession of forced sales at a loss by those who have been trading with capital borrowed for short periods.

Thus it appears that a trader who works on borrowed capital has in one form or another to pay a high rate of interest. But though high, it is not sufficiently high to prevent him from competing with those who trade with their own capital.   On the contrary men trading with borrowed capital seem likely to displace to a great extent those trading with their own.

The reason of this is not far to seek.   A man who has a capital of £50,000 can easily obtain a secure income of £2500 by lending it out.   And very likely he may not care to undergo the labours and anxieties of a business life unless he can get Earnings of Management of £2500, or even £5,000 a year, exclusive of course of Insurance against Trade Risks.   But a man of equal ability who owns little capital, and who therefore cannot live in comfort without working, will be content with lower Earnings of Management.   He may be willing to employ £50,000 of bor-

---

[1] This is done chiefly by "discounting bills."

rowed capital, in addition to his own, even though after allowing for the interest that he actually pays and the indirect risks that he runs through working with borrowed capital, he does not clear more than £1000 a year by the work.   He can therefore afford to sell at a price too low to give that rate of profits which the man of independent means requires.   Thus those who depend on their business for a livelihood, undersell and drive out of trade those who are not so dependent[1].

§ 2.   Again a man may obtain Earnings of Management by carrying on a business with capital, the owners of which take a part at least of the risks of the business.   The simplest way of doing this is the old plan of partnership.   In former times a man of little capital had small chance of getting high Earnings of Management unless he could obtain the confidence of some wealthy man or private firm, who admitted him as a partner.

Again, if a man thinks that he can profitably employ more capital than his own in his business, he often converts it into a joint-stock company.   That is he admits others to shares in his business: they take a share of the risk and a corresponding share of the net proceeds that remain after paying him Earnings of Management according to some plan agreed upon between them[2].   A joint-stock company of this kind which is managed by its chief shareholder or shareholders, may act almost as freely and promptly as a private firm can.   It has some special disadvantages; but under favourable circumstances, it may hold its own even in trades which require ready enterprise and quick action.

The business of a large joint-stock company is however often carried on by Directors, who give it only a little of their time, and General Managers, who give their whole time.   The General Managers are seldom men of much capital, and are contented to work for moderate salaries.   The business of such a company will almost always be managed with less energy and economy than a similar private business in able hands.   As Mill says, it may be possible to secure in hired managers that fidelity which shrinks from a deliberate neglect of duty, but not that zeal which is continually laying schemes by which greater profit may be obtained, or expense saved, and which is ever anxious about small gains and small savings.   If however the

---

[1] This is making English commerce increasingly democratic, and does much harm in preventing "the long duration of great families of merchant princes....But the propensity to variation in the social as in the animal kingdom is the principle of progress." See Bagehot's *Lombard Street*, Introductory chapter.

[2] This is similar in some respects to the old plan of introducing "sleeping partners" into a private firm.   The sleeping partners supply Capital and take a share of the risk, but have no part in the Management.

company is large, and it can afford to pay fairly good salaries to its officers, its affairs are likely to be in many ways better managed than those of a private business in the hands of men of second rate ability. The directors are usually men who can bring a wide and varied business experience to bear in laying down the broad principles on which the affairs of the company are conducted, and in judging the ability and industry of the chief officials under them. So that the management of a large joint-stock company, though generally far from perfect, is seldom very bad except where there is wilful wrong doing.

The publicity of joint-stock companies helps more than it hinders them in trades in which it is necessary to obtain public confidence, as for instance in banking and insurance. They have a monopoly of railways and other undertakings which require enormous capitals, and they are fast pushing their way in all businesses in which large capitals can be managed chiefly by routine and in which there is little need for bold and speculative enterprise. For they can thrive with a much lower rate of profits than will remunerate a wealthy capitalist for under-going the worry and fatigue of business. The growth of Joint Stock Companies offers great opportunities to those who have business power, to obtain the control over capital.

§ 3. We may next inquire how the Earnings of Management of a business are related to the capital employed in it. Is the Normal rate of profits for all capitals employed in trades of the same difficulty the same whether the capitals be large or small?

If two businesses in different trades are equally difficult and disagreeable, and require equal capitals, there will of course be a constant tendency to equality of their Earnings of Management. There may indeed be great differences between the Earnings of Management of two men with the same capital in the two trades; but so there may in one and the same trade. These differences arise from inequalities in ability or good fortune, just as do those between the earnings of successful and unsuccessful medical men or barristers. Again it is true that an able business man who starts in life with a great deal of capital and a good business connexion is likely to obtain higher Earnings of Management than an equally able man who starts without these advantages. But there are similar, though smaller, inequalities between the earnings of professional men of equal abilities who start with unequal social advantages.

What is meant then is that competition tends to equalise the Earnings of Management of men of average ability and good fortune in two occupations in which equal capitals are employed, and which are equally difficult and disagreeable. The profits in each case are to be found by adding the Earnings of Management to the interest on the capital employed. And since the amount of capital employed is the same, and the rate of interest to be allowed is, under the modern system of banking, practically the same for all trades, the amount of interest is the same in the two cases. Therefore when the Earnings of Management tend to equality in the two cases, the profits of the businesses tend to equality. So that :—

> The profits on equal capitals tend continually to equality in trades which involve equal risks, discomforts and exertions ; and which require equally rare natural abilities and an equally expensive training.

It has however already been noticed that if £100 has been invested in the production of a thing two years before it is ready for sale, we must allow twice, or rather more than twice as much under the head of interest as if the £100 had been invested only one year before it was ready for sale : but the amount to be allowed under the head of Earnings of Management on the £100 will be nearly the same in the two cases. So that the annual rate of profits will be much lower in the former case than in the latter. For this reason the annual rate of profits on the total capital employed is, as a general rule, lower in trades which make great use of Fixed capital, than in trades in which nearly all the capital is Circulating.

§ 4. We have next to examine the consequences of the fact that the management of a large capital in any trade almost always requires rarer natural abilities and a more expensive training than the management of a small capital requires. We have seen that a man who conducts a large business must look far ahead, and wide around him ; and that he must be continually on the look out for improved methods of carrying on his business, while the man who manages a small business may be content to follow the lead that is given to him by his neighbours. The former pays subordinates to do the work on which the latter spends the greater part of his time ; and devotes all his energies to planning, and organizing, to forecasting the future and preparing for it. He must have a knowledge of men and the power of managing them. He must select his subordinates well, and while keeping the control of the business in his own hands, he must give them the freedom which will call forth their energy and sense of responsibility. Those who cannot do this, are incapable of building up a large business, or even of keeping one together, if inheritance or other accident should put them in possession of it.

A man who has all the rare qualities that are required for managing a large business will, unless he is specially unlucky, make a high rate of profits on his capital. These profits will increase his capital, and will encourage him to devise and carry out bold plans on a broad basis. The confidence that others have in him will enable him to borrow capital easily; and thus, because he has the faculties which are one condition of getting high Earnings of Management, he will rapidly acquire that control of a large capital which is the other condition.

We see then, firstly, that higher faculties are required for the management of a large than of a small capital; and secondly that there is a process of selection continually going on by which those who have some capital and great business power, soon get control over a large capital; while on the other hand those who have not business power will speedily dissipate a large capital if they happen to get control over it. These facts shew that the Earnings of Management in large businesses must be on the average higher than those in small; and they even give some reason for thinking that the average Earnings of Management in different businesses in the same trade vary almost in proportion to the capital employed. There is however an independent and stronger reason for believing that there is often the same average rate of profits on different capitals in the same trade.

Let us suppose for instance that A and B are proprietors of neighbouring cotton factories which are alike in every respect excepting that A's is twice as large as B's. They hire labour and they buy their raw cotton, machinery, building materials, &c., in the same market and at the same price. There may indeed be a few slight economies in A's business of which B cannot avail himself; and on the other hand A may have to pay subordinates for doing some of the work that B with his smaller business finds time for doing himself. But if these differences be neglected, all the Expenses of production, other than profits, of a yard of A's calico will be the same as those of a yard of B's; and since they sell in the same market at the same price, the profits made on each yard of calico will be the same for A as for B. The rate of A's profits will be the same as that of B's: A's Earnings of Management will be twice those of B.

The results which theory thus indicates are confirmed by experience. Experience and theory alike tell us that as a general rule there is a constant tendency to equality of the rate of profits not only on equal capitals, but also on unequal capitals in the same trade, and in trades that are equally disagreeable and difficult. But there are three important exceptions to this rule.

§ 5. The first exception arises from the fact that the head of a large business often pays wages to subordinates to do a great deal of work that the head of a small business does for himself, and the payment for which is reckoned among his profits. For instance the average rate of profits made by small farmers is higher than that made by large; because the small farmer's profits include the wages of the work of his own hands, and of supervising hired labour more closely than the large farmer can. Again the rate of profits on a shopkeeper's capital, particularly in some of the clothing trades, is generally higher for a small than a large capital, even where the two sell to the same class of customers. For the small shopkeeper includes among his profits the earnings that he gets by attending carefully to the special wants of each customer; but the large shopkeeper has to pay high wages for this work.

The second exception is closely connected with the first. There are many trades in which small makers and dealers are able to sell at a higher price than the large dealers can, because they get access to a different class of customers. One familiar instance of this is the fact that village shopkeepers generally get a very high price for their goods. Their capital is very small; and their profits, though at a high rate on their capital, are so small in amount as not to attract competition. Again in money lending, the smaller the scale on which the business is transacted, the greater is the charge that is made for the loan of money. A man who troubles himself to lend money by a few pounds at a time, can often obtain a very high rate of interest for it. To take an extreme case, there are men in London and Paris and probably elsewhere, who make a living by lending money to costermongers. The money is often lent at the beginning of the day for the purchase of fruit, &c., and returned at the end of the day, when the sales are over, at a profit of ten per cent.; there is little risk in the trade, the money so lent is seldom lost. Now a farthing invested at ten per cent. a day would amount to a billion pounds at the end of a year. But no one can become rich by lending money in this way; because no one can lend much money in this way. The profits on the capital really consist almost entirely of the wages of work for which few capitalists have a taste.

The third exception arises from the influence of the Law of Increasing Return. In many industries a large capital can avail itself of great economies that are out of the reach of a small capital; and the large manufacturer can make higher profits than the small manufacturer. These industries would rapidly be concentrated in the hands of a few wealthy firms, if a man whose practical genius has created a large business, could ensure that his successors for several generations should have a like genius. But in the whole course of history we meet with but very few instances of private firms which have been managed with eminent genius for three generations in succession. The sons and grandsons of a successful man of business have seldom that rare combination of ability and assiduity which would enable them to carry on his work. And there are many instances in which a vast inherited business has been quickly destroyed by men who could have managed a small business well.

In some industries large capitals have completely driven their smaller rivals from the field, and afterwards their competition among themselves has reduced the rate of profits very low. In rolling mills for instance there is little detail which cannot be reduced to routine, and a capital of £1,000,000 invested in them can be controlled by one able man. A rate of profits of 20 per cent., which is not a very high average rate for some parts of the iron trade, would give the owner of such works Earnings of Management amounting to more than £150,000 a year. And since iron-masters can with so little additional effort get the Earnings of Management on an increased capital, wealthy men remain in the trade longer than in most others; and the competition of the great iron-masters with one another is said to have reduced the average rate of profits in their trade below the ordinary level.

§ 6. We are now in a position to sum up our inquiry as to the way in which Normal Earnings of Management are determined.

Firstly, with regard to the demand for business power. It is true that this demand is not measured by any definite market price list of Earnings of Management, such as that which states that carpenters' wages in a certain town are ninepence or tenpence an hour; and it is true that the fluctuations of Earnings of Management are greater than those of wages, because the fluctuations of trade prosperity exert a more direct and a greater influence on the incomes of employers than on those of the employed. But yet the demand for the aid of business power in production is fundamentally of the same kind as the demand for the aid of skilled labour. For instance if a manufacturer can improve the method of carrying on his business so that the work of four hundred men produces as much as that of five hundred men did previously, then he will gain an addition to his Earnings of Management equal to the wages of a hundred men. Thus the Earnings of Management of a manufacturer represent the value of the addition which his work makes to the total produce of capital and industry: they correspond to the effective demand that there is for the aid of his labour in production, just as the wages of a hired labourer correspond to the effective demand for his labour. The Law of Demand tells us that the value in exchange of anything is the measure of its Final value in use; that is, of its value in use to those who are only just induced to purchase it; and that this Final value in use diminishes as the supply of the thing increases. So it is with regard to skilled labour of any kind; every increase in the supply of it tends to diminish the Final value in use of the work it does, and therefore to lower its wages. And so it is with regard to any order of business power; every increase in the supply of it tends to diminish the Final value in use of the work it does, and therefore to lower its Earnings of Management.

Secondly, with regard to the supply of business power. Returning to the case of the manufacturer who obtained high Earnings by an improvement in his methods of manufacture, we see that his success will induce others to follow in his steps, and that their competition will force down his Earnings. The extent to which they will be forced down depends upon the number of those who are able to do the work ; and this will depend on the Earnings to be got by it on the one hand and on its difficulty on the other. Thus the rarity of the natural abilities and the expensiveness of the special training required for the work play the same part in determining Normal Earnings of Management that they do in determining the Normal wages of skilled labour. In either case a rise in the income to be earned sets in operation forces tending to increase the supply of those capable of earning it ; and in either case the extent to which the supply will be increased by a given rise of income, depends upon the social and economic condition of those from whom the supply is drawn.

The conditions which determine the Normal demand for, and the Normal supply of each kind of business power being known, its Normal Earnings of Management are determined as those which will equate supply and demand in the long run. Thus the Law of Normal Earnings of Management is similar to that of the Normal wages of skilled labour, and similar also to the Law of Normal value for commodities[1] ; and is :—

The Normal supply of each kind of business power is that to which the field of employment will just afford the Earnings of Management which are required to call forth this supply : and the rate of the Earnings of Management so determined is the Normal rate for this order of business power.

The conditions which thus determine this Normal rate vary from place to place and from age to age ; but since business power is easily transferred from place to place, variations of the Normal Earnings of Management between different places are less important than those which occur from age to age.

§ 7. But in spite of the fundamental similarity between the Law of Normal Earnings of Management and that of Normal wages of skilled labour, there are several important differences between the two cases. Firstly, the Earnings of Management which a business man gets, depend upon the capital with which he has started, in the same way as, but to a greater extent than, the income of a professional man depends on the start in life which the social position of his parents gives him. And a

---

[1] Comp. Book II., ch. v., § 3.

business man working with his own capital includes among his Earnings the equivalent of that Insurance against Personal Risks which must be allowed for, in some form or other, by those who work with borrowed capital.

Secondly, business men are chosen by a process of natural selection from among many millions of competitors. For many employers of labour, in some parts of England more than half, have risen from the ranks of hired labour. Every artisan who has exceptional natural abilities has a chance of raising himself to a post of command, and is in fact a candidate for the prizes that may be earned by success in business; and the average of these Earnings of Management is high, partly because the class of employers contains, in addition to the able men that have been born within its ranks, a large share of the best natural abilities that have arisen among the lower ranks of industry. While *Profits* on capital invested in education is a specially important element in the incomes of professional men, *Rent* of rare natural abilities is a specially important element in the incomes of business men.

The total amount of the Earnings of Management got by business men in a country may be found by subtracting interest on the whole amount of their own capital from their total net incomes after allowing for all expenses and losses : and, even after allowance has been made for Insurance against Personal Risks, this amount certainly gives a very high rate of wage for the skill and ability of business men. But this rate is not so high as at first sight appears; for great deductions must be made on account of those who have lost their capital in trade. The earnings of the labour that these men have wasted, together with all the capital that they have lost, must be deducted from the Earnings of Management got by successful men before the average Earnings of Management can be found. Those who fail are quickly lost from sight and memory; but their number is very great. It is said that in America three-fourths of those who engage in trade become insolvent in the course of the first five years[1].

§ 8. The supply of skilled labour is increasing faster than that of unskilled labour, and the supply of business power is increasing faster than that of the lower kinds of skilled labour. Thus the competition of business power for the aid of the lower orders of labour in production is increasing. And as a consequence the Earnings of Management that can be got by doing work of a given order of difficulty—the *Task-Earnings* of Management—are diminishing. The continual increase in the complexity of business, and the continual increase in the amount of capital that can be employed in business

---

[1] Bowen, *American Political Economy*, ch. x.

under a single management, are indeed giving to business ability of the highest order the opportunities of obtaining greater Earnings of Management than were ever heard of in earlier generations. But the total amount of the Earnings of Management is not so high in proportion to the amount of capital employed as it used to be. And the ratio which the Earnings of Management of a business bear on the average to the capital employed in it is diminishing; and will probably continue to diminish. For the growth of education will increase rapidly the supply of business power that is competing for the aid of hired labour in production ; and this competition will prevent the Earnings of Management from growing as fast as capital is likely to grow.

Since the Normal rate of Interest is likely to fall, and the ratio which Normal Earnings of Management bear to capital is likely to fall, and since profits are composed of interest and Earnings of Management, therefore the Normal rate of profits is likely to fall. It will not fall rapidly for a time, and then remain stationary at a *minimum*. But subject to some oscillations, its fall will probably be continuous, though increasingly slow, so long as the world is inhabited by men of the same nature with ourselves.

CHAPTER XIII.

RELATION OF NORMAL TO MARKET VALUE.

§ 1. WE have seen that "every producer of a commodity calculates the price which he will be able to obtain for it, and the Expenses of producing it, and determines by this means to what extent it is his own interest to increase or diminish his production. If there is free competition, his interest leads him to act in the same way as he would if his only object were to regulate the amount produced so that it could just be sold off at a price equal to its Expenses of production." Thus the Normal value of a thing—that toward which the Market value continually tends—is equal to its Expenses of production. These Expenses of production may ultimately be resolved into wages and profits, or rather into earnings and interest.

We have seen how each Expense of production *measures* that effort or abstinence which is the corresponding element of Cost of production. We have seen that the interest which can be got by abstaining from the immediate consumption of £100 worth of wealth and saving it to be used as capital, is a practically fixed and uniform amount at any given time and in any given country. This Normal rate of interest depends on the one hand on the field that there is in that time and country for the employment of capital, and on the other hand on the supply of capital; this supply depends on many causes, one of which is the rate of interest that has hitherto prevailed in the country.

The Normal wages of *unskilled labour* in any time and country depend on the scope for its employment on the one hand and on its supply on the other. The scope for its employment depends partly on the natural resources of the country, partly on the amounts of capital, of skilled labour and of business power that are seeking its aid in production. The supply of labour depends, as regards both quantity and quality, on many causes, the chief of which is the rate of wages. It is true that things which are luxuries in one stage of civilization are regarded as necessaries in another, and that all such changes affect the Normal wages of unskilled labour. But in any given phase of civilization the Normal Task Wages of unskilled labour are nearly constant.

So with regard to the earnings of *skilled labour*, including the incomes of professional men, and of all others who render skilled service for payment. The earnings of each kind of skilled labour depend on the scope for its employment on the one hand, and on the supply of it on the other. The expensiveness of the education, and the rarity of the natural qualities required for it are the chief of the conditions which determine the supply that will be called forth by any given rate of wages ; so that the supply is governed by laws similar in many respects to the Law of Normal Supply of commodities. The Normal wages of skilled labour of any given degree of difficulty, may vary slowly. But at any time and place they are determined by the social and economic condition of the people, and they may be said to *measure* the efforts involved in the work. The fact that Earnings of Management can be obtained only by those who have the control of capital, does not prevent their Normal value from being determined substantially in the same way as the wages of skilled labour. That part of the Normal Earnings of Management which can be got by a man who works with borrowed capital, measures the difficulty of his business. A man who conducts a similar business with his own capital obtains in addition the equivalent of Personal Risks.

Thus the Cost of production of a thing is measured by its Normal Expenses of production. If the difficulty of producing a thing, or its Cost of production is independent of the amount produced, Cost of production determines Expenses of production and therefore determines Normal value. But when the amount produced is increased, the Cost of production may increase according to the Law of Diminishing Return, or may diminish according to that of Increasing Return. In order to cover these cases, the Law of Normal Value must be stated thus :—"The Normal supply of the commodity is such, that its Normal Expenses of production equal the value, which will call forth a demand for this amount ; and the price so determined is the Normal value." Normal value still measures Cost of production, but is not determined simply by it.

[§ 2. This is an instance of the rule that in Nature changes generally react on one another. For instance it is not true that the state of a man's lungs is determined by that of his heart, or *vice versa;* but subject to external influences, the conditions of his heart, lungs and other parts of his body determine one another. So when two unequal balls A and B are put into a smooth basin, it is not right to regard A's position as determining the position of B. For though it is true that if we know exactly where A is, we can tell at once where B is, it is equally true that if we know where B is, we can tell where A is. The positions of A and B are determined simultaneously by the action of the Law of Gravitation.

So it is with regard to Normal value. It is true that in the exceptional case in which the difficulty of production of a thing is fixed independently of amount produced, Cost of production determines Normal value. But as a rule the Cost of production of a thing is not fixed : the amount produced and its Normal value are to be regarded as determined simultaneously under the action of Economic Laws.

It is then incorrect to say, as Ricardo did, that Cost of production alone determines value : but it is no less incorrect to make utility alone, as others have done, the basis of value. It is certainly true that utility is a condition of value always ; and that in cases in which the supply of the commodity is fixed, utility determines price. It is true that the price of every commodity must be the measure of its Final utility; that is of its value in use to those who are only just induced to purchase it. But it is not true that this Final utility determines value : for it changes itself, according to the Law of Demand, with every change in the amount of the commodity that is offered for sale. This amount, and therefore the Final utility of the commodity, depend upon the relation between the circumstances of supply and those of demand.]

§ 3. We have now to pass from the theory of Normal value to that of Market value. Normal results are those which would be brought about by competition if it acted freely, and always had time to cause those effects which it has a tendency to cause. Market results are those which actually are brought about by the complex social and economic forces of the world in which we live.

We have compared Normal value to the Normal growth of a tree. Let us now compare it to the Normal tides which there would be if there were no disturbing wind, and no irregularities of coast line. Observation tells us that waves driven by the wind over the sea make its surface rapidly rise and fall; and that the irregularities of coast line pile up the tidal waves in some places ten times as high as they are in the middle of the ocean. The theory of the Normal tides does not tell us what is the highest point that the tide reaches at any place in (say) the Bristol Channel. We cannot find out this without examining the special circumstances of the case, and allowing for the influence of the winds, and the peculiar nature of the shores. But on the other hand we can make no progress in explaining the movements of the sea unless we first understand which of them are due to local or transitional causes, and which to the

Normal influence of the attractions of the Moon and Sun. And we cannot do this until we have first worked out the abstract theory of the tides that would be formed in a world in which there were no disturbing winds and no irregular shores.

So with regard to the theory of Normal value. It does not tell us what will be the wages of a certain work, or the price of a certain thing at any particular time. We cannot discover the Market value of a thing without allowing for the fluctuations of supply and demand, and for the resistance which local obstacles oppose to the free movement of the stream of competition. But on the other hand we can make no progress in explaining the movements of wages and prices, unless we first understand which of them are due to local or transitional causes, and which to the Normal action of free competition. The theory of Normal value is the starting point from which we must set out to explore all the various irregularities and unevennesses of Market values. It teaches how the great tidal waves of wages and prices would move if every one were careful to forecast the future, and deliberately to shape his course so as to obtain the greatest economic advantages for himself and his family. It puts us in the right position for examining how man's action is modified by custom, or apathy, or generally by motives other than the desire for wealth.

We can then apply our theory to explain facts, so far as it will go; and those facts which cannot be explained by our theory are "light-giving" facts, and shew us how to correct and enlarge our theory. Thus the science of Economics progresses step by step, alternately applying theory in the search for and explanation of new facts, and applying new facts in correcting and broadening and strengthening theory.

BOOK III.

MARKET VALUE.

CHAPTER I.

CHANGES IN THE PURCHASING POWER OF MONEY.

§ 1. THROUGHOUT the discussion of the Theory of Normal value it was assumed that the purchasing power of money remained unchanged[1]; so that a rise or fall in the exchange value or general purchasing power of a thing could always be shortly expressed as a rise or fall of its price. We must now inquire briefly how the value or general purchasing power of money changes from time to time. But a full discussion of the theory of the value of money belongs to the "Economics of Trade and Finance."

The most obvious of the causes that affect the purchasing power of the precious metals in a country is the quantity of them that is available for use as money. If this increases very fast, there will be more than is wanted to carry on the business of the country at the old prices, and prices will rise. On the other hand, if the amount of the precious metals remains stationary while the population and wealth of the country increases, there will be a great demand for money to carry on the business of the country; the purchasing power of the precious metals will rise, and prices will fall.

For instance at the beginning of the sixteenth century when the new supplies from the American silver mines made themselves felt, the purchasing power of silver began to fall; and early in the seventeenth century prices in London were on the average three times as high as they were in 1500. Again prices were high at the beginning of the present century. But no

---

[1] Bk. II. ch. i. § 4.

important fresh supplies of metals came from the mines till 1850. During that time the stock of precious metals was being diminished by their use in the industrial arts and by wear and tear; and meanwhile population and wealth were increasing rapidly. So the purchasing power of gold rose; and prices fell to about half what they were in 1800—10. About 1850 the gold mines of California and Australia were discovered, there was a great increase in the supply of the precious metals, and prices rose again.

§ 2. But though the amount of the precious metals in circulation is the most obvious of the causes that affect the purchasing power of money, a no less important cause is the growth of artificial substitutes for the precious metals as a medium of exchange.

The most familiar of these substitutes are bank notes. They pass freely from hand to hand, and exert nearly the same influence over prices as an equivalent amount of coined money does. But in England this influence is not as important as that exercised by cheques, which have displaced both coin and bank notes in nearly all wholesale and in many retail transactions.

A cheque does not circulate freely, but is generally given by the person who receives it to his banker, who demands payment of it for him. But though cheques do not act as substitutes for coin in the same way as bank notes do, yet the total amount of them is so great as to exercise a very powerful influence over prices. Again the modern system of credit enables a man who has neither money nor anything that immediately represents money, to obtain from a banker or other money dealer the means of purchasing goods. He can do this not only on his own credit (as when a bank allows him a "Book credit"), but on the credit of others who have undertaken to pay him money at a future date (as when he "discounts a Bill").

The business of the civilized world has increased very rapidly during the present century; and an enormous amount of coin would have been required to carry it on with the present prices. If credit had not found substitutes for coin, there would have been so great a demand for the precious metals, that their purchasing power would have become many times as great as it actually is; prices would have been very low. The growth of credit supplies a permanent substitute for the precious metals, and therefore affects their Normal values. But credit fluctuates, and each fluctuation alters their Market values.

For instance, an expansion of credit coincided with the influx of precious metals consequent on the discovery of the Californian and Australian mines, and increased the upward tendency of prices. But in 1857 there was a *crisis;* that is, many trading firms were unable to pay their debts, credit was violently contracted, and prices fell, although the store of precious metals in the country was growing as rapidly as ever. After a time credit began to expand again, and prices rose till 1866 when there was another crisis, and prices fell. Again credit expanded, and prices rose till 1873; when, though there was no crisis, a gradual contraction of credit set in which has continued till 1879. The lowest point which prices reached between 1857 and 1866 was much higher than the level of 1850; and the lowest point between 1866 and 1873 was higher still. But since then there has been a slight check in the supply of gold; and a great deal of gold has been absorbed by the adoption of a gold currency in Germany and other causes; and prices, measured in gold, are now (1879) as low as they were in 1850.

§ 3.   The beginning of a period of rising credit is often a series of good harvests. Less having to be spent in food, there is a better demand for other commodities. Producers find that the demand for their goods is increasing; they expect to sell at a profit, and are willing to pay good prices for the prompt delivery of what they want. Employers compete with one another for labour; wages rise; and the employed in spending their wages increase the demand for all kinds of commodities. New public and private Companies are started to take advantage of the promising openings which shew themselves among the general activity. Thus the desire to buy and the willingness to pay increased prices grow together; Credit is jubilant, and readily accepts paper promises to pay. Prices, wages and profits go on rising: there is a general rise in the incomes of those engaged in trade: they spend freely, increase the demand for goods and raise prices still higher. Many speculators seeing the rise, and thinking it will continue buy goods with the expectation of selling them at a profit. At such a time a man, who has only a few hundred pounds, can often borrow from bankers and others the means of buying many thousand pounds' worth of goods; and every one who thus enters into the market as a buyer, adds to the upward tendency of prices, whether he buys with his own or with borrowed money.

This movement goes on for some time, till at last an enormous amount of trading is being carried on by credit and with borrowed money. Old firms are borrowing in order to extend their business; new firms are borrowing in order to start their business, and speculators are borrowing in order to buy and hold goods: trade is in a dangerous condition. Those whose business it is to lend money are among the first to read the signs of the times; and they begin to think about contracting their loans. But they cannot do this without much disturbing trade. If they had been more chary of lending at an earlier stage, they would simply have prevented some new business from being undertaken ; but when it is once undertaken, it cannot be abandoned without a loss of much of the capital that has been invested in it. Trading companies of all kinds have borrowed vast sums with which they have begun to build railways and docks and ironworks and factories ; prices being high they do not get much building done for their outlay, and though they are not yet ready to reap profits on their investment, they have to come again into the market to borrow more capital. The lenders of capital already wish to contract their loans ; and the demand for more loans raises the rate of interest very high. Distrust increases, those who have lent become eager to secure themselves ; and refuse to renew their loans on easy or even on any terms. Some speculators have to sell goods in order to pay their debts ; and by so doing they check the rise of prices. This check makes all other speculators anxious, and many rush in to sell. For a speculator who has borrowed money at interest to buy goods may be ruined if he holds them a long time even while their price remains stationary ; he is almost sure to be ruined if he holds them while their price falls. When a large speculator fails, his failure generally causes that of others who have lent their credit to him ; and their failure again that of others. Many of those who fail may be really "sound," that is their assets may exceed their debts. But though a man is sound, some untoward event, such as the failure of others who are known to be indebted to him, may make his creditors suspect him. They may be able to demand immediate payment from him, while he cannot collect quickly what is owing to him ; and the market being disturbed he is distrusted ; he cannot borrow, and he fails. As credit by growing makes itself grow, so when distrust has taken the place of confidence, failure and panic breed panic and failure. The commercial storm leaves its path strewn with ruin. When it is over there is a calm, but a dull heavy calm. Those who have saved themselves are in no mood to venture again ; companies, whose success is doubtful, are wound up ; new companies cannot be formed. Coal, iron, and the other materials for making Fixed capital fall in price as rapidly as they rose. Iron works and ships are for sale, but there are no buyers at any moderate price.

Thus the state of trade, to use the famous words of Lord Overstone, "revolves apparently in an established cycle. First we find it in a state of quiescence,—next, improvement,—growing confidence,—prosperity,—excitement,—over-trading,—convulsion,—pressure,—stagnation,—distress,—ending again in quiescence."

⟦§ 4. After every crisis, in every period of commercial depression, it is said that supply is in excess of demand. Of course there may easily be an excessive supply of some particular commodities; so much cloth and furniture and cutlery may have been made that they cannot be sold at a remunerative price. But something more than this is meant. For after a crisis the warehouses are overstocked with goods in almost every important trade; scarcely any trade can continue undiminished production so as to afford a good rate of profits to capital and a good rate of wages to labour. And it is thought that this state of things is one of general over-production. We shall however find that it really is nothing but a state of commercial disorganization; and that the remedy for it is a revival of confidence.

To begin with, it is clear that, as Mill says, "What constitutes the means of payment for commodities is simply commodities. Each person's means of paying for the productions of other people consist of those which he himself possesses. All sellers are inevitably, and by the meaning of the word, buyers. Could we suddenly double the productive powers of the country, we should double the supply of commodities in every market; but we should, by the same stroke, double the purchasing power. Everybody would bring a double demand as well as supply; everybody would be able to buy twice as much, because every one would have twice as much to offer in exchange."

But though men have the power to purchase they may not choose to use it. For when confidence has been shaken by failures, capital cannot be got to start new companies or extend old ones. Projects for new railways meet with no favour, ships lie idle, and there are no orders for new ships. There is scarcely any demand for the work of navvies, and not much for the work of the building and the engine-making trades. In short there is but little occupation in any of the trades which make Fixed capital[1]. Those whose skill and capital is Specialised in these trades are earning little, and therefore buying little of the produce of other trades. Other trades, finding a poor market for their goods, produce less; they earn less, and therefore they buy less; the diminution of the demand for their wares makes them demand less of other trades. Thus commercial disorganization spreads, the disorganization of one trade throws others out of gear, and they react on it and increase its disorganization.

The chief cause of the evil is a want of confidence. The greater part of it could be removed almost in an instant if

---

[1] The causes which specially affect such trades will be further considered in ch. ii. § 6.

confidence could return, touch all industries with her magic wand, and make them continue their production and their demand for the wares of others. If all trades which make goods for direct consumption agreed to work on and to buy each other's goods as in ordinary times, they would supply one another with the means of earning a moderate rate of profits and of wages. The trades which make Fixed capital might have to wait a little longer, but they too would get employment when confidence had revived so far that those who had capital to invest had made up their minds how to invest it. Confidence by growing would cause itself to grow ; credit would give increased means of purchase, and thus prices would recover. Those in trade already would make good profits, new companies would be started, old businesses would be extended; and soon there would be a good demand even for the work of those who make Fixed capital. There is of course no formal agreement between the different trades to begin again to work full times and so make a market for each other's wares. But the revival of industry comes about through the gradual and often simultaneous growth of confidence among many various trades ; it begins as soon as traders think that prices will not continue to fall : and with a revival of industry prices rise[1].]

[§ 5.   The connexion between a fall of prices and a suspension of industry requires to be further worked out.

There is no reason why a depression of trade and a fall of prices should stop the work of those who can produce without having to pay money on account of any Expenses of production. For instance a man who pays no wages, who works with his own hands, and produces what raw material he requires, cannot lose anything by continuing to work. It does not matter to him how low prices have fallen, provided that the prices of his goods have not fallen more in proportion than those of others. When prices are low, he will get few coins for his goods ; but if he can buy as many things with them as he could with the greater number of coins he got when prices were high, he will not be injured by the fall of prices. He would be a

[1] The most plausible of all the plans that have been suggested by Socialists for the artificial organization of industry is one which aims at the "abolition of commercial risk." They propose that in times of depression Government should step forward, and, by guaranteeing each separate industry against risk, cause all industries to work, and therefore to earn and therefore to buy each other's products. Government, by running every risk at once, would, they think, run no risk. But they have not yet shewn how Government should tell whether a man's distress was really due to causes beyond his own control, nor how its guarantee could be worked without hindering that freedom on which energy and the progress of invention depend.

little discouraged if he thought that the price of his goods would fall more than the prices of others ; but even then he would not be very likely to stop work.

And in the same way a manufacturer, though he has to pay for raw material and wages would not check his production on account of a fall in prices, if the fall affected all things equally, and were not likely to go further. If the price which he got for his goods had fallen by a quarter, and the prices which he had to pay for labour and raw material had also fallen by a quarter, the trade would be as profitable to him as before the fall. Three sovereigns would now do the work of four, he would use fewer counters in measuring off his receipts against his outgoings ; but his receipts would stand in the same relation to his outgoings as before. His net profits would be the same percentage of his total business. The counters by which they are reckoned would be less by one quarter, but they would purchase as much of the necessaries, comforts, and luxuries of life as they did before.

It however very seldom happens in fact that the expenses which a manufacturer has to pay out fall as much in proportion as the price which he gets for his goods. For when prices are rising, the rise in the price of the finished commodity is generally more rapid than that in the price of the raw material, always more rapid than that in the price of labour ; and when prices are falling, the fall in the price of the finished commodity is generally more rapid than that in the price of the raw material, always more rapid than that in the price of labour. And therefore when prices are falling the manufacturer's receipts are sometimes scarcely sufficient even to repay him for his outlay on raw material, wages, and other forms of Circulating capital ; they seldom give him in addition enough to pay interest on his Fixed capital and Earnings of Management for himself.

Even if the prices of labour and raw material fall as rapidly as those of finished goods, the manufacturer may lose by continuing production if the fall has not come to an end. He may pay for raw material and labour at a time when prices generally have fallen by one-sixth ; but if, by the time he comes to sell, prices have fallen by another sixth, his receipts may be less than is sufficient to cover his outlay.

We conclude then that manufacturing cannot be carried on except at a low rate of profit, or at a loss, when the prices of finished goods are low relatively to those of labour and raw material ; or when prices are falling, even if the prices of all things are falling equally.]

[§ 6. Thus a fall in prices lowers profits and impoverishes the manufacturer : while it increases the purchasing power of those who have fixed incomes. So again it enriches creditors at the expense of debtors.   For if the money that is owing to them is repaid, this money gives them a great purchasing power; and if they have lent it at a fixed rate of interest, each payment is worth more to them than it would be if prices were high. But for the same reasons that it enriches creditors and those who receive fixed incomes, it impoverishes those men of business who have borrowed capital; and it impoverishes those who have to make, as most business men have, considerable fixed money payments for rents, salaries, and other matters. When prices are ascending, the improvement is thought to be greater than it really is; because general opinion with regard to the prosperity of the country is much influenced by the authority of manufacturers and merchants. These judge by their own experience, and in time of ascending prices their fortunes are rapidly increased; in a time of descending prices their fortunes are stationary or dwindle. But statistics prove that the real income of the country is not very much less in the present time of low prices, than it was in the period of high prices that went before it.   The total amount of the necessaries, comforts and luxuries which are enjoyed by Englishmen is but little less in 1879 than it was in 1872.]

CHAPTER II.

§ 1. WE have discussed causes that alter permanently or temporarily the purchasing power of money: we may now again assume that the purchasing power of money remains unchanged, unless the contrary is stated ; and may again measure value or general purchasing power in terms of money, and speak of a change in general purchasing power as a change in price.

We have next to consider how the market value of a commodity oscillates up and down on either side of the Normal value, while that Normal value itself may be rising or falling slowly.

Producers and dealers endeavour to anticipate every fluctuation of market value ; if they expect the price to be high, they increase their supply so as to profit by it; if they expect it to be low, they check their supply so as to avoid losing by it. Thus their action, when they are competing freely with one another, is the same as it would be if their object were to restrain the oscillations of the market value on either side of the Normal value. When they succeed, supply is said to be closely adjusted to demand ; but the market price is likely to deviate far from the Normal price when they err in their calculations, or when they combine with one another artificially to limit supply.

§ 2. The chief source of error on the side of supply is the uncertainty of nature's return to man's effort. A good instance of this is found in the fish market, where the fluctuations are great because the haul of the fishing boats is uncertain, and fish will not keep long. At Billingsgate each dealer posts up a list of the fish that he has for sale ; and knowing what the other dealers have, tries to put such a price on his fish that he may just get them sold before the end of the day. If he fixes it too high, he has fish left useless on his hands in the evening ; if he fixes it too low, he gains less than he might.

Again, the price of corn fluctuates much from year to year.

For as a rule very little corn remains over from one harvest to the next ; so that each year's consumption is almost limited to the supply of the previous harvest. If the harvest is scanty there is a dearth of food, and hunger forces people to give a very high price for it. Here we may notice that fluctuations in supply cause great variations in the price of necessaries of life, but only small variations in the price of those things for which substitutes can be readily found, or which can be easily dispensed with altogether. If fish is dear, people are content to buy little of it, so that even if the supply is very short, its price is not forced up very high. But however dear corn is, every one buys it or has it given to him ; so that a small falling off in the supply of corn will cause a great rise in its price[1].

In uncivilized countries the transport of grain for any considerable distance is practically impossible except along rivers, and on the sea coast. Even in Europe in the Middle Ages, "each locality depended as a general rule on its own produce and that of its immediate neighbourhood. In most years accordingly there was, in some part or other of any large country, a real dearth. Almost every season must be unpropitious to some among the many soils and climates to be found in an extensive tract of country ; but as the same season is also in general more than ordinarily favourable to others, it is only occasionally that the aggregate produce of the whole country is deficient, and even then in a less degree than that of many separate portions ; while a deficiency at all considerable extending to the whole world is a thing almost unknown. In modern times, therefore, there is only dearth, where there formerly would have been famine, and sufficiency everywhere when anciently there would have been scarcity in some places and superfluity in others . . . . This effect is much promoted by the existence of large capitals, belonging to what are called speculative merchants, whose business it is to buy goods in order to resell them at a profit. These dealers naturally buying things when they are cheapest, and storing them up to be brought again into the market when the price has become unusually high ; the tendency of their operations is to equalise price, or at least to moderate its inequalities. The prices of things are neither so much depressed at one time, nor so much raised at another, as they would be if speculative dealers did not exist[2]."

---

[1] In the middle of last century, it was calculated that "a deficit of

1 tenth			3 tenths
2 do.			8 do.
3 do.	raises the price of corn		16 do.
4 do.			28 do.
5 do.			45 do."

Mill, Book IV. ch. ii. § 4.

In recent times the action of merchants and dealers in equalising prices has been much aided by the steamship, the railroad, and the telegraph. Not long ago news from distant markets was many months in coming, now it comes in a few minutes. Merchants can even telegraph instructions to ports at which their ships are to call; so that a scarcity in a market many thousands of miles away can be met in a few days by the arrival of English ships[1].

§ 3. The market price of many things is settled from day to day by the action of dealers rather than by that of producers. Many kinds of raw produce can only be produced at certain times of the year; and the immediate effect of a rise in the price of such things is not to increase the production of them, but simply to induce dealers to bring forward larger quantities for sale, and perhaps to import fresh supplies from distant places. If we go into any corn, or wool, or cotton market, we shall see dealers selling readily on one day, and holding back on another. The amount which each of them offers for sale at any price is governed by his calculations of the present and future conditions of the markets with which he is connected. There are some offers which no dealer would accept; some which no one would refuse. There is some price which will be accepted by those who can least afford to wait, and by those whose expectations of the future condition of the market are least sanguine; but not by others. The higher the price that is bid, the larger will be the sales.

For instance, the conditions of a certain corn market may be such that a price of 50s. would induce dealers in it to sell 500 quarters during the day; while they would be induced to sell 700 quarters by a price of 51s., 1000 quarters by a price of 52s., and so on. Thus in any market, at any time, there is some price at which each particular amount will be offered for sale. And in the same way there is some price at which each particular amount will find purchasers. Perhaps the millers and the speculators in corn who attend the market would between them buy 900 quarters if they could be got for 50s. each, 700 if they could be got for 51s., but only 600 if they could not be got for less than 52s. If everyone knew exactly the state of the market, exactly how eager buyers were to buy and sellers to sell, the price would be fixed at once at 51s., and 700 quarters would be sold off during the day at this price: this would be the price which would equate supply and demand. But in fact the price would oscillate up and down during the day, and even at the same moment bargains would be struck at slightly different prices in different parts of the same corn-exchange;

---

[1] Comp. Crump's *New departure in Political Economy.*

the average price for the day would be about 51*s*., and the total amount sold would not differ far from 700 quarters.

Thus the Normal price of corn varies from one age to another under the slow action of economic changes : meanwhile in each age the average price between successive harvests varies from year to year, owing to the failure of producers to adjust the supply of corn to the demand for it : and the daily price in each market is swayed backwards and forwards on either side of the average price for the year by the calculations and bargainings of dealers.

In the case of corn the demand is pretty well known before-hand ; and the rapid fluctuations that occur in its price from week to week and from day to day, are chiefly due to imperfec-tions in the estimates that dealers form of the stocks in existence at any time, and to changes in their forecasts of the coming harvest. There are many other things, such as coal and iron, the prices of which fluctuate from day to day chiefly in conse-quence of the estimates that dealers form of the present and coming demand for them. But whatever be the nature of the calculation by which the bargainings of dealers are chiefly governed, these bargainings, except when dealers combine to keep prices artificially high, tend to make the market price such as to equate supply and demand in the market. That is they tend to make the price such, that the amount which people are willing to offer for sale in the market at that price is just equal to the amount which can find purchasers at that price in the market.

§ 4. Let us next consider some fluctuations of price that arise from the failure to forecast changes in demand.

A change of fashion often makes the Market price of some kinds of materials very much higher or very much lower than their Normal price. A manufacturer who is quick in reading the signs of the times, and anticipates the coming demand for stuffs of a particular kind, makes large profits. But in this case supply can be adjusted to the demand very rapidly ; and therefore the price cannot easily be raised much by an increase in demand unless it is very great and sudden.

But it is otherwise with houses, the supply of which cannot be quickly increased to meet a new demand; their value rises and falls with changes in the prosperity of the place in which they are. When Berlin became an imperial city, there was a great demand for house room : house rents rose ex-travagantly, and hod-men earned in a day more wages than agricultural labourers earned in a week. On the other hand the value of houses falls very low in places from which popu-lation is receding. There is more than one place in America in which a town of 20,000 inhabitants has grown up in a year, but in a few more years has been deserted, and the houses in it been left valueless. In some Cornish villages which have been deserted by their mining population, and in some other parts of England, houses can be bought for less than half of what it would cost to build them.

§ 5. Prices are liable to great fluctuations in trades in which there is a great use of Fixed capital. For when prices are at their Normal level, the price of goods not only returns with interest the manufacturer's outlay for raw material and labour, but also gives interest on his Fixed capital with an allowance for its Depreciation, and pays his own Earnings of Management. As long as the price pays him back what he spends in raw material and labour with interest, his desire to keep his workmen together, and to keep up his trade connexions may induce him to go on. Therefore, the more Fixed capital a manufacturer uses, the stronger are his inducements to keep his factory at work even after the price of his goods has fallen a long way below their Normal value, and thus to force down prices further still.

Again, most of the capital that is Fixed is also Specialised. The capital for instance that is sunk in opening a coal mine, cannot be withdrawn from it when the price of coal falls ; and a prudent capitalist will not be induced by a high price of coal to invest money in coal mines, unless there is reason to expect that the price will be sustained for a long while. The price of coal may therefore rise far before any attempt is made to increase the supply by opening up new mines ; and even after that, a considerable time will elapse before the supplies from the new mines can exert any influence. Coal mining requires also a great deal of Specialised Personal capital ; and a sudden increase in the supply of coal cannot be got without suddenly increasing the number of miners. Men who are not familiar with the dangers and discomforts of underground life, cannot be attracted to it except by high wages ; and since their labour is at first very inefficient, the wages paid for raising a ton of coal are very much higher than the Normal wages of the work. And therefore the increased demand is able to raise the price of coal very high without calling forth such an increase of supply as to force the price quickly down again. On the other hand when the demand for coal falls off, the Material and Personal capital that is specialised in coal mining keep up the supply, and the price is forced down very low. The use of coal for domestic purposes varies but little from year to year ; the amount of coal that is wanted for making steam varies a little more ; but by far the most important variations in the demand for coal are due to its use in the manufacture of iron.

§ 6. There are great fluctuations in the price of iron, partly because a rise in price does not increase quickly the supply of the coal and iron ore, and of the Fixed capital that are wanted in its manufacture ; partly because the demand for iron is subject to violent changes, in consequence of its being chiefly used in making machines, railroads, and other forms of Fixed capital. The demand for Fixed capital is liable to more extreme fluctuations than the demand for commodities that are wanted for immediate consumption, and the trades which make Fixed capital are more affected than any others by alternations of commercial prosperity and adversity. For while credit is expanding, the extra purchasing power which credit gains goes chiefly to traders and trading companies, who, whether they want it to begin or to extend their business, are sure to spend a great part of it on machinery, buildings, ships, railway material, and other forms of Fixed capital. On the other hand where credit is contracting many find their means of purchasing altogether cut off, while those whose means are not straitened do not care to invest in Fixed capital until they think prices have nearly reached their turning point.

The price of pig iron was doubled, and the price of some kinds of coal was quadrupled in the years 1870—1873, but now their prices are lower than in 1870 ; the wages of labour in the iron trades rose fifty per cent. in the years 1870—1873, and have again fallen ; and similar changes have occurred with each fluctuation of general prosperity. The price of iron in England and other countries rose more rapidly than almost any other prices in the years preceding each of the crises of 1837, 1847, 1857, and 1866 ; and it fell more rapidly than most other prices in the years following each of these crises ; so that not only the price, but also the value or general purchasing power of iron rose and fell at each of these periods. Nearly the same may be said of the building trades as of the iron trades, the wages of navvies and of masons, bricklayers and carpenters have risen rapidly before, and fallen rapidly after, almost every crisis.

In some periods of commercial depression almost the only demand for Fixed capital comes from manufacturers who do not like to close their works for alterations while trade is brisk ; but who, when trade is slack, and the prices of building and machinery are low, take the opportunity of making such extensions and repairs as may enable them to profit by the revival of trade when it comes. But this demand is not nearly sufficient to make up the deficiency that arises from the general contraction of credit, from the failure of old firms and public companies, and from the absence of new companies.

The present depression of trade has been accompanied by a great falling off of England's exports, but not by a corresponding diminution of her imports. This is partly due to the fact that

Englishmen, having suffered great losses in foreign investments, have been bringing home a great deal of their capital from abroad. When English capital is lent to foreign countries much of it is generally spent on railway lines and machinery that are bought in England. This was especially the case in the years of prosperity that preceded 1873; and the subsequent decline of England's exports injured the iron trade more than other English trades. But it did not affect the building trades, because they do not make things for exportation. On the other hand the capital which Englishmen brought home could not be invested here without leading to a demand for building in various forms, and so somewhat sustaining the building trades. This explains why it was that after 1873 prices fell very rapidly in the iron trade, but were kept up for a long time in the building trades.

§ 7. One cause of an increase in the demand for a commodity is a failure in the supply of something for which it can be substituted. Thus the failure of the supply of cotton during the American war increased the demand for wool. Again, one cause of an increase in the supply, and consequent fall in the price of anything, is an increase in the demand for something that is produced with it. The prices of the gas and the coke that are got from a ton of coal, must together be enough to cover their joint Expenses of production. If the demand for gas rises, more coke will be produced, and its price must fall, so that the increased supply may be taken off the market. The rise in the price of gas must be sufficient to cover this fall in the price of coke, and also to cover the increase, if there is any, in the joint Expenses of production of gas and coke. Again, since the repeal of the Corn Laws much of the wheat consumed in England has been imported, of course without any straw. This has caused a scarcity and a consequent rise in the price of straw, and the farmer who grows corn looks to the straw for a great part of the value of the crop.

The value of straw then is high in countries which import corn, and low in those which export corn. In the same way the price of mutton in the wool-producing districts of Australia was at one time very low. The wool was exported, the meat had to be consumed at home; and as there was no great demand for it, the price of the wool had to defray almost the whole of the joint Expenses of production of the wool and the meat. Afterwards the low price of meat gave a stimulus to the trade of preserving meat for exportation, and now its price in Australia is higher.

Similar remarks apply to that part of the Expenses of production of a thing which depends upon transport, whether of the raw material to the place of manufacture, or of the finished commodity to the place of sale. The expense of making and keeping in repair roads and railways is shared among the different things that pass over them. When the discovery of mines in a district leads to the making of railways to it, the inhabitants at once find that they get a higher price for everything that they produce to be sent away to distant markets, and that they have to pay a lower price for things which they buy from a distance. Again the exports from England being less heavy and bulky than those from America the competition for freights from England is so great as to keep them very low, and thus to throw the greater part of expense of working the ships on the freight of goods from America. Any increase in the American demand for the heavier and bulkier kinds of English goods increases the competition of ships for freights from America, and so tends to lower the price of American goods in England. Again, if a commodity which is heavy but not bulky, is exported in the same ships with another which is bulky but not heavy, the freights which either of them has to pay may be very small or very great according as the demand for the other of them is very great or very small. For instance, ships whose chief cargo consists of iron rails, often carry light Staffordshire potteries for very low freights. And tin is brought from Australia in wool ships as ballast, almost the whole expenses of the ships for the double journey being borne by the wool : but if the production of minerals in Australia were to increase, and that of wool to decline, the wool might be carried for very low freights.

§ 8. When an increase in the demand for a commodity raises its price, the gain at first goes almost entirely into the hands of the manufacturers. But soon their eagerness to extend their business leads them to compete with one another for the hire of labour, and gradually wages rise till a large part of the gain is transferred from the employers to the employed. Conversely when the demand slackens and the price of the commodity falls, the burden of the fall is at first borne entirely by employers ; but gradually it is in a great measure transferred from them to the employed. The manner in which wages rise in the one case and fall in the other, and the distribution of the rise or fall among the various classes of workmen who are employed in producing the commodity, are a good deal influenced in England at the present time by trade combinations ; and they will be most conveniently discussed at a later stage.

But it may be noticed here that movements in wages almost always follow, and scarcely ever occasion, movements in prices. A rise in price is occasioned by an increased demand : after a time wages rise ; still the demand increases, and still the price rises; but the further rise in price is occasioned as the first rise was by the fact that demand has increased more rapidly than supply. It is true that the rise in wages seemed to play some part in sustaining the upward movement of prices; for if wages had remained low, and the whole gain of the high prices had gone to profits, capital would have been attracted into the trade more rapidly, the supply would have increased faster, and therefore prices would not have risen so much. But still each rise in wages is caused directly by a rise in price.

The upward movement in wages is scarcely ever so great in proportion as the upward movement of prices, and therefore scarcely ever so great as the upward movement of the Earnings of Management. One cause of this is that the rise in price goes in the first instance, as has just been said, entirely into the pockets of the employer; and the rise in wages seldom begins until the rise in profits has called forth increased competition among employers. But another cause is that a great deal of risk is involved in bringing additional capital into a trade to meet what is not unlikely to be only a temporary increase in demand; and part of what appears as a rise in profits is really only insurance against this risk.

In just the same way when the demand slackens, prices begin their downward movement first; the fall of wages begins later on; it is occasioned by and is not the cause of the fall in prices; and the fall in price and the consequent fall in profits is much greater in proportion than the fall in wages. At such times indeed there is often no profit at all, but a great loss of capital. This loss may be unequally distributed among the various producers, but taking trade as a whole, it may be regarded as paid out of that insurance fund which was got together in times of high prices and high profits.

[§ 9. When the wages of any class of labourers have been raised by a rise in the price of the commodity produced by them, the rapidity with which an additional supply of labour comes into the trade depends on the relation in which these wages stand to those of other trades. If the wages in this trade are abnormally high relatively to others, the rise is likely to attract so much additional labour, as to prevent the upward movement of wages from going very far, and to make them fall fast and far when the time of depression comes. On the other hand, if, before the rise came, the wages were below their Normal level relatively to other trades, the rise may go on for a long time without bringing in much additional labour, and whatever rise is gained will probably be maintained.

Thus we see how the Law that Normal value is determined by Normal Expenses of production is consistent with the fact that market fluctuations of value are the cause and not the consequence of market fluctuations of Expenses of production. If Ricardo and Mill had taken more pains to make clear the distinctions between the theory of Normal value and that of Market value, there could not have been as much controversy as there has been on the question whether value is governed by Expenses of production, or Expenses of production by value.]

CHAPTER III.

LOCAL VARIATIONS OF PRICES AND WAGES. INFLUENCE OF CUSTOM.

§ 1. WHEN seeking for the Law of Normal value of a commodity, we noticed that the same commodity may have different Normal values in different markets. Its Normal value in any market is equal to its Expenses of production there, and among these is to be reckoned the Expense of carrying it there from the place at which it is made, including of course any customs duties that have to be paid on the way. Thus the Law of Normal value contains in itself the following **Laws of Local Variation** of Normal prices:

> If two markets are supplied with a commodity from the same source, its Normal value is higher in the more distant (or less accessible) market by the difference between the expenses of carrying it from the place where it is made to those markets.
>
> If there are two places in which a commodity is made for sale in the same market, its Normal value is lower in the more distant (or less accessible) of these two places by the difference between the expenses of carrying it to this market from the two places.

These laws take it for granted that if the difference between the prices of a commodity in two markets is greater than the expense of carrying it from one to the other, some one will set to work to bring it from the cheaper to the dearer market. They assume that there are men connected with these markets who have the capital and the business habits required for the work; and that the demand for the commodity is on so great a scale as to make it worth while to organize a traffic in it.

These conditions are fulfilled when the commodity is one in general use, and when the markets are large towns in close commercial intercourse with each other; local variations in the wholesale prices of the staple wares of commerce are, with a few exceptions, to be attributed to differences in the expense of transport. The most important of these exceptions occur when some producers are very anxious to force their way into a distant market. The competition of others who are more advantageously placed for supplying this market may induce them to sell at a price so low that, after allowing for the expenses of carriage, it does not afford them the ordinary rate of profits; while perhaps they make up this deficiency by combining with one another to sell at a high price in their own markets. Thus for instance English manufacturers sometimes sell goods in America at a price which, after allowing for taxes and expense of transport, is lower than that at which they sell in England; and some American goods, such as sewing machines, are sold in Canada at a lower price, allowance being made for the customs duty, than in the United States. But the tendency of competition is to remove anomalies of this kind by breaking up local combinations, and compelling the producers to sell in the home market at a price equal to the Expenses of production of the commodity there.

Where there is no organized traffic, prices are not determined by free competition : their local variations are not governed simply by the above laws. Some account then must be given of the local variations of the prices of things that cannot easily be sent long distances to market, and of retail prices generally.

§ 2.   First among the things which cannot be sent to market is land. But railways now enable many kinds of agricultural produce to be sent great distances to market; and thus bring them under the Laws of Local Variations of Normal prices. And since the rent of land is the excess of the price which its produce fetches, over the expenses of raising it and sending it to market, it follows that, if land were always let by free competition for agricultural purposes, rent would be brought under the indirect influence of these laws.

And the value of land is in a great measure determined by its rent. For suppose the rate of interest for safe investment were four per cent., so that people could obtain a secure income of £100 a year from the investment of £2500. Then if rent were the only advantage which land gave to its owner, and if rent were not likely to rise, people would be willing to pay just £2500 for land that would yield them a secure rent of £100 a year. But when people buy land they often look forward to a rise in its rent. The opening up new fields for agriculture in America and increased facilities of transport may indeed check the rise in the value of agricultural produce, and so check the rise in the rent of English farms; but the rise in the rent of land near large towns and in manufacturing districts seems likely to continue without much interruption. This rise, in as far as it is caused by the growth of population and independently of any action on the part of the landlord, has been called an "unearned increment" of the rent of land. When this has been estimated, the amount that is added to the value of the land on account of it, can be found by a simple arithmetical calculation.

But this is an incomplete account of the causes which determine the value of land. For firstly, even where competition is perfectly free, allowance must be made for the other advantages which land affords besides the right to receive its rent. Some people derive a peculiar pleasure from the ownership of land; they love their land as they love their dogs, and they are as willing to pay for the gratification of their affection for the one as for the other. This feeling, and the social position which land gives, raise its value further still. But the amount of this last addition depends on national character and on social arrangements which vary from one country to another and from one time to another; and these variations obey no law.

Secondly, the rent of land is seldom determined by perfectly free competition. The comfort of the landlord, the social position which counts for much in the value of his land, require him to live on cordial terms with his tenants ; and he is seldom anxious to drive hard bargains with them. The competition for a farm is often practically limited to a few families in its neighbourhood, or rather, to those who get on well with the landlord in personal and social and political matters ; and the landlord would often find it difficult, even if he were inclined to do so, to exact the highest rent which the land could be made to pay.

On the other hand it is true now, as it was in Adam Smith's time, that "upon equal or nearly equal profits men will choose to employ their capitals rather in the improvement and cultivation of land than in manufactures or foreign trade." In some parts of the country, in which landlords grant long leases to their tenants, and enable them to invest their capital securely in the land, competition raises rents so high as to make the farmer's rate of profits lower than that in almost any other trade.

§ 3. The hindrances to the free play of competition in determining the rent of land are relics of the past. In the village communities of our Germanic forefathers, and in the similar communities that still exist in India, we find no such thing as private property in land ; the price of land is not ruled by competition, because it has no price. Custom determines the price of everything that is made and sold in the village. It is only in the case of those few things which the villagers buy from outsiders, or which they make to be sold to outsiders, that price is determined by bargaining and free competition, and is affected at once by economic changes. An influx of precious metals into the country would raise the price of these things at once; but for a long while it would hardly affect the prices of those things that each village made for itself. In the course of time however the villagers would find that they earned much more by making things to be sent away and sold at the new high prices, than by making things to be sold for use at home at the old customary prices. They would slowly seek the more profitable work; the things wanted for home consumption would become scarcer, and in spite of custom their prices would gradually rise. The more secluded a village was, the less trade it had with distant places, the longer would it be before its prices were affected by the influx of the precious metals.

The influence of custom has not yet died out in civilized countries. In agricultural districts there are many villages which, at all events until quite recently, have had scarcely any intercourse with the rest of the country. Before the development of railways, towns drew most of their supplies from the country lying immediately around them, and the remoter districts often did not feel the influence of social and economic changes in the life of the towns until more than a generation after they had occurred.

Habits of enterprise grow slowly. Those parts of the country which till recently had scarcely any communication with other places, still shew little eagerness to avail themselves of the means that are now within their reach of sending their produce to distant markets. But they are being roused from their lethargy by the enterprise of townsfolk who are organizing the supply of dairy produce and other perishable things from remote districts to large towns. The sluggishness of some farmers, their unwillingness to read newspapers connected with their trade, and their habits of suspicious secrecy towards one another, prevent there being a uniform wholesale price for dairy produce; and it often happens that two farmers living side by side sell their milk at unequal prices. But competition is much more effective than it used to be: "beef, mutton, veal, butter, eggs and poultry for example have risen about twenty-five per cent. in the London market, but they have risen a hundred per cent. above their rates a few years ago in the inland parts of Ireland and Scotland on the new lines of railway. The common price of meat in the towns in the interior of Ireland before they were connected with the ports and the English market by railways, was from $3\frac{1}{2}d.$ to $4d.$ a pound, and now it is from $7d.$ to $8d.$[1]"

An interesting example of the more intimate relations in

[1] Cliffe Leslie's *Essays on Political and Moral Philosophy*, p. 277

which the rural districts now stand to the towns is found by comparing the way in which the new supplies of the precious metals distributed themselves over town and country after the discoveries of American mines at the end of the fifteenth, and in the nineteenth century. In the former case two centuries elapsed before the full effect of the new supplies was felt all over Europe. The new silver remained almost entirely in a few towns and commercial centres, "prices rising enormously in London for example, while wholly unaffected in parts of the Highlands of Scotland and of the West of Ireland, and but little affected even in some parts of England not far from the metropolis[1]."

But now it is the country districts, those which have recently been opened up by railways which have absorbed the chief share. A good instance of this is to be found in Germany; for while some parts of the country have recently gained good railway communication, there are vast tracts which are still very little affected by the new means of transport. New supplies of gold have poured in and the banking system has grown rapidly; and just before 1873 prices rose generally. But while the change was very great in some parts, it was very little in others; and Mr Cliffe Leslie, after a careful study of price lists when the movement was at its height, concluded that the immediate effect of the change was on the whole not to diminish, but to increase local inequalities of prices. He divided Germany into four monetary regions, and found that prices remain very low in places in arrear of the world's progress in respect of their means of locomotion as in other respects; that they have risen considerably in places communicating by steam with good markets, but not themselves the sites of much enterprise or possessing any special attractions; that they have risen rapidly in places which unite the best means of communication with local activity or considerable resort from without; and most rapidly of all in those places which besides having these advantages, lie near the traffic and movement of western Europe[2].

The special causes which affect retail prices will best be considered in connexion with local variations in the earnings of retail dealers. And we now proceed to enquire into the local variations of wages and profits.

§ 4. Adam Smith tells us that "man is of all sorts of luggage the most difficult to be transported." And Brentano goes to the root of the matter when he says that what distinguishes labour from all other wares is "the absolutely indissoluble union between the labour and him who offers it for

---

[1] Cliffe Leslie's *Essays on Political and Moral Philosophy*, p. 327.
[2] *Ib.* p. 331.

sale[1]." The seller of a commodity generally cares little where, and to whom he sells, so long as he gets the best price for it. But it is altogether different with the labourer. During the whole time for which he has sold his labour, he himself must be in that place, and with those companions, and subject to that authority, which the employer may prescribe; and when his work is over, he is still confined to the society of those who live in the neighbourhood of his work. He refuses therefore to leave his home in search of higher wages, unless he expects these wages to compensate him not only for any discomforts that his work may bring, but also for the separation from his friends and relations and from the familiar scenes and associations of his native place. It has already been said that in reckoning the Net Advantages which draw men to an occupation and exert an influence on its Normal wages, account must be taken of its incidental comforts, of its healthiness, its cleanliness and its social repute. It must now be added that among the Net Advantages which bind a man to an occupation in one particular place, and so influence its Market wages, these personal friendships and affections and old associations are among the most important. It is to this, no less than to apathy and ignorance, that we must ascribe the real inequalities that there are in the wages of the same trade in places not very distant from one another. But such inequalities are often much less than they would appear if we looked at Time-wages alone without allowing for local variations in the average efficiency of labour. In fact when Task-wages are equal, an inequality of Time-wages is no real inequality: at all events it is not one of those inequalities which competition tends to remove.

We have already noticed how a rise in the rate of wages in a district may lead in the course of a generation, if not sooner, to such an increase of efficiency that labour is no dearer to the employer; he has not to pay higher Task-wages than before the change[2]. For instance, in 1770 the average weekly wages of agricultural labourers were 7s. 6d. in the southern counties of England, while they were only 6s. 9d. in the northern. The growth of manufactures in the northern counties has drawn away labourers from the land, and by causing a scarcity of labour has raised agricultural wages to an average of 11s. 6d. in 1850, and to an average of 18s. now. Meanwhile the average wages in the southern counties have only risen to 8s. 6d. in 1850, and to about 15s. now. But the higher wages have so increased the average strength and efficiency of the

---

[1] *Arbeitergilden*, Vol. II. p. 6.
[2] See Bk. II. ch. vii. § 2.

northern labourer, that the Task-wages in the North are no higher than in the South.

[§ 5.   In considering the influence of wages on the efficiency of the labourer, we ought of course to look not at money or Nominal wages, but at Real wages; that is, the necessaries comforts and luxuries which wages will procure for the labourer. But comforts and luxuries and the opportunities of such an education as makes bright and intelligent workers, are generally scarce where necessaries are plentiful.   So that the money wages of labourers in different parts of the world are a better measure than at first sight appears of the energy which their children are likely to have when grown up.   And Mr Brassey asserts that the money cost of navvies' work, such as digging a railway trench, its Task-wages measured in money, are nearly the same all over the civilized world.   The chief exceptions to this rule are to be found in new countries, and in parts of old countries which have recently developed great industrial activity; for the economic condition of these districts resembles that of new countries in many striking respects.   Both Time and Task-wages are generally high in such places until there has been time enough for them to be reduced to their Normal level by the growth of population.]

[§ 6.   Another cause which tends to equalise Task-wages in different places is the competition of goods made in different places but sold in the same market.

For instance English and Belgian locomotives are sold at the same price in markets about equally accessible to England and Belgium.   The natural advantages of the iron trades in the two countries are about equal and the rate of interest is nearly the same, so that the share of the price which goes to capital, and therefore the share that remains to industry must be about the same in the two cases; and the earnings of English and Belgian producers of iron must be about equal for the same efficiency.   But since the average efficiency of the English ironworker is higher than that of the Belgian, whatever tends to equalise the Task-wages of the two tends to make their Time-wages unequal.

The producers of iron consist of many various classes of workers such as coal miners, iron miners, puddlers, engineers, &c., and employers; and if it happens at any time that the Task-wages of miners are higher in England than in Belgium, while the Task-wages of puddlers and engineers are correspondingly higher in Belgium than in England, these inequalities will not be directly affected by the competition between English and Belgian locomotives.   But here comes into play the movement from one employment to another in the same district, and the selection by parents for their children of the most advantageous employment within their reach. These causes, as we have seen, establish Normal relations between the wages of different trades in the same district. If in England puddlers' wages are abnormally low relatively to those of miners, while in Belgium miners' wages are abnormally low relatively to those of puddlers, there will be in each place local changes at work tending to remove these inequalities. And if the wages of the various classes of workers engaged in the production of iron stand in about the same relation to one another in England as they do in Belgium, then the competition of their manufactures in neutral markets will tend to make the Task-wages of each class equal in the two countries.

This competition affects indirectly other trades. Take for instance the case of English bricklayers who do not compete directly with foreigners. The wages of bricklayers tend to bear a certain Normal relation to those of puddlers in each country ; and therefore competition in the iron trade, by tending to equalise the Task-wages of puddlers in England and Belgium, tends also to equalise the wages of bricklayers, in the two countries. This indirect tendency towards the equality of Task-wages in two places which compete in neutral markets often escapes attention. It acts silently, but it acts always, it acts everywhere, and it affects every trade.]

§ 7. A striking instance of local variations of wages is afforded by the wages of women. Man is difficult of transport ; but woman has even less power of choosing the place in which she works ; she is more bound by family ties, and she cannot seek her fortunes in the world as freely as he can. The competition of those coming from a distance has not lowered the wages of women in the textile districts as rapidly as it has the wages of men in similar cases. And since women cannot easily move to the factories, cotton factories have sprung up in iron districts to take advantage of the labour of the wives and children of the ironworkers. Perhaps the strongest instance of the local variations of Task-wages is to be found in the case of domestic servants. Their wages are rising rapidly in England under the influence of a growing dislike to the loss of personal freedom which their work involves. This dislike is so strong in some new countries that few but immigrants will enter domestic service, and they often get very high wages; but in backward countries people are willing to do the work of servants for low wages.

In England many women get low wages, not because the value of the work they do is low, but because both they and their employers have been in the habit of taking it for granted that the wages of women must be low. Sometimes even when men and women do the same work in the same factory, not only the Time-wages, but also the Task-wages of the women are lower than those of the men.   In so far as this inequality is due to custom, it will disappear with the progress of intelligence and of the habits of competition.   But more of it than at first sight appears, is due to causes that are likely to be permanent. Employers say that if a man and a woman are equally good workers, the woman is of less service in the long run. For although she is generally more anxious than a man is to merit the approval of the employer or overlooker,—she does not give up her whole mind to her work in the same way as a man does : her work is more liable to be interrupted than that of a man, and she is less likely to continue at it during her whole life : partly for these reasons, her thoughts are occupied more about her home and less about the place in which she works than his are, and she has on the whole less persistence, and less judgment and resource in cases of difficulty.   Thus though the accuracy with which women follow their instructions is very serviceable in some branches of the work, the employer often prefers to have men, because he can select from them foremen and overlookers as well as workers in those branches of the business in which discretion is wanted.   Again many kinds of work which are generally regarded as light, occasionally require the use of great physical strength, and perhaps the working overtime in special emergencies ; and for such work women are at a disadvantage. Thus the occupations for which women are well fitted are few, and therefore overcrowded and badly paid.   And this influences custom and general opinion, and causes women to be underpaid when they are doing difficult work well.

But the progress of science and machinery is opening out to women many new occupations in which very little physical strength is required.   Telegraphy is a good instance of these ; and in all the lighter metal trades women are, with the aid of machines, doing work that used to belong exclusively to men, and being paid for it wages at all events much higher than the average wages of women used to be.   Meanwhile the progress of education is fitting women to do more difficult work, and is making them more ready to demand, and employers more ready to grant them higher wages for it : and it is much increasing their employment in the higher part of the work of education itself.   Prejudice, and trades union rules, have kept them out of a very few occupations for which they are well fitted ; but the progress of enlightenment is breaking down this opposition generally, and in particular in that case in which it has been most detrimental to the public weal, namely the medical treatment of women and children.   The experience of France shews that much more of the work of business management might safely be entrusted to women than is yet done in England ; and there is every reason to believe that there will be a gradual increase in the number of cases like that of one of the largest and most successful brass works in Birmingham, in which the post of general manager is filled by a woman.

§ 8.   Local variations of profits may be caused by local variations of interest, or by local variations of the Earnings of Management.   We have seen that the growth of the modern system of credit has equalised the rate of interest throughout England ; and that a man of business has in some respects greater facilities than any other class of workers have, for moving from a place where there is a poor market for his abilities to one where there is a good market.   It is true that by a change of place he may lose some capital which has been sunk either in establishing a good local trade connexion, or in erecting buildings and other plant that cannot be removed ; but his habits and resources fit him for learning what is going on in distant places and for taking advantage of his knowledge.   And on the whole the Task-earnings of Management, the earnings that are got by ability of a given order, do not seem to vary very much from one place to another.   But a tendency towards the equality of Task-earnings of Management in two places is a tendency towards the inequality of the average rate of profits when the average ability in one of them is higher than in the other.   A good instance of this is seen in the case of farming.

Where the population is vigorous and enterprising, farmers and labourers have a high standard of efficiency and get high earnings ; so that we should expect to find that farmers' Earnings of Management are high where labourers' wages are high, and low where wages are low.   And observation shews that this is the general rule.   We should also expect to find that where land is rich the population is well fed and vigorous : and that therefore where rents are high farmers' earnings and the wages of labour are generally high.   This rule is subject to much greater exceptions than the preceding one ; because the vigour of the population and the current rates of wages and farmers' earnings are often more affected by the neighbourhood of manufactures than by the richness of land: they are high in the North of England where the land is poor, and they are low in the South of England where the land is rich ; and again they are very high in new countries where land can be got for nothing and no rent is paid.   But if we compare different parts of Europe which are under equally favourable conditions in other respects, and which are not near manufacturing or mining districts, we find that the rule holds fairly well[1].

§ 9.   There is however one class of occupations in which

---

[1] Comp. Cliffe Leslie, *l.c.*, pp. 365—370.

the local variations of profits are great. The Earnings of Management got by small shopkeepers vary a great deal from one country to another. For instance they are very low in Germany, and they are very high in America. For there are many Germans who have the little capital and education that a small shopkeeper requires, and who like an easy life. But in new countries those who have a little capital hope to work hard and make their fortunes; so they will not keep a shop unless they can get a good income from it. The difference between retail and wholesale prices is therefore greater in England than in Germany, greater in America than in England; and as another consequence of the same causes, large capitals have displaced small capitals in the retail trade in America more than in England, and in England more than in Germany.

We may next consider the question:—how is it that retail prices often differ much in different parts of the same town, that they are for instance higher in the West-end than in the East-end of London? The answer is not the same for all kinds of trades. In trades that deal in things the selection of which requires taste, the shopkeepers of a fashionable neighbourhood must be men of taste themselves. They must always be well provided with the goods that are coming into fashion; they must promptly rid themselves, even at a loss, of all goods that would lower the general character of their stock; and as they must offer their customers a large choice, their stock of goods must be very great in proportion to their sales. High prices will always be charged in such shops; and high prices will not deter the rich from going to them. But it is different with shops which sell provisions and other goods, in the selection of which little or no taste is required. There is nothing to prevent a shopkeeper who can get a wide reputation for selling ordinary things of a good quality and at a low price, from absorbing a large part of the trade of his district; though of course he cannot attract the custom of those who purchase through their servants and do not pay their bills promptly. Such people will always support a special class of shops where high prices are charged from which to deduct a commission for the servants, interest on all debts, and insurance against bad debts.

Retail prices fluctuate less than wholesale prices. The reason of this is that the retailer can keep his customers if he satisfies them that on the whole his prices are fair. They do not watch the market closely, they do not know whether in each separate charge he has made proper allowance for the fluctuations of the market. But in large wholesale transactions the purchaser examines each bargain on its own merits. In important transactions the higgling and bargaining of the market are a fit occupation for business men; but in most retail transactions it is a waste of time and energy to bargain.

[It is often said that the high rent which a West-end shop-keeper has to pay compels him to charge high prices. But this is an instance of the error of mistaking cause for effect, which is often made with regard to rent. If a shop is so situated that a shopkeeper who has sufficient capital and understands his business can make large net profits in it, its rent will be high: otherwise not. The shopkeeper may make these large profits in either of two ways. If his shop is in the West-end he can hope for custom even though his prices are high, and perhaps he would not much increase his sales by selling cheaply; so he charges high prices and pays his rent out of them. If his shop is in the East-end, he knows that he must sell cheaply, or not sell at all; and he has to be content with a low rate of profit each time he turns over his capital; but if he is in a first-rate position he can turn over his capital many times a year, so his annual net profits may be very great, and he may be willing to pay a very high rent. Prices are low in many of the most highly rented shops in London; and they are very high in some of the quiet streets in the fashionable parts of London where rent is not very high, and in many villages where rent is very low. Rent does not then enter into retail price any more than it enters into wholesale price[1]; but some advantages of situation cause high rents and high prices, and others cause high rents and low prices.]

[1] See Book II. ch. iv.

CHAPTER IV.

MONOPOLIES. COMBINATIONS.

§ 1. IN examining market fluctuations and local variations of prices and wages, we have so far supposed each man to fashion his own course without any special agreement with his neighbours in the same trade. But now we are to discuss the influence exerted by trade combinations. These may be organized into formal societies with definite rules, or they may simply adhere together under the influence of custom or of a real or supposed community of trade or class interests.

If the producers of a commodity are many in number and act without any concert, it is to the interest of each of them to increase his supply of it whenever he expects to obtain a price greater than its Expenses of production. So that the price of a commodity cannot long exceed its Expenses of production, if there is free competition among its producers. But where there is not this free competition, where the whole of the production is in the hands of one firm, or where it is in the hands of several firms who combine together to limit the supply, the price may be maintained at a good deal above its Normal level; when the price is thus kept at a higher level than the Expenses of production of the commodity it may be called a **Monopoly price.**

A man has a complete monopoly of a commodity if no one but himself can produce it. Complete monopolies are for instance conferred by the ownership of a valuable mineral spring, or of a patent which prohibits any one but its owner from making a certain thing. The question which such a monopolist has to settle in order to determine at what price he shall sell, is a very simple one, supposing him to consult only his own interest. He calculates the price at which he can sell each particular amount of the commodity, and also what the Expenses of producing it will be. He thus determines what will be the total net profits that he will make by offering it for each particular price; and then fixes his price so as to make these total net profits as large as possible[1].

A producer who has established a reputation for making something particularly well, often has a partial monopoly. But in deciding at what price to sell, he must consider the risk that a high price will attract the competition of rival producers. It may be his best policy to secure himself in possession of his partial monopoly by charging a price which allows only a low rate of profits on his capital; for if he gets even low profits on a very large capital, his Earnings of Management will be high.

§ 2. When the production of a commodity is in many hands a combination among dealers seldom aims at obtaining a complete monopoly. But combinations for raising prices by limiting supply have been made in every age, in every country, and in almost every trade. In India each trade forms a caste by itself which is generally in a very efficient though not formally organized combination. Within the villages indeed custom rules, but the price which is charged to Europeans is often deliberately fixed at a higher rate than that charged to natives, and it is very seldom that any one can be found to sell to a European at the lower price.

But in a country in which there are no castes, a trade combination in any market has to contend with great difficulties. If those who produce for the market are many in number and scattered over a wide area, it is not easy to form and keep together a trade combination. The difficulty is greatest in those trades in which a great deal of Fixed capital is used. For the combination will aim at keeping the price at all events sufficiently high to cover all the Expenses of production: while it may be the interest of any member of the combination to force a sale of his goods at any price which is more than enough to return to him his actual outlay on them, without allowing anything for interest on his Fixed capital, or for other permanent charges which cannot be avoided however little be produced. But the more likely individual producers are to continue their production and force down prices below their Normal level, the greater is the gain which the trade as a whole may get, at the expense of consumers, by a successful combination to limit production and sustain prices. And the trades in which much Fixed capital is used, are those in which the greatest efforts have been made to form such combinations.

For instance, the Normal fares and freights of a steamship

---

[1] If he calculates that at a price y, an amount x can be sold, and that for this amount the Expenses of production would be z per unit of the commodity, he will try to fix the price so as to make $xy - xz$ a *maximum*.

company must be enough to give profits on the vast Fixed capital employed, as well as to cover the working expenses; but if a ship is not full, the expense incurred in carrying an additional passenger or an extra ton of goods will be very much less than the Normal rate. And when two lines of steamers compete for the traffic between two places, they often lower their fares and freights much below their Normal or "paying" rates. If one company is much richer than the other, it may choose to continue this competition till it has ruined its rival, and obtained a monopoly of the traffic. But generally it is to the interest of both companies to agree upon a tariff of fares and freights; and if there is room enough for both of them, they may make for a time large monopoly profits by charging rates considerably above their Normal level; that is, considerably more than sufficient to pay all the working expenses and give the Normal rate of profits on all the capital employed. But when the combination is made, each of the companies will be under a strong temptation to make indirect concessions which will have the effect of attracting customers, without openly lowering the tariff. A suspicion that something of this kind is being done is a frequent cause of the disruption of such combinations. In this way a great many combinations have been made and broken up and made again in most branches of the carrying trade, but particularly in the trade between England and America, and in the American coasting and river traffic. The recent history of the trunk lines, which run from Chicago and the Mississippi valley to the Atlantic, has been full of such combinations and has contained many startling and romantic episodes[1]. And the great coal companies of Pennsylvania and New England have at various times bound themselves to one another under pecuniary penalties not to exceed a certain output, which is fixed from time to time by a central committee: it is more difficult to evade this regulation than one which fixes the price at which the goods should be sold.

§ 3. Next, with regard to the difficulty of excluding the competition of new rivals from a distance. This varies much with different commodities. A combination of Swiss cotton manufacturers for instance could have but very little effect upon the price of cotton in the markets of the world. An agreement among English cotton manufacturers to limit supply might raise the price appreciably in a time of great commercial activity; but since every one wants to make hay while the sun shines, every one would be anxious to get a large share of the abnormally high profits that were then being made, and the combination would almost certainly be broken through. If on the other

---

[1] See *The Railway Problem*, by F. J. Adams, junior.

hand an attempt to limit the produce of English mills were made when trade was bad, and many of the mills of other countries were standing idle, the effect of the limitation would be to set foreign mills to work instead of English; England's foreign rivals would reap the full benefit of any little rise in price there might be, and have a larger sale for their goods. Moreover such a combination would, as has just been pointed out, have to bear a heavy strain because of the large amount of Fixed capital employed in it. The Lancashire workmen, when they wished their employers to limit production, proposed to relieve this strain by agreeing not to work full time for any employer until prices rose again.

§ 4. If a commodity cannot be easily brought from a great distance, a local combination of its producers may find it to their advantage to limit the supply. For instance, a local combination of the makers of ices could fix the price where they chose, because ices cannot be brought from a distance; though they probably would not fix it very high for fear of checking the consumption. But a combination of corn-dealers in a place to which corn could not be easily imported would not be restrained by any such fear; and in the Middle Ages when the trade in corn was not organized, when the news of high prices did not pass quickly from one place to another, and when the transport of heavy things by land was very expensive, a local combination of corn-dealers often forced up the price very high. After a while the price might be lowered by fresh supplies, and some part of their stocks might have to be sold at a loss. But at the worst the corn could be kept till next year; and if, as might easily happen, they had sold half their stocks at more than twice the price at which they had bought them, they could afford to destroy the rest[1].

Even now combinations among corn-dealers occasionally cause local disturbances in its price. A great deal of the corn that is consumed in England comes from Chicago viâ New York; and if competition were perfectly free the price of corn ought to be higher in England than in New York by the expense of carrying it across the Atlantic, and higher in New York than Chicago by the expense of carrying it nearly half-way across

---

[1] See the tables quoted above, Book III. ch. ii. It seems, therefore, that Mill is mistaken when he argues, following Adam Smith, that "if a speculator has bought a great quantity of corn, and by withholding it from the market has raised the price ten shillings a quarter, just so much...will the price be lowered by bringing it back." Book IV. ch. ii. § 5. The mediaeval laws and edicts against those who combined to "engross" the supplies of food in particular markets, and to "retail" or "regrate" them at an extravagant price, though they certainly did more harm than good, were not so foolish as is often supposed.

the American continent. But it is said that combinations of dealers sometimes keep up its price in New York nearly as high as that at which the competition of other countries forces them to sell it in England; and that the Chicago corn-factors often succeed in charging the baker as much in Chicago as in New York.

Again, the price of a commodity in a market can be artificially raised when there is a practical monopoly of the means of carrying it there. Coal is cheap in places to which it can be easily carried by water; but it is generally dear in an inland place, which is at the mercy of a single railway company.

§ 5. We may now summarize the conditions of success of a trade combination to raise the price of a commodity in a market by limiting its supply :—Those who start the combination must be able to obtain the adhesion of nearly all the traders who can conveniently supply the market. The combination must be able to impose social or pecuniary penalties on any who are not faithful to it; and the commodity must be one that is in urgent demand, so that its consumption will not be much checked by a rise in its price.

There is a close correspondence between these and the conditions of success of a combination of buyers to force down prices. The buyers who start the combination must be able to induce nearly all those who frequent the market to join the combination. The combination must be able to impose social or pecuniary penalties on any who are not faithful to it; and the commodity must be difficult of transport, or there must be some other cause which excludes new buyers from the market. Lastly, the circumstances of the producers and dealers in it must be such that the supply will not be much checked by a low price. These conditions are perhaps fulfilled in a few cases in which the buyers are wealthy merchants who buy the goods for sale at a distance, particularly where the sellers are poor men, such as fishermen, or where they belong to uncivilised races. And they are often fulfilled when the buyers are employers of labour, and the sellers are labourers in an over-peopled district, who have scarcely any choice as to their means of earning a livelihood.

§ 6. Ever since wages ceased to be fixed by custom, and began to be arranged by contract, combinations among employers to lower wages have been common; and in many places they have had all the conditions required for success. Take for instance the case of the farmers in a part of England which is far from all large towns and seats of manufacture. The farmers are few in number, most of them have known one another from childhood, and there is generally a tacit understanding among them as to the rate at which they are to pay their labourers. If any of them were to break through this understanding, particularly if he were to do it with the object of drawing men away from another farmer, he would suffer in the esteem of those for whose opinion he cares most. In fact "there is rarely much competition for labour on the part of employers *within* a trade in a particular place unless there be competition for it from *without*[1]." And unless there is a manufacturing industry in the neighbourhood, competition from without seldom makes its appearance in an agricultural village.

On the other hand labourers are in the position of sellers of perishable commodities : in some cases they may like to rest from work for a while and have a "play-day"; but if they are kept long from work and wages they all, and particularly the married men, suffer much from losing the price of part of their labour. Agricultural labourers seldom think of seeking work outside the parish in which they were born; and thus are sometimes at the mercy of a few farmers who may perhaps decide at a market-dinner what wages to allow.

The meetings in which farmers decide on such matters are generally informal, and little is known of them except by the farmers themselves. But we can read in any newspaper how the Association of West Lancashire Coal Owners or of Fall River Manufacturers met on a certain day, and voted that wages should be raised or lowered 10 per cent.; or how "meetings of employers were held at Blackburn and Preston to consider proposals with regard to the rate of wages made by the North and North-East Lancashire Association of Master Cotton Spinners."

Combinations of employers in trades that are carried on in towns cannot however be managed as easily as combinations of farmers. For in a town or manufacturing district there is generally some sort of competition from without for the labour in a trade, and town labourers are more apt to change their occupation and their abode, and to look about them for the best occupation for their children than farm labourers are. So that if a combination of employers succeed in forcing down wages in a trade much below their Normal level, the supply of labour in the trade will be diminished ; the price of the commodity will be raised by the limitation of its supply; and the employers, buying their labour cheaply and selling their goods dearly, will make very high profits. Each of them will have much to gain by attracting more men to himself, even at a somewhat higher wage, and extending his business just at the time when the selling-price of his goods is much above their Expenses of production. Very strong penalties are therefore

---

[1] Cliffe Leslie, *Land Systems*, p. 371.

required to prevent each manufacturer from pursuing his own interests, and bidding against his rivals in the labour market. But the social penalties which a combination of manufacturers can inflict upon an unfaithful member are not generally very heavy; for he seldom depends for society on those in his own trade as much as a farmer does. And therefore such combinations often fix a scale of pecuniary penalties for breaking the rules, and require from each member a bond for the due payment of them. Such combinations seem to be on the whole gaining strength; but few of them are yet very strong.

CHAPTER V.

TRADES UNIONS.

§ 1. TRADES UNIONS are modern representatives of a series of movements that have exercised great influence over the growth of the people of England, and indeed of all other countries of Western Europe. For the spirit which leads the members of a trade to combine together and concert action for their common benefit, has been present throughout the whole period in which modern civilization has grown up. The wayward savage or the wandering freebooter may submit to some sort of rude military discipline; the passive Oriental may acquiesce in government imposed upon him by the superior energy of a dominant caste; but the highest forms of civilization have existed only where the people have had the energy, the patience, and the strength of will that are required for a resolute and enduring self-government. These qualities have been most highly developed among the Teutonic races that have peopled Western Europe, and especially among the English; but unfortunately these races have often taken a narrow, almost a bigoted view of the meaning of the term "neighbour." They have generally been more anxious to be true to those whom they have regarded as their friends, than to avoid inflicting unnecessary injuries on others around them.

§ 2. We have already seen how the citizens of the Middle Ages formed themselves into town gilds, in order to defend themselves against the oppressions of lawless barons. They did many noble and self-sacrificing deeds until they had achieved their freedom: but afterwards they sank into a habit of harsh exclusiveness towards their inferiors. The oppressed craftsmen formed themselves into gilds, which, after a struggle of some centuries, overthrew the old town gilds, took the rule out of their hands, and governed the towns in their place for many generations.

In early times so little capital was required in production that the distinction between the capitalist employer and the hired labourer hardly existed.   Each craftsman supplied himself with what little capital he wanted, and worked with his own hands.   He was generally aided by an apprentice, who would in due course become a craftsman, and often by his own family and perhaps one or two hired servants. Fashions changed slowly, new inventions were rare; his servants were generally hired by the year, it was to his interest to keep them employed even when there was not a good demand for his wares, so he did not wait for orders but worked steadily, and made things for stock.   The even tenour of the craftsman's life was seldom disturbed save by famines and plagues, by wars and the tyranny of kings or barons.   The craft gilds fostered honesty of work and brotherly kindness, they defended the oppressed and relieved the distress of the unfortunate.

As time went on the complexity of trade increased, more capital was required for production, the craftsman became a small master.   It was then ordered on the authority, partly of the gild and partly of the state, how many apprentices each master might have; how many hired labourers, and what wages he should pay them; and how many hours he should work. Gradually as riches increased the masters ceased to work with their own hands and to associate with their hired servants; and in some cases regulations with regard to apprentices made the members of a gild almost an exclusive caste.

§ 3.   This social separation between masters and men went on steadily but somewhat slowly until the latter part of last century, when a great impulse was given to it by a series of the most important inventions the world has known.   Between the years 1760 and 1770 Roebuck began to smelt iron by coal, Brindley connected the rising seats of manufactures with the sea by canals, Wedgwood discovered the art of making earthenware cheaply and well, Hargreaves invented the spinning jenny, Arkwright utilized Wyatt's and High's inventions for spinning by rollers, and applied water-power to move them; and Watt invented the condensing steam-engine.   Crompton's mule and Cartwright's power-loom came shortly after.   These inventions took manufacture away from houses and cottages, and gave it to factories and large workshops.   Armies of workmen came together under the management of capitalist employers, and the modern Wages-question made its first appearance.

It seems that many of the earlier manufacturers were harsh and uncultivated men, who made a bad use of their newly-acquired power.   They crowded their factories with apprentices, many of whom they took from the parish with a premium of £5 each.   The factories were so unhealthy, and the children worked so hard and for such long hours as to be seriously injured physically and morally.   The workmen did not yet know how to protect themselves; and at the beginning of the present century their means were straitened by the great rise in the prices of food and clothing that was caused by an extraordinary series of bad harvests, and by the taxes and restrictions arising from the great French war. A Parliamentary report of 1806 says that "the opulent clothiers make it a rule to have one-third more men than they can employ, and thus these have to stand still part of their time." The working men groped about for a remedy against their adversities. For a long time they could think of no better plan than that of petitioning parliament to enforce some ordinances that were framed by the great statesmen of the times of the later Tudors. In particular they urged the enforcement of two statutes passed in 1555 and 1562[1], which limited the number of looms each master weaver might have, which ordered that the number of apprentices in a shop should not exceed by more than three the number of journey men, and which reiterated the injunctions that wages should be periodically fixed by the Justices of the peace. The first trades-unions were associations of workmen formed with the purpose of petitioning parliament to enforce these rules, and their efforts met with a partial and temporary success. But though such ordinances probably did more good than harm in the times of the Tudors, they would have imposed unendurable shackles on the growth of modern industry. At length it became evident to the unions that they would look in vain to the government for aid, and that they must rely, as the gilds before them had relied, upon their own energies. From that time they no longer approached government with the purpose of inducing it to interfere in their behalf; but they petitioned and agitated for the cessation of government inter-ference against them. Step by step the combination laws have been repealed: until now nothing is illegal if done by a work-man, which would not be illegal if done by anyone else. And nothing is illegal when done by a combination of workmen, which would not be illegal when done by a combination of other people.

Free to work out their own destinies, the trades-unions have grown very much on the lines laid down by the old gilds. The good and evil of the gilds, their individual self-sacrifice and their class selfishness, are reproduced in modern unions. And even in matters of detail there is scarcely a single regulation of the unions to which a parallel cannot be found in the history of gilds.

Two generations ago unions were chiefly managed by

[1] Philip and Mary 2nd and 3rd, cap. 11; and Elizabeth 5th, c. 4. See Brentano on *Gilds*, pp. 99, 103.

ignorant, rude men.   The law had made a crime of what was no crime, the agreement to refuse to work in order to obtain higher wages; and "men who know that they are criminals by the mere object which they have in view, care little for the additional criminality involved in the means they adopt."   They knew that the law was full of class injustice: destruction of life and property, when it was wrought for the purpose of enforcing what they thought justice, seemed to them to have a higher sanction than that of the law ; and their moral sense became in a measure reconciled to crimes of brutal violence.

In many of the smaller unions there remains to the present day much of the folly and ignorance and selfishness, and a little of the violence of earlier times.   But we may trust that those faults which are not now found in the largest and best managed unions, will, with the course of time and the diffusion of knowledge, disappear altogether.   It is true that even the best unions do not always act up to the principles of unionism as they are expounded by their most enlightened members. But as when dealing with the economics of trade we do not trouble ourselves to discuss at length the guiles of dishonest merchants ; so when dealing with the economics of unionism, we may accept its principles as they are put into practice by the most enlightened unionists.   Let us then enquire into the constitution, the resources, the aims and the methods of action of the best unions of the present time.

§ 4.   A union is an association of workmen in the same trade.   Its principal objects are "(1) to procure for their members the best return for their labour in the shape of higher wages, shorter hours of labour, and the enforcement of certain restrictions as to the conditions of employment, which could not be accomplished except by means of combination; (2) to provide mutual assurance for the members by means of pecuniary assistance in case of sickness, accident, death, out of work, superannuation when disabled by old age, loss of tools by fire, and emigration[1]."

Every member of a trade is invited to join its union provided he can shew that he has complied with its regulations as to apprenticeship, where such exist; that he is fairly steady in his habits, and that he is capable of earning the current wages of the district where he seeks admission.   The ceremony of initiation retains much of the dignity and solemn courtesy, and some even of the forms which it had among the old gilds.

§ 5.   Originally unions were confined to single towns or small districts, and many are so still; but there is a strong

---

[1] *The Conflicts of Capital and Labour*, by George Howell, ch. III. § 45.

tendency towards uniting local unions belonging to the same trade. Sometimes, particularly in the case of miners, the bond of connexion is a slight one; the local unions form themselves into an Associated or Federated union. That is, each local society remains "self-governing, self-supporting, keeping its own funds, controlled by its own rules, directed by its own officers and committees, and fixing its own payments and benefits, but in other respects acting in concert, especially in all matters affecting time, wages, conditions of labour, security of life and limb, and supporting each other in all cases of strikes, lock-outs, or disputes with their employers [1]."

More commonly different unions in the same trade join to form an Amalgamated union, which has a central committee of management, or executive, elected by the whole body. On all matters for which the rules of the union do not make clear provision, the executive give decisions which are binding till the next general meeting of delegates from the local branches. When a union has several branches the ordinary expenditure of each is governed by the general rules of the society, which prescribe what payments are to be made as "donation" to those out of work, though not on strike; as help to those who are travelling in search of work; as superannuation allowance; or in case of sickness, accidents, or death. A branch may not make any payment out of the general funds on its own responsibility for the purpose of supporting a strike. "The method of procedure with a view to obtain an advance of wages, a reduction of the working hours, or any other special benefit sought by the members of a given union, or branch of a union, the refusal of which by the employers may lead to a strike, is as follows :—The movement originates with the workmen in some particular shop, firm, or place; the proposal has then to be submitted to the local branch or lodge, where it is discussed in all its details; if the motion be carried by the members of the local branch, it has to be sent to the executive of the union [2]." It must be accompanied by full details as to the numbers of unionists and non-unionists affected, the state of trade and of feeling in the district, and the chance of success. If the executive approves the proposal, it circulates this full statement, with comments of its own, to every branch ; and all members of the society have equal votes in deciding on it. Thus it is voted on by those who will derive no direct benefit from the success of the strike; but who will have to pay a share of the strike allowance. Consequently many such applications are refused every year.

[1] *Ib.* § 36.
[2] *Ib.* § 26, and Appendix VI.

Once a quarter there is a general audit and "equalization" of funds among the different branches. That is to say, the balance of the income of each branch over its authorized expenditure is added into the general reserve of the society, and this reserve is divided out among the different branches in proportion to their numbers ; so that, with the exception of a few extraordinary local levies, all the income of each branch is paid into the common purse, and no payments can be made from this purse except by the authority of the whole union. Thus a large union has all the strength of an organized republic, in which the most intelligent members are sure of having their opinions heard, but in which every important step is ruled by the votes of the whole body. It is daily becoming more true that the "higgling and bargaining" which determine market fluctuations of wages, are not between individual employers and individual men, but between a group of employers and a group of men.

§ 6.   The total number of unionists is about 1,250,000 ; and more than half of these are represented at the Trades-union Congress that is now held every year in some large town. The discussions at these Congresses have a very wide range ; but their action is almost confined to pursuing the original aim of the union, that of influencing legislation in matters that specially affect working men.

A proposal has been made to organize a general federation of unions for active purposes : but there seems to be no probability of this being done, unless as a defensive measure in case the " National Federation of Employers " should become strong.   In almost every large town there is a Trades Council elected by the local unions and branches of unions.   They have little power, but they take action in some matters of general interest ; and they sometimes arbitrate between different unions. When one union wants aid from others in carrying on a strike, the local Trades Council generally investigate the case ; and either collect subscriptions for the strikers, or recommend them to close the strike on the best terms that can be got.

§ 7.   Though unions do not yet contain nearly half the working men in the country, they do contain more than half of the most skilful and intelligent and steady workers in almost every skilled trade.   There are no doubt some energetic men, anxious to raise themselves in life, who find the rules of a union burdensome.   But more are excluded from unions because they are below the union's standard of efficiency as workmen, or because they are unwilling to subscribe to its funds.

It may be well to inquire how it is that unions have so strong a hold on the best workmen. Firstly, as in the days of the old gilds, men delight in the notion of self-help and self-defence-by union. The best employers admit that if the unions never allowed their policy to be influenced by mean men and shirks, they would do very little harm: and the best unionists admit that if there were no unjust or harsh employers, unions might become mere benefit-societies; as it is, many feel their duty to their union to be a kind of patriotism. Again, non-unionists very often enter into a strike as heartily as unionists; but having no resources of their own, consent to be supported by the union: and when the strike is over those of them who have any honourable feeling join the union. Lastly, unions get a powerful hold on those working men who dread nothing so much as becoming dependent on the parish. For it can promise to maintain a man comfortably whenever he is out of work. But any provident society which did not consist of men in the same trade with himself, would fail if it attempted to do this: for it could not test the truth of his statement when he said that he could not get work at a reasonable wage.

§ 8. Next with regard to the *cost of strikes.* We may add together into one sum all the expenses incurred by working men in strikes, including the wages lost while they were idle. We may add together into another sum all the wages they have gained *directly* by strikes, whenever these have been successful in obtaining a rise and preventing a fall of wages. We shall then certainly find that the former sum is very much larger than the latter. But this does not prove that strikes cost more to working men than the benefits gained by them are worth. It would be as reasonable to argue that the £16,000,000 which England spent on the Abyssinian war was badly spent, because we brought back from it very little booty except King Theodore's umbrella. Whether the expenditure was prudent or not, depends on the very difficult question whether it was worth £16,000,000 to give one more hint that other nations may not illtreat a British subject with impunity. And the unionists maintain that their expenditure is prudent because it makes employers feel that they cannot lower wages or harass their men wantonly without a risk of suffering for it. The function of an army is not to make war, but to preserve a satisfactory peace; war is a proof that the army has failed of its first object. And though there is always a war party in a union, its cooler and abler members know that to declare a strike is to confess failure. The number of strikes would be diminished if all unionists reflected that six years' work at a rise of a shilling a week is required to balance the loss of ten weeks' wages at thirty shillings a week.

But many strikes are not part of a deliberate policy; and in fact the trade quarrels of the smaller unions, as of the gilds of old days, have been far more often caused by irritated personal or class feelings, than by disputes about wages. The organization of the larger unions generally enables them to prevent a personal quarrel from maturing into a strike.

§ 9.   Let us next look at the chief rules in which the policy of the unions is embodied.   The restless changes of modern industry make it very difficult to enforce strict regulations as to *apprentices*.   This is perhaps the most important matter which most unions find it best to leave to be decided by local trade custom.   No doubt a system of apprenticeships supplemented by a good system of technical schools, may greatly promote the education of the country; provided that the apprentice is put to work under a man who is paid to teach him, or who is in some way interested in making him a good workman, and that the apprenticeship rules are not used as a means of artificially limiting the numbers of those who are brought up to skilled occupations.   We have seen that one of the chief causes of the origin of unions was the belief that the masters were flooding their factories with apprentices, who, when their service was over, could not get employment at any reasonable wage; and perhaps a few cases of the kind now exist.   But there can be no justification for such rules as that which the boiler-makers profess to enforce, viz. that there shall be only one apprentice to every five journeymen, or the still severer rules of the hatters. If such a rule were acted on generally by the skilled trades of England, the proportion of skilled labourers to unskilled would steadily grow less.   In spite of the improvements in the arts of production, the total produce of industry would increase but slowly or would diminish ; the improvement in the intelligence and the income of the average English workman would be stopped ; and compared with other countries, where such restrictions were not known, England would become poor and ignorant.   It seems however that a candidate for admission to a union is seldom asked for his indentures, even where they might be called for under the rules ; and that scarcely 10 per cent. of those now admitted as members of trades unions have been properly apprenticed[1].

§ 10.   Trades-unions aim at enabling the men in the trade to bargain as one compact body with their employers.   They have generally decided that this end cannot be attained, without their insisting that, if wages are paid by time, there must be in each district a *minimum* rate of wage, that is a rate below which no member of the union may work till the rule is altered; and that if wages are paid by the piece, a detailed tariff for such payments must be agreed upon.

Firstly with regard to payment *by time*.   Beginners, sick men, and old men are often allowed to work for less than the

---

[1] Howell, ch. v. § 71.

fixed rate : but if the union as a body is to make any bargain about the day's wages, there must be some rate fixed for the time as a minimum rate for those who cannot shew that they are an exceptional case. Of course a specially able man may earn more than this rate. This minimum is not the same in all parts of the country; and some unions publish in their annual reports a statement of the current rate of wages in every district in which they have a lodge. For instance, the carpenters in 1873 report 20*s.* a week at Barnstaple and Taunton, about 28*s.* at Bristol, 28*s.* or 30*s.* at various northern towns and 37*s.* at London. Where the wages are high, the standard of efficiency which a man must attain in order to earn the current wages of the district is high. If then a member of the union at Bristol cannot get 28*s.* a week, he will be forbidden to work for less there, but the union will pay the expense of his going, say, to Taunton where he will be able to get employment at the current wages. On the other hand an exceptionally able carpenter in Taunton is likely to migrate to Bristol or London to get higher wages. By thus sending inefficient men to places where the standard of efficiency is low, and indirectly at least helping efficient men to go to places where it is high, unions help to perpetuate, if not to intensify, local inequalities of efficiency and therefore local inequalities of Time-wages.

Secondly with regard to *piece-work*. Where the work varies in character from day to day, so that no tariff can be agreed upon for it, the unions object to the system of piece-work. For under it the workman must be left unaided to make his bargain with his employer for each separate job : unless indeed he has to bargain with a piece-master who contracts with the employer to find the labour for doing a certain job[1]. Of the two the latter plan is the more distasteful to the unions; but they object to both. However even where no tariff can be fixed, the system of piece-work is making its way in spite of the opposition of the unions. For the ablest and strongest masters generally insist on it as necessary to enable them to carry out their plans freely, and to get their men to use their best energies; and such employers naturally beat in the race those who yield to the unions on this and other points. Where a tariff can be agreed upon, the unions do not generally oppose the system of piece-work. Piece-work is adopted almost universally in trades that make goods for exportation, partly because in many of them tariffs can easily be framed, partly because the stress of competition is severest in these trades.

[1] This plan must not be confounded with the system under which a sub-contract is taken by a gang of workmen with one of their members to act as spokesman. This system is a form of co-operation, and is not objected to by unions. See Book III. ch. ix.

Unionists however maintain that the system of piece-work sometimes makes men overwork and become prematurely old, and that it causes work to be done badly. These disadvantages really exist in a few trades, though seldom to any great extent. They say further that by increasing the amount of work done by each man it decreases the demand for labour, and so lowers wages. If the resistance to piece-work on this ground extends to all trades, it is an attempt to diminish production, and therefore to diminish the Wages-and-profits Fund, and therefore it can have no other end than that of diminishing wages generally: for there is no such thing as general overproduction[1]. If however it is confined to one trade, the temporary scarcity of labour in that trade may in a few cases cause it to gain at the expense of others. But this gain can only be temporary and must involve a greater injury to others[2].

§ 11.   Exactly the same three disadvantages are said to be inherent in long *hours of labour*. A man who labours habitually twelve or fourteen hours a day at work from which he gets no enjoyment might almost as well not live; it is better that he should work less and earn less. Unions desire that the Normal day's work should be short ; and that when a man works over-time he should be paid at a higher rate than for his Normal day. This plan would contribute much to the moral and social progress of the world. But its general adoption is hindered by the fact that where it has been introduced, the best workmen often insist on working overtime in order to earn high wages; so that an employer who does not habitually work overtime, loses his best men. This is a case in which the collective will of the union is overridden by the individual wills of its members.

Another obstacle to its adoption is that a continually in-creasing part of the outlay of the employer consists of interest on Fixed capital, and a sinking fund to replace such machinery as is superseded by new inventions. This part of his outlay is independent of the number of hours in the day's work. It is to be feared that English workmen will not succeed in obtaining more rest and recreation without a great sacrifice of their incomes, unless they overcome their repugnance to one heroic remedy. That remedy is the gradual adoption of double shifts in trades in which much Fixed capital is employed. Many manufacturers admit that if they could get two sets of men to work their machinery for eight hours a day each, they could afford to pay the men as high daily wages for the eight hours' work as they now pay for ten hours, and yet make a better

---

[1] See Book III. ch. i. § 4.
[2] See Book III. ch. vii.

profit. No doubt certain practical objections can be urged against the plan: for instance, a machine is not so well cared for when two men share the responsibility of keeping it in order as when one man has the whole management of it; again, there would be a little difficulty in readjusting the office arrangements to suit a day of sixteen hours. But employers and their foremen do not seem to regard these difficulties as insuperable; and experience shews that workmen soon overcome the repugnance which they feel at first to double shifts. One set might end its work at noon, and the other begin then; or what would perhaps be better, one shift might work, say, from 5 a.m. to 11 a.m. and from 1.30 p.m. to 3.30 p.m., the second set working from 11.15 a.m. to 1.15 p.m. and from 3.45 p.m. to 9.45 p.m.; the two sets might change places at the end of each week or month. There is not enough labour in England to allow such a plan to be adopted at once in all the workshops and factories for which it is suited: but as machinery is gradually worn out or antiquated, it might be replaced on a smaller scale. On the other hand, much new machinery that cannot be profitably introduced for a ten hours' day, would be introduced for a sixteen hours' day: being once introduced it would be improved on: the art of production would progress more rapidly; the Wages-and-profits Fund would increase; working men would be able to earn higher wages without tempting capital to migrate to countries where wages are lower, and all classes of society would reap benefit from the change.

§ 12. There seem to be very few unions that try to control the amount of work that each man does. But in many workshops social pressure is brought to bear on any one who works so hard as to set a standard of work higher than the others like; and no doubt the organization of unions often increases this social pressure. Again a foreman, if a member of the union, is apt to conceal the faults of the unionist workman, and to give them an undue preference over abler non-unionists. The control of a branch of a union has sometimes got into the hands of men who have used its machinery to obtain full wages for very little work; and though such cases are rare, the mischief which they cause is perhaps greater than that due to other kinds of union action which have attracted a larger share of public attention.

§ 13. Unions are rapidly growing out of the habit of *rattening*; that is of hiding, stealing or destroying the tools of an employer or a workman who offends against their rules. There is no sign of the disuse of the habit of *picketing* a place where the men have struck; that is of surrounding all entrances to it with men appointed to represent the interests of the union; but cases of intimidation on the part of these pickets are become rarer:

they now confine themselves almost entirely to explaining to workmen who may be seeking employment, the nature and cause of the strike. The pickets appeal to their feelings of class patriotism, and endeavour to dissuade them from siding with the employers against the employed ; offering them on the part of the union the repayment of all the expenses to which they may be put by abandoning their purpose.

The leaders of the unions have done good service in dissuading their followers from resisting the introduction of improved processes and machinery in many trades, particularly in those which are subject to foreign competition. When an employer displaces by a machine the special skill which men have spent their lifetime in acquiring, and which constitutes their whole capital, he generally exerts himself to prevent their sinking down to the level of unskilled labourers : if this were universally done the last plea for resistance to machinery would be removed. It is said that a union as intelligent as that of the compositors is inclined to resist the introduction of type-setting machines. And it is said that lawyers, who though not formally organized, are yet a more powerful body than any trades union, are not as energetic as they might be in the endeavour to simplify legal processes.

So far nothing has been said of the ambition which some unionists have to *regulate trade* so as to make it less liable to extreme fluctuations. It is quite true that if a plan for doing this can be discovered, working men are more likely to exert themselves to carry it through than employers are. For employers are very unwilling to submit to the restraint and control that would be necessary for carrying out such a plan ; and, while vicissitudes of trade bring nothing but evil to working men, the excitements and the chances of sudden gains which they afford have an attraction for some employers. But no such plan has yet been proposed which seems to have any chance of success.

CHAPTER VI.

INFLUENCE OF TRADES UNIONS ON WAGES.

§ 1.   WE have already seen how there is a continual contest between the different industrial classes as to the distribution of the produce of their joint labour; we have now to inquire how this contest is affected by trade combinations.   Let us neglect for a time the conflicting interests of different classes of hired labour; and suppose that producers can be divided into one great class of employers and another of employed.   And let us inquire whether it would be possible for the employed by combining among themselves to raise wages generally at the expense of profits.

We know that, other things being equal, it will be to the interest of an employer to pay wages equal to the net value of the labourer's work, if he cannot get a sufficient supply of labour on cheaper terms.   If a farmer for instance calculates that the work of an additional labourer would add to the produce of his farm enough to repay with profits the outlay of 14*s.* a week in wages, it will be to his interest, other things being equal, to offer these wages rather than go without the extra assistance. But other things are very likely not to be equal.   If the current rate in the parish is 12*s.* a week, he could not bid 14*s.* without incurring odium among his brother farmers, and perhaps tempting the labourers already in his employ to demand 14*s.* So he will probably offer only 12*s.*, and complain of the scarcity of labour.   The price of 12*s.* will be maintained because competition is not perfectly free; because the labourers have not much choice as to the market in which they sell their labour, and because they cannot hold back their labour at a reserve price equal to the highest wage which the employer can afford to pay.

The disadvantage under which labourers lie in such a case as this, may be seen by considering the position of a shopkeeper in like circumstances.   As a rule a shopkeeper fixes the price of his goods; and if the customers who come into his shop on one day refuse to pay that price, he waits till others come who will pay it. But if at any time he were compelled to sell off his goods quickly, taking whatever offers he could get, and not holding back for any reserve price, he might have to sell them at much less than their real value, at all events if he had access to only a few buyers. For these few might not happen to have much occasion for his goods, so that it might not be worth their while to pay him a good price; and they might even combine to take advantage of his necessity, and force him to sell at a lower price than it would have been worth their while to pay[1].

In the same way, if the labourer has no savings of his own, and does not belong to a trade combination, he may have to sell his labour at whatever price the employers in his neighbourhood may agree to offer; and this price may be considerably less than they would have been willing to pay rather than go without his labour. If these local agreements among employers are common to nearly all places and nearly all trades, profits in all trades alike may be a little higher and wages a little lower, than if they had been determined by that perfectly free competition which is assumed in the theory of Normal value. It is true that profits could not be very much higher than their Normal value, because if they were, the inducement to employers to extend their businesses by hiring more labour at a higher price, would be very strong ; the tacit agreements among employers would continually be broken through, and wages would rise and profits would fall nearly to their Normal level. But still it is clear that if the labourers throughout a country have been in the habit of selling their labour without reserve, they may have received among them a smaller share of the Wages-and-profits Fund than they would have got if there had been perfectly free competition among employers, or than they would have got if they had been able to offer their labour at a reserve price.

If then the labourers enter into local trade combinations, and refuse to sell their labour except at a reserve price, it is quite possible that they may increase their share of the Wages-and-profits Fund, and raise wages at the expense of profits.

[1] If there are very few buyers in a market. it may make a great difference whether goods are sold by Dutch or English auction. In a Dutch auction the salesman starts with a high price and lowers it till he comes to a price, say 20s., which some one is willing to pay rather than go without the thing. But in an English auction, the salesman would have started with a low price, and raised it till no one would bid any higher: and if there had been only one person willing to pay 18s., and he bid 18s., no bid beyond this would be made, and the thing would have been sold for 2s. less by English than by Dutch auction. See Thornton *On Labour*, 2nd ed. pp. 56, 7.

But to what extent can they do this? Will their action so check the demand for their labour as to cause a reaction in which profits rise at the expense of wages?

§ 2. To answer this question we must start from the fact that wages are labour's share of the Wages-and-profits Fund, which is the net produce of land, labour and capital, after deducting rent and taxes. Therefore a rise in wages is at all events in some danger of bringing about its own destruction, if it is obtained in such a way as to diminish this Fund. Now the rate of profits is one of many causes that govern the accumulation of capital; and a fall in the rate of profits, unless counteracted by some other cause, tends to diminish the Wages-and-profits Fund, or at least to check its growth.

It is true that this diminution may be of little importance for some years; and meanwhile the advantage which combination gives labourers in bargaining with their employers, may possibly enable them to get so large a share of the diminished Fund as to maintain their wages. But though the effects which the fall in profits exerts on the Wages-and-profits Fund may be small at first, they will increase steadily, unless the rise in wages exercises some compensatory effect. If in one year they cause the Fund to be one per cent. less than it otherwise would have been, this loss will have increased to two per cent. at the end of the second year, to three per cent. at the end of the third year, to ten per cent. at the end of the tenth year, and so on[1]. While this loss increases steadily year by year, there will be no corresponding increase in the advantage which combination gives to labourers in their bargaining; and sooner or later the competition of capital for the aid of labour in production will be diminished; wages will fall, and will probably go on falling until the removal of the causes which checked the growth of the Wages-and-profits Fund.

It is then clear that if a rise of wages is obtained simply at the expense of profits, if it lowers profits without exerting any compensatory effect on the Wages-and-profits Fund, it must

---

[1] The case in the text is understated. Even if the rate of profits remained unchanged without any further fall throughout the ten years, the loss to the Wages-and-profits Fund would increase in geometric, not in arithmetic progression. But further, wages could not be kept at their raised level without throwing a continually increasing burden on profits; and therefore the diminution (or check to the growth) of the Wages-and-profits Fund would be very much greater in the second year than in the first, very much greater in the third year than in the second, and so on. Further, a fall in the rate of interest promotes the use of machinery, and tends to increase Auxiliary-capital at the expense of Wage-capital, and thus to lower wages. An exact treatment of the problem here indicated requires the aid of mathematics.

be self-destructive in the long run. It must lead in time to such a scarcity of capital and of business power that the total Wages-and-profits Fund will be insufficient to afford high wages to labour, even while capital is getting a low rate of interest, and business power is receiving low Earnings of Management.

§ 3. But it is not necessary that a rise of wages which labourers may obtain by the aid of their combinations, should be self-destructive. For even if it is got at the expense of profits in the first instance, it may be used in such a way as to prevent any diminution of the Wages-and-profits Fund, and to throw no permanent burden on profits.

Firstly, if labourers saved as large a part of their income as capitalists and employers do, a rise of wages at the expense of profits would scarcely affect the accumulation of capital. But the working classes consume nearly the whole of their income on their immediate wants. The wages of hired labour in the United kingdom amount to nearly £500,000,000; or about one half of the total net annual income of the country. But their annual savings, even when allowance is made for the houses and furniture which they buy, and for their contributions to provident societies, form a very small part of the two hundred and forty millions which are added yearly to the wealth of the country. It is true that in those parts of England in which wages have long been high, many artizans own their own houses : and a rise in wages leads in the course of time to an increase in the will to save, as well as in the power to save. Still it must be admitted that the immediate effect of a rise of wages at the expense of profits will be to check the growth of Material capital.

Secondly, we have seen that an increase in Time-wages, if it leads to such an increase of efficiency that Task-wages are no higher than before, will not lower profits, but raise them. In other words a rise in wages almost always leads to an increase of Personal capital; and the increase of the Wages-and-profits Fund depends on the Personal as much as on the Material capital of the country.

A rise of wages may then to a great extent be devoted to adding to the Material and Personal capital of the working classes, and increasing their efficiency : and if so spent, it will not lead to any diminution of the Wages-and-profits Fund, it will not be self-destructive even though it has been obtained at the expense of profits in the first instance.

It must however be noticed that in supposing the rise of wages to increase the efficiency of labourers, it has been taken for granted that the measures by which they obtain the rise do not to any great extent diminish their efficiency. It has been taken for granted that they do not insist on such regulations with regard to apprenticeships as tend to prevent the number of skilled labourers from increasing; that they do not oppose improvements in machinery, in the process of manufacture, or in its arrangements; and lastly that they are able to attain their ends without many strikes. Of course the expense which workmen incur in a strike must be deducted from their gains before the real value of the rise can be found. But a further and perhaps more important deduction must be made on account of the indirect injury which strikes and the fear of strikes inflict on production. For production is checked, and therefore the Wages-and-profits Fund is diminished, by everything that hampers the enterprise of employers, or that makes them design timidly and carry out their designs imperfectly: the more their energy is diverted from their proper work in production to vexatious controversies with those whom they employ, the less will be the Wages-and-profits Fund.

We conclude then that it is not impossible for trades unions to enable labourers to obtain a general rise of wages which they would not have otherwise got; but that this rise will itself bring into operation causes which will lower wages, and that it cannot be permanent, unless it be obtained by means which do not seriously hinder production, and unless it be used in such a way as to largely increase if not the Material yet the Personal capital of labourers, and to add a great deal to their efficiency.

[§ 4. This result helps us to interpret the proposition:— "Industry is limited by capital[1]"—a proposition which has been often used as a way of stating what has been called *the Wages-Fund theory*. This theory has been much misunderstood, and has been the occasion of many popular fallacies. But even as explained by its ablest and most careful exponents, it seems to be unsatisfactory; because it rests on the assumption that all wages are paid out of wealth that has already been set by as capital. This was first assumed for the sake of simplicity, rather than with the intention of being made a basis of economic science. But from the habit of using it for convenience, some economists drifted into the habit of thinking and writing as though it were a necessary law of nature that wages should be paid entirely out of wealth that has been set by as capital. Starting from this basis they shewed that the circumstances of the country determine in what proportion capital is divided into the two parts, Auxiliary and Remuneratory. They called the Remuneratory capital in the country its "Wages-Fund;" and they argued that no change could increase this Fund, unless it either increased the total amount of capital in the country, or caused the Remuneratory capital to increase at the expense of the Auxiliary.

[1] See Book I. ch. iii. § 3.

When therefore trades unions claimed to be able to raise wages at the expense of profits, the upholders of the Wages-Fund theory answered that the action of unions cannot increase, but must rather diminish capital ; that they cannot alter the circumstances that determine the ratio in which capital is divided into Auxiliary and Remuneratory[1]; that as they can do neither of these things, they cannot increase the Remuneratory capital which forms the Wages-Fund ; and that therefore any rise that their efforts may obtain in the real wages of one trade, must be compensated by a fall of at least equal amount in the wages of other trades. In fact as Mill says, "In the common" or Wages-Fund "theory, the order of ideas is this. The capitalist's pecuniary means consist of two parts—his capital, and his profits or income. His capital is what he starts with at the beginning of the year, or when he commences some round of business operations : his income he does not receive until the end of the year, or until the round of operations is completed. His capital, except such part as is fixed in buildings and machinery, or laid out in materials, is what he has got to pay wages with. He cannot pay them out of his income, for he has not yet received it. When he does receive it, he may lay by a portion to add to his capital, and as such it will become part of next year's wages-fund, but has nothing to do with this year's.

"This distinction, however, between the relation of the capitalist to his capital, and his relation to his income, is wholly imaginary…. His own income…is advanced from his capital and replaced from the returns, *pari passu* with the wages he pays. If we choose to call the whole of what he possesses applicable to the payment of wages, the Wages-Fund, that fund is co-extensive with the whole proceeds of his business, after keeping up his machinery, buildings and materials, and feeding his family ; and it is expended jointly upon himself and his labourers. The less he expends on the one, the more may be expended on the other, and *vice versâ*."

This is the reason which Mill gives for wishing to introduce into the theory of wages contained in his Political Economy "those qualifications and limitations which are necessary to make it admissible." Instead of holding that there is a certain amount of wealth deliberately set by to be used as Remuneratory capital, he regards wages and profits alike as coming from that net produce of land, labour and capital which, after deducting rent and taxes, we have called the Wages-and-profits Fund : he

---

[1] We have seen that a fall in the rate of interest increases the use of machinery and other fixed capital, and therefore tends to increase Auxiliary capital relatively to Remuneratory. But the exponents of the Wages-Fund Theory seem generally to have overlooked this argument on their side.

argues that it is the division of this Fund into the two parts of profits and wages which determines how much of the produce shall become Remuneratory capital.

The difference between the new doctrine and the old can be well illustrated by the case of immigration of labour into a country. According to the old doctrine wages have to be paid out of wealth that has already been set apart as capital: and since the labourers will require some raw material and implements to work with, there must be an increase of Auxiliary capital, and therefore a diminution of Remuneratory; and therefore the total amount of wages got by the larger number of labourers must be less than that which has been got by the smaller. According to the new doctrine this result will not necessarily follow: indeed the opposite result is the more probable. For the increase in the supply of labour will increase the net produce of capital and labour, and therefore the Wages-and-profits Fund. It is true that employers will compete less keenly than before for the hire of labour, partly because there is more labour to be hired; and partly because it will answer their purpose to divert some of their means from hiring labourers to providing more Auxiliary capital; and therefore the rate of wages will fall. But it is not certain, nor even very probable, that the whole share which labour gets of the Wages-and-profits Fund will amount to less than before[1].

The old method of stating the wages problem led working men to regard their wages as paid out of a fund of capital already stored up, the amount of which is, for the time at least, fixed independently of their exertions. The new doctrine shews how their wages depend not only on the capital which others have stored up, but also, and to a greater extent, on the efficiency of their own work.]

[1] Cairnes (*Leading Principles*, Part II. ch. i.) has argued that there was no sufficient reason for Mill's changing his position. He has ably restated Mill's old theory and guarded it against some common misinterpretations; but he has not caught the point of Mill's new argument, as is shewn by his going on to contend that "an increase...in the supply of labour, when it is of a kind to be used in conjunction with Fixed capital and raw material," would cause the Wages-Fund to undergo "diminution as the number who are to share it is increased."

On the other hand Professors Jevons, Cliffe Leslie, Hearn and Francis Walker, and Mr Shadwell, have all adopted the same general idea that wages are the share of the produce which the laws of supply and demand enable the labourer to secure (see Jevons' *Theory of Political Economy*, second edition, preface, p. 50). Professor Walker has collected some instructive instances in which it is the labourer who lends his labour in advance to his employer, and not the employer who advances his wages to the labourer. See also Thornton *On Labour*.

CHAPTER VII.

§ 1. WE have seen that it is not impossible for labourers, by forming themselves into trade combinations, to obtain a general rise in wages; and that this rise may be maintained, provided it is so used that the Wages-and-profits Fund is not diminished. The next point to be observed is that when a combination in any trade obtains a rise of wages, this rise is seldom entirely at the expense of profits; the employers are almost always able to shift nearly the whole of the burden on to others. Part of it falls on the consumers of the things produced by the trade, and many of these generally belong to the working classes; part falls on other trades which are directly or indirectly associated with this trade in the process of production.

For instance when carpenters by a strike or a threat of a strike get their wages raised, the master builders seldom bear the chief part of the burden. The rise is generally got when the price of houses is rising; and by checking or threatening to check the supply of building it causes a further rise in the price of building; and this rise in price checks the demand for building. A check in the demand for building checks the demand for the labour of bricklayers, masons, plasterers, painters and other workmen who are directly associated with the carpenters under the same set of employers; and also for the labour of brickmakers, quarrymen and others who, though not working under the same employers with the carpenters, are indirectly associated with them in the work of production. In fact the interests of the carpenters are related to those of the bricklayers and masons, and to those of the brickmakers and quarrymen, in very much the same way as they are to those of the master builders. In matters that affect the demand for building and its price, the interests of all these classes are in harmony; and in questions connected with the way in which this price is shared, the interests of carpenters are very nearly as much in opposition to those of bricklayers and masons, and to those of brickmakers and quarrymen, as they are to those of master builders. Given the price which employers can get for their buildings, the cheaper they buy their bricks and the cheaper they can get them laid, the more building will they undertake, and the greater will be their demand for the labour of carpenters. And *vice versâ* a fall in the wages of carpenters, other things being equal, will increase the demand for brickmaking and bricklaying.

To take an instance from another branch of production : a fall in the wages of iron-workers may induce iron-masters to take contracts that they would otherwise have refused; and this will tend to prevent a fall in the wages of the coal-miners who raise the coal for the ironworks. On the other hand a fall in the price of iron has to be borne partly by the different classes of employers, partly by the different classes of workmen whose labour contributes to the production of iron ; the greater the share that is borne by one, the less is that which has to be borne by each of the others. There is thus a conflict between the interests of the coal-miners and iron-workers which has once or twice brought about an open conflict between their unions; the iron-workers refusing to work until the coal-miners would raise the coal at a cheaper rate. Such feuds between unions are sometimes very bitter and of long standing ; so that one of the chief uses of Trades-councils is to "prevent a union from incurring the odium of a strike through some misunderstanding or petty jealousy between two sections of one trade, which, in the end, if it had taken place, would not only have injured both parties to the dispute, but would also have been ruinous to the employer, although he was in no way concerned in the cause of the quarrel[1]."

§ 2. But yet this opposition between the interests of associated groups of workmen does not very often attract the attention of the workmen themselves. When one group strikes for higher wages, the others give moral if not material support to the strikers. In each of our great industries the employers are often seen arrayed on the one side, while several classes of employed are arrayed in a strike on the other, and the remaining classes are observing a friendly neutrality towards the strikers.

The causes of this fact are not far to seek. Firstly, the employers are regarded as the representatives of capital. They receive as profits the difference between the price of their goods and their outlay on wages, on raw material, and on keeping up their buildings, machinery, &c. Even though it may be known that they do not own nearly all the capital which they use, the distinction between the interest on it and their Earnings of Management does not obtrude itself; and the large sums which

---

[1] Howell, ch. X. § 20.

they receive seem to be a plentiful store from which higher wages may be paid to labour. These large sums really include not only interest and Earnings of Management, but Insurance against the loss of capital. When an employer fails, his losses are soon forgotten by others; but success, as long as it lasts, forces itself on every one's observation. And it is not to be wondered at that in trades in which success is unevenly distributed, some working men should forget the failures which have kept down the average rate of profits, and have prevented the average Earnings of Management from being more than a fair return for the difficulty and strain of the work: while they look greedily at the few large fortunes which have been amassed, as it were, out of their toil.

Secondly, although there is a well-marked class distinction between skilled and unskilled labourers, and although in some districts more than half the employers have risen from among the employed, yet the great social division of the ranks of industry is that between employers and employed. A working man's friends and relations are seldom to be found among the employers, they are generally scattered about the trades which are associated with his own; and he himself is much more likely to pass over to one of these trades than to become an employer.

Thirdly, although a rise in the wages of one trade tends to hinder a rise in the wages of other trades that are associated with it in the same process of production, yet the wages of all these trades are continually seen to rise together when the demand for the produce of their joint industry increases, and to fall together when it diminishes. It is true that the profits of the employers are generally rising or falling at the same time; but in this case the correspondence is not quite so close; and as the profits of an employer can only be guessed at, while the wages of a workman are definitely known, it is not nearly so obvious. Again the circulation of labour, which tends to keep the earnings in different occupations in their Normal relations to one another, acts much more quickly between two groups of associated workmen than between them and their employers. If the wages of carpenters are abnormally high relatively to those of masons, the supply of carpenters will soon begin to increase relatively to that of masons, and the inequality will be redressed. There is in fact a belief among the working classes that if the wages of one trade rise, there will be, and in fairness ought to be, a corresponding rise in the wages of others associated with it in the same process of production; and this belief is itself a great force. If carpenters' wages had risen more rapidly than masons', it would be thought fair and reasonable that the masons should take the first opportunity of demanding a rise, while the carpenters might get but little sympathy from other trades if they demanded a second rise. In physical science we may investigate the laws of nature without making any allowance for the influence of popular opinion; but in Economics and in other moral sciences we cannot do this : for in the moral world, the belief that a change ought to occur and will occur, tends to make it occur.

§ 3. We have seen in successive chapters[1]; (i) what are the general conditions on which the power of a combination to raise prices depends; (ii) what are the constitution and modes of action of trades unions; (iii) what are the limits which the Laws of Normal wages and profits impose on attempts of combinations of labourers to raise wages generally at the expense of profits; and (iv) how a rise in the wages of any trade affects the interests not only of their employers and of the consumers of the commodity which they help to produce, but also of the trades which are associated with them in producing it. We may now collect together the conditions on which the power of a union to obtain a rise of wages for its members depends.

Firstly, with regard to the immediate result of any particular trade dispute.

This depends partly on the number and action of the non-unionist members of the trade and on the difficulty of bringing men from other trades into it; partly on the pecuniary position of the union, on the amount of its reserve fund, and of the contributions which can be levied in support of a strike from those not engaged in it; partly on the resolution of the unionists, and the belief which they and others have in the justice of their demands. The immediate effect which a check to the supply of labour in the trade will have upon the price that can be got for it, depends partly on the strength of any combination there may be among employers; partly on the strength of will and the resources of individual employers; and partly on the loss which they would incur by suspending work. The amount of this loss depends on the margin which the state of the market affords between the price of the commodity which they produce and the outlay of Circulating capital required for producing it : other things being equal, this margin will be the greater, the lower are the wages of the other groups of labourers whom they employ, and the larger the extent to which the Normal Expenses of production of the commodity consist of permanent charges and of the interest on Fixed capital. In estimating the state of the market for the commodity, account must be taken of the stocks which employers have in hand, and

---

[1] Book III. ch. iv.—vii.

of the competition which they must meet from others who are not affected by the dispute.

The immediate issue of any trade conflict which a union undertakes may therefore depend upon the character and the personal relations of those who play a leading part in it, and upon a variety of other accidents, much more than upon the action of the Laws of Normal wages and profits.

Secondly, with regard to the permanent effects of the policy of a trades union.

If the commodity which the trade produces can be easily brought from great distances, a single union can seldom succeed in causing a great scarcity of it; and the competition of distant producers in the same or other countries exerts an influence on Task-wages against which the union can make but little way[1]. But when no such competition is to be feared it is doubtless true that if a union can keep the number of those in the trade permanently less than it otherwise would be, the price of the commodity which they help to produce may be so raised by its scarcity, as to make it worth while for employers to pay them permanently very high wages.

There are cases in which unions have pursued this end with some partial success, by means of stringent regulations which hinder anyone from joining the trade who has not served an apprenticeship, and which limit the number of apprentices who may be taken. But though such regulations may easily be enforced by a trade whose wages are abnormally low, it is a very difficult thing to enforce them when the wages of the trade are abnormally high relatively to those of others. For then both employers and those workmen who wish to enter the trade have so much to gain by evading them, that no regulations can succeed for a very long time in preventing a large influx of new comers. If its Net Advantages are already up to the level of other trades of equal difficulty in the neighbourhood, it cannot succeed in obtaining a permanent rise in its wages, unless there is a corresponding rise in the wages of other trades.

It follows then that no course of action can be permanently advantageous to any one trades union, unless the general policy of which it is a part tends to raise the wages of all trades. So that if we consider only ultimate and permanent effects, we may apply to the case of a single union the rule which we obtained in the last chapter. We there saw that labourers cannot succeed in getting a general rise in wages by means of trade combinations except on certain conditions. And we may now conclude that a single trade cannot obtain a permanent rise of wages except on the same conditions; that is, unless the rise

---

[1] See Book III. ch. iii. § 6.

is got by measures which do not seriously hinder production, and unless those who get the increased wages use them so as to increase their efficiency and to add largely to the amount, if not of Material, yet of Personal capital in the country. No trades-union policy is likely to be permanently successful which prevents people from making the most of their faculties, and doing the best work they can; or which hinders the adoption of improved methods of production; or which much increases the uncertainty of business, or in any other way inflicts great injury on employers and capitalists; or lastly, which leads to a great increase of consumption on those passing enjoyments that leave no permanent good behind them. This is almost the same as saying that it cannot be to the permanent interests of a union to adopt a policy which is injurious to the general well-being, and therefore morally wrong.

But unfortunately the pecuniary interests of those who are at any particular time members of a union, are often very different from the ultimate and permanent interests of the union; for they may not live long enough for the full working out in their time of those results which, according to the law of Normal wages and interests, must ultimately follow from their action. If they can artificially limit the numbers in their trade so as to keep up the wages in it abnormally high for several years, it will be to their pecuniary interest to do so; even though the regulations by which they attain their end tend to bring about a fall of wages in the long run. Men cannot be dissuaded from making such regulations by arguments addressed to their prudence, as distinguished from their sense of duty.

§ 4. "Except[1] on matters of mere detail, there are perhaps no practical questions even among those which approach nearest to the character of pure economic questions which admit of being decided on economic premises alone[2]," and it is alike un-scientific and injurious to the public welfare to attempt to discuss men's conduct in industrial conflicts without taking account of other motives beside the desire for pecuniary gain. The communists assumed that no one should desire to gain at the expense of an equal loss of happiness to others; but the world is not yet ready for applying in practice principles of so lofty a morality as this. The world is however ready, and working men among others are ready, to endeavour to act up to the principle, that no one should desire a gain which would involve a very much greater loss of happiness to others. Of course the loss of £1 involves much less loss of happiness to a rich than

---

[1] The remarks on economic method (Book I. ch. i. §§ 2 and 3) should be read in connection with this section.

[2] Preface to Mill's *Political Economy*.

to a poor man. And it would not be reasonable to ask working-men to abstain from a measure which would give them a net gain of £1 at the expense of a loss of 30s. to profits, unless it could be shewn that this loss would react on wages in the long run. But many of them are willing to admit that no union should adopt a course which will raise its own wages at the expense of a much greater total loss of wages to others ; and if this principle be generally adopted as a basis of action, then nearly all the evil that still remains in the policy of unions can be removed by such a study of economic science, as will enable them to discern those remote effects of their action "which are not seen," as well as those immediate results "which are seen."

Much would be gained if all workmen knew that each trade's production constitutes a demand for the labour of other trades : that since about half of all the things that are produced are bought by working men, working men as a body have to bear about one-half of the loss that arises from any check to production ; and that, though one trade may sometimes gain a higher price for what work it does, by diminishing production, yet one-half of this increase in price has generally to be borne by other members of the working classes : that there cannot be general over-production, though there is sometimes a disorganization of industry which looks very like it : that if, under the fear of over-production, each trade diminished its production by, say, one-third, the Real wages of labour, the necessaries, comforts and luxuries which working men are able to purchase, would be diminished by about one-third.

Much would be gained if all working men would reflect that unnecessary hindrances in the way of those who wish to learn a skilled trade are wrong ; and that it is almost always wrong for one union to seek to obtain a rise in wages by a line of conduct, the general adoption of which would diminish the production of wealth, and therefore cause in the long run a general fall of wages.

Unfortunately working men are able to say with too much truth that many of their superiors in the commercial world sometimes speak and often act as though nothing more were to be expected in business transactions than that a man should avoid dishonesty and pursue his own interests. It is of course true that employers have sometimes no choice except between limiting their production and incurring very heavy losses ; but they are as liable as workmen are to combine to limit production even when there is no such urgent occasion, and thus to seek a small benefit for themselves at the cost of a great loss to the rest of society. And, as workmen are sometimes tempted to enter into a contest to get wages much above their Normal level, wages which can only be maintained even temporarily by harsh regulations and continual conflicts, involving a great diminution of the Wages-and-profits Fund, and inflicting grievous injury on society; so employers are sometimes under a like temptation to strive by arbitrary means for unduly high profits.

The duties of different classes of industry to one another may profitably be discussed from the pulpit, in Social Science Associations, in Chambers of Commerce, in Trades Councils, and in Trades-union Congresses. And there is much to be gained from all movements which tend to bring employers face to face with their employés, to talk over peacefully the economic and moral grounds of any claims that may be advanced: this is the work of Boards of Conciliation.

CHAPTER VIII.

ARBITRATION AND CONCILIATION[1].

§ 1. DISPUTES relating to the carrying out of contracts between employers and employed have long been settled in France by Conseils des Prud'hommes, that is, by boards of an equal number of representatives from the two classes with a chairman appointed by Government. Mr Mundella improved on this plan by inducing employers and employed in his own trade of hosiery at Nottingham to agree to refer their disputes, not only as to the interpretation of past contracts, but as to the terms on which new contracts should be made, to a board of Conciliation. This board, started in 1860, has been in successful work ever since, and a great many others have been framed on its model. Each of them consists of equal numbers of representatives of employers and employed in the same trade, with a chairman chosen by the board. If he has a casting vote, he is often practically arbitrator; and Mr Mundella is probably right in thinking that the board should generally discuss without voting. Each side should listen to the arguments of the other, and endeavour to work towards a solution to which the whole board can agree without a vote. If no such agreement can be arrived at, the question should be referred to the arbitration of a referee who is a member of the board, but who is summoned to its meetings only when a satisfactory conclusion cannot be obtained without his aid.

Thus the work of boards of conciliation is to remove the causes of trade quarrels by friendly intercourse. But when there is no such board, and a quarrel is already beginning, the best thing to be done is generally to refer the dispute at once to the decision of an Arbitrator or a court of Arbitration. Mischief having already begun, the work of arbitration must be done quickly, and generally without the knowledge required for dealing with the subtler intricacies of the trade; an arbitrator

---

[1] On the subject of this chapter consult Crompton, *Industrial Conciliation*.

could hardly fix, as Mr Mundella's board does, a list of piece-work wages for six thousand different tasks. But though arbitration is in many ways inferior to systematic conciliation, it is more elastic and more easily introduced; and it is the only resource in a trade in which habits of mutual forbearance and confidence and openness have not yet made much progress; and it prepares the way for conciliation.

The progress both of arbitration and conciliation depends on the fidelity with which employers and employed conform to the decisions. The unions can generally answer for all the unionists concerned, and their action indirectly controls that of the non-unionists. There have been very few instances in which either masters or men have refused to abide by the award of those to whose decision they have submitted their case.

§ 2. The considerations on which the decision of a board of conciliation or of an arbitrator must be based, are as various as human life itself. But yet there is one broad principle which must underlie their work. They must, as the earlier economists would have said, conform to Nature. That is, they must not set up by artificial means arrangements widely different from those which would have been naturally brought about. For if they do, their work will be in strong conflict with natural forces, and it will be destroyed. They must follow the example of Rennie, who when he had to construct a breakwater in Plymouth Sound, first set himself to discover the slope at which the natural action of the waves of the sea would arrange a bank of stones. He then let stones drop into the water so as to form such a slope, and the force of the waves, instead of overthrowing his work, only built it compact together and strengthened it. He controlled Nature because he guided her forces, while conforming to her laws. And this is the proper work of industrial conciliation and arbitration.

We have seen that there is a Normal value about which the wages of each kind of labour tend to fluctuate. This value may indeed change with the growth of civilization and the progress of invention, and with changes in man's habits and character. But yet at any given place and in any given age the Normal relations of the wages of one trade to those of others are determined by the operation of economic laws; and any attempt to keep wages much above or much below their natural level will be opposed by strong natural forces, and will fail.

Again, the awards should follow the tendency of natural laws to raise wages when trade is good, and lower them when it is bad. But the fluctuations in the wages of labour are naturally less violent than those in the prices of goods; and as variations of wages introduce a harmful uncertainty into the workman's life, conciliators and arbitrators should aim at making these fluctuations as small as they safely can, without holding out to either side a strong inducement to repudiate or evade the award. Mischief almost always results in the long run from an award which gives to one side terms much worse than those which it knows it could obtain by a strike or a lock-out.

§ 3. Boards of conciliation can meet frequently and adjust wages to each passing change of the market ; but yet it is often best that they should adopt a self-adjusting *sliding scale*. And courts of arbitration have no other means of making a settlement that shall give peace to a trade for a long time to come. To form such a scale it is necessary to take as a starting-point some period at which prices, profits and the wages of the various branches of the trade were by general agreement considered to be " fair," that is at their Normal value. These prices, profits and wages being taken as the *Standard* prices, profits and wages, the next step is to arrange that every important change in the price of the goods produced shall be followed without any special award by a corresponding change in the wages of each branch. It has just been said that the aim should be to make the fluctuations of wages as small as possible ; and therefore the rule should not be that wages should always bear a fixed proportion to the selling price ; but for one trade the rule might be that when the price is ten per cent. above or below the Standard price, wages should be five per cent. above or below the standard wages, and so for other variations ; while other trades might have other rules different in detail, but similar in general character. A sliding scale must not be expected to work for a very long time together without alteration ; it must at all events be recast whenever any considerable change occurs in the manner of carrying on the trade.

The provisions of a sliding scale must be definite and unmistakable ; but perhaps more harm than good is done by trying to make them extremely simple. Nature is not simple but complex ; and a sliding scale that aims not at resisting but at guiding the working of natural laws must sometimes be complex too. Thus it should generally take account not only of the price which the manufacturer gets for his goods, but also of that which he pays for his raw material. For instance, the Standard price in the iron trade, instead of being the price of a ton of a certain kind of pig iron, might be the excess of this price over the price of the iron stone and coal that are used in making it. And the Standards in the cotton trade should have reference to the price which manufacturers have to pay for their raw cotton, as well as to those which they get for their finished goods[1].

[1] This plan seems to evade the objections to sliding scales urged by Mr Crompton, *Industrial Conciliation*, p. 88.

§ 4.   There is great difficulty in obtaining the facts on which
the decisions of a trade dispute should depend ; it is often difficult for working men even to ascertain the real price at which
the produce of their labour is being sold. One of the advantages
of boards of conciliation is that in them trusted representatives
of the working men may learn from their employers, in some
cases perhaps under the seal of confidence, so much of the
actual condition of the trade as may enable them to enter into
the difficulties of the employers ; to yield when the necessities
of the case require it, and to stand firmly when they can prove
that the employers' case, on the employers' own shewing, is not
a strong one.   And meanwhile employers and employed are
brought nearer to one another not only by the general influences of social intercourse, but by learning that one another's
motives are not so bad as they appear to be when looked
at from a distance through the distorting atmosphere of industrial conflict.

But there is another, and a more thorough means by which a
class of working men can get to understand the hidden work-
ings of the trade in which they are engaged.   They can start
an establishment with their own capital; and by having complete control over it, receiving its profits and bearing its losses,
they can get access to nearly all the mysteries of the trade.
The knowledge thus obtained enables them to tell better than
they could by any other means when a rise in wages would
so disturb trade as to do more harm than good, and when it
may "fairly" be demanded ; when a proposal to lower wages
is not really called for by the circumstances of the trade, and
should be resisted as "unjust." In this and many other ways,
the allied movements of the extension of economic knowledge
and the improvement of industrial morality will be much promoted by co-operative production.

CHAPTER IX.

CO-OPERATION.

§ 1. THE ideal which the founders of the Co-operative movement had before them, was that of regenerating the world by restraining the cruel force of competition, and substituting for it brotherly trust and association. They saw that under the sway of competition much of men's energy is wasted in the endeavour to overreach one another. They saw the seller, whether of commodities or labour, striving to give as little, and that of as poor a quality as he could. And they saw the buyer always trying to take advantage of the seller's necessity, and thus forcing the seller, and especially the seller of labour, to struggle against a reduction of price, even when, if the buyer were more open with him, he might see that the reduction was necessary. The " Co-operative Faith " is rather felt than clearly expressed, but it is earnestly held by shrewd practical men. It is that these evils can be in a great measure removed by that spirit of brotherly trust and openness, which, though undeveloped, is yet latent in man's nature. It looks forward to a time when man shall have so far progressed, that there shall be no needless secrecy in business, and each one shall think of promoting the general well-being as much as of protecting his own interests.

Thus its ultimate aim has a resemblance to that which prevailed in the early Christian Church, and which led then to a community of goods. Co-operation is divided from most modern socialistic schemes by advocating no disturbance of private property, by insisting on self-help, and by abhorring state-help and all unnecessary interference with individual freedom. But in other respects co-operation has much sympathy with, and has learnt much from the enthusiasts of socialism. In fact the greatest of English socialists, Robert Owen, was the founder of co-operation ; and many of the most earnest co-operators can trace their faith to him. The extravagance of some of his opinions wrecked his best enterprises. But his unbounded belief in the latent goodness of human nature and in the possibility of forming noble characters, his earnest desire to bring out whatever power of right action men have by trusting them and appealing to their reason, his carelessness about his own interests, the unrivalled business genius and insight by which he acquired vast gains, and the generosity with which he shared them with his operatives, and otherwise devoted them to his great social aims—all these traits had a great fascination for many of those working men of the generation now passing away who have exercised the profoundest influence over others[1].

The work which co-operators have set themselves to do for the present, may be classed under three heads. They attempt to remove or diminish the secrecies and discords that exist, firstly between employers and employed (or, as is inaccurately said, between capital and labour), secondly between retail dealers and private customers, and thirdly between retail and wholesale dealers and producers. While pursuing these ends, they aim at enabling working men to employ their own capital in trade and manufacture, and to save out of the profits "joint capital by joint action for joint purposes[2]."

§ 2. Mr Babbage was the first who clearly explained how industrial co-operation would diminish discord and bring out the energy and zeal of the workers[3]. One of the forms of co-operation which he advocated was *Industrial Partnership*. In this system the organizing and managing power remains in the hands of the employers, who provide the greater part of the capital required; but the wages of the employés depend in some measure upon the profits of the business. The system under which each of the clerks at Mr Smith's bookstalls receives a percentage on all that he sells, but has no direct pecuniary interest in the general success of the concern, has been quoted as an instance of Industrial Partnership: it is really a case of paying wages by piece-work: but it is very important to notice that there is an element of co-operation in this and every other plan for paying wages by piece-work. The system of Industrial Partnership is well illustrated in Mr Leclaire's house painting establishment in Paris. " Besides himself there are two other partners in the concern—a Mr

---

[1] Karl Marx, who thinks co-operation too mild a remedy for the diseases which affect society, is proud to point out how the great Socialist invented and put into working the limitation of the hours of factory labour, the sending to school of factory children, and the system of co-operation; how all these notions of his were called Utopian and Communistic, and laughed to scorn by almost all respectable people; and how respectable these notions have since become (*Das Kapital*, p. 277).

[2] Professor Stuart's *Address to the Co-operative Congress*, 1879.

[3] *Economy of Manufactures*, ch. XXVI.

Defournaux and a Provident Society composed of all the other persons (apparently about two hundred) employed. Each of these three partners has a capital of 100,000 francs invested in the business. Messrs Leclaire and Defournaux receive each 6000 francs (£240) as wages of superintendence and divide one half of the net profits equally between themselves. The other half goes to the workpeople, two-fifths of it being paid to the Provident Society, and the other three-fifths being distributed among the individual members. Mr Leclaire however reserves to himself the right of deciding who shall share in the distribution, and to what amount; only pledging himself never to keep back any part, but to pay to the Provident Society whatever fraction of the workpeople's quota may not have been awarded to individuals[1]."

§ 3.   The term "Co-operative production" in its stricter use is however confined to cases in which the working men and women employed supply a part at least of the capital required for the business, and take some share in its management. In former times, Mr Holyoake says[2], "Capitalists hired labour, paid its market-price, and took all profits. Co-operative labour proposes to reverse this process. Its plan is to buy capital, pay for it its market-price, and itself take all the profits." Thus a co-operative workshop is one "in which labour hires capital, devises its own arrangement and works for its own hand[3]." "Workmen who intend commencing one, first save, accumulate, or subscribe all the capital they can as security to capitalists from whom they may need to borrow more, if their own is insufficient... They hire, or buy, or build their premises; engage or appoint managers, engineers, designers, architects, accountants, or whatever officers they require, at the ordinary salaries such persons can command in the market, according to their ability. Every workman employed is paid wages in the same way. If they need capital in excess of their own, they borrow it at market rates according to risks of the business—the capital subscribed by their own members being paid for at the same rate. Their rent, materials, salaries, wages, business outlays of all kinds, and interest on capital, are the annual costs of their undertaking. All gain beyond that is profit, which is divided among all officers, and workmen, and customers, according to their services. Thus in lucky years when 20 per cent. profit is made, a manager whose salary is £500 gets £100 additional; a workman whose wages are £100 a year takes £20 profit, in addition to the interest paid him for his proportion of capital in the concern.

[1] Thornton *On Labour*, 2nd ed. pp. 366—7.
[2] *History of Co-operation*, vol. II. p. 88.
[3] *Ib.* p. 122.

There is no second division on capital; the workers take all surplus, and thus the highest exertions of those, who by labour of brain or hand create the profit, are secured, because they reap all the advantage. This is the distinctive principle of a co-operative workshop[1]."

A good instance of such a workshop is the Hebden Bridge Fustian Co-operative Society. Here every worker, man or woman, must be a shareholder, some shares are held by other co-operative societies and some by "outside" individuals, chiefly workmen engaged in the same trade in the neighbourhood. All shareholders have equal votes, and all are ready to co-operate by giving counsel in cases of difficulty where their technical knowledge can be of avail. This society seems to have most of the conditions which are favourable to the success of a co-operative workshop; and these conditions may now be enumerated.

§ 4. The work by which an employer gets Earnings of Management is of two kinds. The first is that of organizing the production; of determining what shall be made and how it shall be made; and of deciding where and when to buy and sell. We may adopt an American term, and call this *Engineering* the business. The second part of his work, which may be called that of *Superintendence*, consists in providing for the proper carrying out of his instructions. It may be laid down as a general rule that co-operative workshops are not likely to succeed in those trades in which the work of Engineering is difficult and important[2].

For in such trades a board of business men is at a great disadvantage in competing with a single individual, and a board of working men would have to depend almost entirely on their manager. But no co-operative workshop has yet offered a sufficient salary to retain the services of a manager of first-rate ability, unless he is so much under the influence of the Co-operative Faith as to be willing to work for the Cause at a less salary than he could get in the open market. Thus Co-operative workshops have not succeeded in the past, and they are not very likely to succeed in the future in businesses that require much inventive power, such as many kinds of machine-making trades; or that depend much upon passing opportunities and so require much knowledge of what is going on, together with quick decisions and bold action, such as trades for making materials for ladies' dresses in which the fashion changes quickly; or that require a large capital, such as iron rolling-mills; or in which the profits are made chiefly by successful speculation.

---

[1] *Ib.* pp. 123—4.
[2] Compare Brassey *Lectures on the Labour Question*, pp. 126—130.

But in trades that easily fall into a regular routine, so that the employers' work is chiefly mere Superintendence, co-operation can make great savings by preventing the greater part of this work from having to be done at all. For co-operators can keep one another to work, they can secure the efficiency of their own foremen and other subordinate managers, and they can prevent waste and mismanagement in many matters of detail. Thus co-operative workshops have the best chance of success in trades in which there is a steady demand, in which changes are slow, and fluctuations of price slight, and in which the capital is small in proportion to the labour employed. Co-operative work has succeeded in many trades that supply the ordinary wants of the working classes; and seems likely to succeed in many more: and it has done well in small trading ships and whale ships and other fishing vessels.

Co-operation has hitherto made but little progress in agriculture; although most of the conditions for its success are present there. But agricultural labourers, even if they can get command over the capital required for stocking a farm, can seldom stand the brunt of several bad harvests in succession: and what is more important, their narrow school and social education unfits them to some extent for co-operative work: for co-operation is the child of confidence; and ignorance is the parent of mistrust. The "Communities" in America are chiefly agricultural, and many of them are very successful; but they own the land which they cultivate, and which supplies most of their simple wants; they have a good deal of practical ability, and a religious enthusiasm which includes a spirit of brotherhood and mutual trust.

§ 5.   But even in trades the general management of which is beyond the reach of co-operative effort, workmen may co-operate in taking sub-contracts. When the sub-contractor is a middleman, skilled perhaps in little but hard bargaining and severe ruling, workmen complain that the system of sub-contracts, though it may cheapen production, often does much harm to the workman[1]. But trades unions do not oppose, and co-operators should do all that they can to extend the use of the plan in which a sub-contract is taken by a set of workmen, who supply their own tools, share the whole responsibility among themselves, and are under the orders of men chosen and paid by themselves. This system has long been in use among navvies and miners and quarrymen, and in the shipbuilding trades; and it seems capable of almost unlimited extension. "On a long line of railway every cutting, bridge, tunnel, embankment and station is executed by one or more separate sub-contractors;

---

[1] See Howell, ch. VI. §§ 3, 4.

and thus the co-operative system may readily be applied to the construction of every section of the largest undertaking, after it has been sufficiently subdivided[1]." And in many factories in which a room with all its machinery is let out to a middleman who hires the requisite labour, and contracts to do a certain piece of work for a given price, the middleman might with advantage be displaced by a co-operative gang.

§ 6.   Co-operative *credit associations* have had great success in Germany; partly because the system of work in large factories has made much less progress than in England, and there are vast numbers of working men who require the use of some little trading capital.   Groups of these workmen, with a few in other social ranks, have formed themselves into associations, each of which has a nucleus of capital of its own, and by pledging this as well as the whole property of all its members, borrows more capital at the market rate of interest.   It then makes loans to its members at a rate which would seem high to the wealthy borrower, but which is very much lower than that at which a single working man can borrow in the ordinary course of business; for the risk, that the workman may get ill or abscond before the loan is repaid, prevents him from getting it at any moderate rate.   The margin between the interest which the association pays, and that which it receives, is almost always sufficient to give very large profits on its capital, after allowing for all expenses and losses; and out of these profits fresh capital is accumulated, so that the association trades every year more with its own, and less with borrowed capital.   The losses are not large, because the principle of co-operation is thoroughly applied in the constant testing of each member's character and conduct by the other members, many of whom are neighbours of his and know all about him.   A high standard is maintained, not only when a man applies for admission, but afterwards when he wants to borrow; and, as no loan is made for more than three months, this process of testing is constantly going on.   These associations did not grow spontaneously as the English workman's co-operative stores did; they were planned and in great measure built up, by the foresight and energy of Dr Schulze-Delitzsch.   He started the first of them in 1849 in the little town of Delitzsch, and in 1877 he reported that there were 1827 credit associations, that they contained over 1,000,000 members, that they owned £8,000,000 capital and had £20,000,000 more on loan; and that they did business to the amount of £110,000,000[2].

---

[1] Brassey, *l. c.* p. 137.
[2] English readers may learn more of these Associations, and other co-operative movements in Germany from Mr R. B. D. Morier's paper

§ 7. Co-operation endeavours "to promote the practice of truthfulness, justice, and economy, in production and exchange. 1. By the abolition of all false dealing, either (*a*) direct, by representing any article produced or sold to be other than what it is known to the producer or vendor to be; or, (*b*) indirect, by concealing from the purchaser any fact known to the vendor material to be known by the purchaser, to enable him to judge of the value of the article purchased. 2. By conciliating the conflicting interests of the capitalist, the worker, and the purchaser, through an equitable division among them of the fund commonly known as profit[1]."

And we now pass to consider the work of co-operation in endeavouring to put the relations between retail dealer and consumer on a better footing. The work of co-operative stores is humbler than that of co-operative workshops; but, partly for this reason, its success has been greater. The way was pioneered by twenty-eight working men in Rochdale, who in 1844 subscribed a pound apiece to buy flour, oatmeal, sugar and butter at wholesale prices. One of their number acted as a salesman, and the profits went to increase the capital of the store. It grew steadily from this small beginning till in 1878 it had 10,187 members, £292,053 share-capital, and sold goods to the amount of £298,679. The example of the working men of Rochdale has been followed by working men in many other towns; and between them, these working men's stores own nearly £5,000,000 of share-capital, and do business amounting to about £14,000,000 annually. These figures do not include the stores started by the middle classes, which are indeed called co-operative, but in which there is very little of the true co-operative spirit.

§ 8. The workmen's stores have followed closely in the steps of the Rochdale pioneers, and one general description will serve for all. They charge the ordinary retail prices of the neighbourhood; from the gross profits at the end of each quarter are deducted interest on capital, and an allowance for depreciation and extensions; and, in the best stores, $2\frac{1}{2}$ per cent. is set by for reading-rooms, libraries, lectures, and educational purposes generally. The remainder would, if the leaders of the movement had their way, be divided among all the persons employed and members of the store in proportion to the amount

in the appendix to the eleventh report of the Trades Union Commissioners, and from an appendix by Mr Neale to the report of the Co-operative Congress for 1879. The relations between co-operation and socialistic schemes for state aid and guarantee may be studied in Dr Schulze-Delitzsch's *deutscher Arbeiter-catechismus*; in Lassalle's answer *Herr Bastiat-Schulze von Delitzsch*; and in Schulze's reply *Die Abschaffung des geschäftlichen Risico durch Herrn Lassalle.*

[1] Rules of the Co-operative Union.

of their wages or of their respective purchases during the quarter. But a movement begun with high aims often suffers from its own success; and even at Rochdale the new comers, who have been attracted to the store by the desire of gain, have out-voted the older members, and divide the whole net profits among the members without giving any share to labour.

Much of the good done by these stores is due to their plan of charging a full price at first, and returning to the consumer a share of the profits in a lump sum at the end of the quarter : for the workman is thus induced to put away week by week part of his earnings almost without knowing it. He may then with-draw his savings, perhaps to buy a sewing-machine, or some important piece of furniture ; and thus he is often led to aim at having a well-ordered home in which to take pride. If he has already such a home, the best thing he can do with his " di-vidend" is not to withdraw it, but to take his part in " saving joint capital by joint action for joint purposes." In such stores there is much real co-operation : many of the members take an active interest in the way in which the business is carried on, are ready with help and advice whenever it can be useful, and take part in the selection and the supervision of the officers of the society. They themselves are educated by this work; and are led on to discuss and undertake bolder co-operative enterprises partly by the sense that they have funds at their disposal which may fitly be used for the purpose, partly by their intercourse at the stores with others in whom the Co-operative Faith is strong.

Their zeal is stimulated in annual Co-operative Congresses ; a Co-operative Board, Union, and Gild are continually at work, endeavouring at once to consolidate and to broaden the great movement; and co-operators are learning that if "education is desirable for all mankind, it is life's necessity for co-operators[1]."

§ 9. The advantages which co-operative stores have in com-petition with shopkeepers may be classed thus :

i. They have adopted cash payments as a principle. No customer is offended at being refused credit at a store : but shopkeepers find that even if they start with the cash system, they can hardly avoid meeting exceptional cases by giving cre-dit, and soon the exceptional cases become the rule. The credit system not only leads to many bad debts, but it inverts the natural order of loans. It is reasonable that the trader who expects trade profits on his capital should borrow directly or indirectly from the private individual who can only get interest on it. But on the credit system the customer borrows the use of capital from the shopkeeper.

---

[1] This truth is ably worked out in Professor Stuart's address.

ii. The stores in which the co-operative element is strong, sell unadulterated goods ; and others are believed to do the same.

iii. A store can do a large business without spending much on advertisements, or on an expensive site. A large store likes to have an imposing front : but this answers for a great many departments one above the other.

iv. When competing with the small shopkeeper it has the advantage of buying in larger quantities, and therefore more nearly direct from the producer than he can.

v. Those who have an interest in the success of the store, will wait more patiently to be served than the customers at a private shop : and therefore the amount of business done is larger in proportion to the number of those who stand behind the counter in the store than in the shop.

The great difficulty that the stores have to contend with in seeking the custom of the working classes, arises from the fact that a working man who is not a unionist generally wants to borrow from shopkeepers when he is out of employment ; and that even unionists, when excited by a struggle for victory, are sorely tempted to accept the offer of friendly shopkeepers to advance the means of sustaining the strike for some time longer. And there are many in other ranks of life who cannot, or who think they cannot, avoid spending their income before they receive it.

§ 10. It is probable that there will always be some shopkeepers who will carry on their business on the old plan, and who will retain those customers who are willing to pay high prices, on condition of receiving credit, of having assistants always ready to attend on them without delay and to shew them innumerable things which they do not want to buy, and of having every little trifle which they buy delivered at their houses at once. But all these services cost more to the shopkeepers than they are really worth to the great majority of customers. And the success of co-operative stores has proved that there is a great demand for traders who will act on the business principle of not doing any thing for the customer which must in the long run cost the customer more than it is worth his while to pay for it. But there is no reason why shopkeepers who adopt this principle should not be able to hold their own against all stores except those in which there is so much true co-operation as to be a great source of strength. With equal advantages the professional trader with trained skill and specialised taste can hold his own against joint-stock companies managed by amateurs. And since in the long run the Earnings of Management of shopkeepers are governed by the Laws which were discussed in the second Book, they will, when the new system is fairly in operation, obtain as good incomes as they would have done if the old system had continued.

The change will benefit shopkeepers by freeing them in a great measure from their dependence on small bodies of customers whose humours they have to consult; they will have the sound position that comes of doing business in a business-like way. But the change will of course diminish the number of shopkeepers whose work is required[1]; and the process of thinning out must be painful; the suffering need not however be great if shopkeepers adapt themselves quickly to the requirements of the new age, and urge all young men who have not special reasons for becoming shopkeepers to choose some other occupation. The general prosperity of the country will be much increased when the capital and labour that are now wastefully employed in the retail trade, are set free for other work.

§ 11. The third work of co-operators is to diminish the discords between retail and wholesale dealers and producers. For this purpose they have started a Wholesale Co-operative Society, which aims at doing for the retail stores what the retail stores aim at doing for the individual consumer. It buys directly from the producer, or importer; it imports some things itself, and it has its own works for making biscuits, shoes, and soap. The retail stores who deal with it share in its profits; and however little they buy, however little they understand the business of buying, they can, it is asserted, buy from it on the most favourable terms.

There is a plan for making this society the centre of a grand Federation of Co-operators. It is proposed that co-operative consumers should guarantee to co-operative producers a steady market for their wares[2]. Having uninterrupted employment, the co-operative producers would, it is argued, be free from anxiety, and be able to get high wages for themselves, while they produced at a low price on the average; and the co-operative purchasers would gain by buying their goods cheaply in the first instance, and also by receiving a share of the net profits of the co-operative workshops. For it is assumed that the net profits of the co-operative workshops would be divided between the labour employed in it and the customers. The total demand of co-operative consumers is of course not constant from year to

---

[1] It has been calculated by Mr Neale (*Economics of Co-operation*) that there are 41,735 separate establishments for 22 of the principal retail trades in London. If for each of these trades there were 648 shops, that is 9 to the square mile, no one would have to go more than a quarter of a mile to the nearest shop; there would be 14,256 shops in all. Assuming that this supply would be sufficient, there are in London 251 shops for every 100 that are really wanted.

[2] See Book III. ch. i. § 4.

year; and therefore perfectly uninterrupted employment could not be guaranteed to the workshops if their annual produce exceeded the amount which the Stores were willing to purchase in the most unfavourable years. And the prices and wages in the workshops would have to fall whenever they fell in the outside markets : for otherwise the trust of co-operators would be put to too great a strain.

The plan will require much exercise of the Co-operative Faith ; but it will be a gain to the world if many wish for it, and a great gain if they achieve it.

INDEX.

CAMBRIDGE: PRINTED BY C. J. CLAY, M.A. AT THE UNIVERSITY PRESS.

Printed in Great Britain by
Antony Rowe Ltd, Chippenham, Wiltshire